IMAGE   COMICS   PRESENTS

F L I G H T ™

V O L U M E   O N E

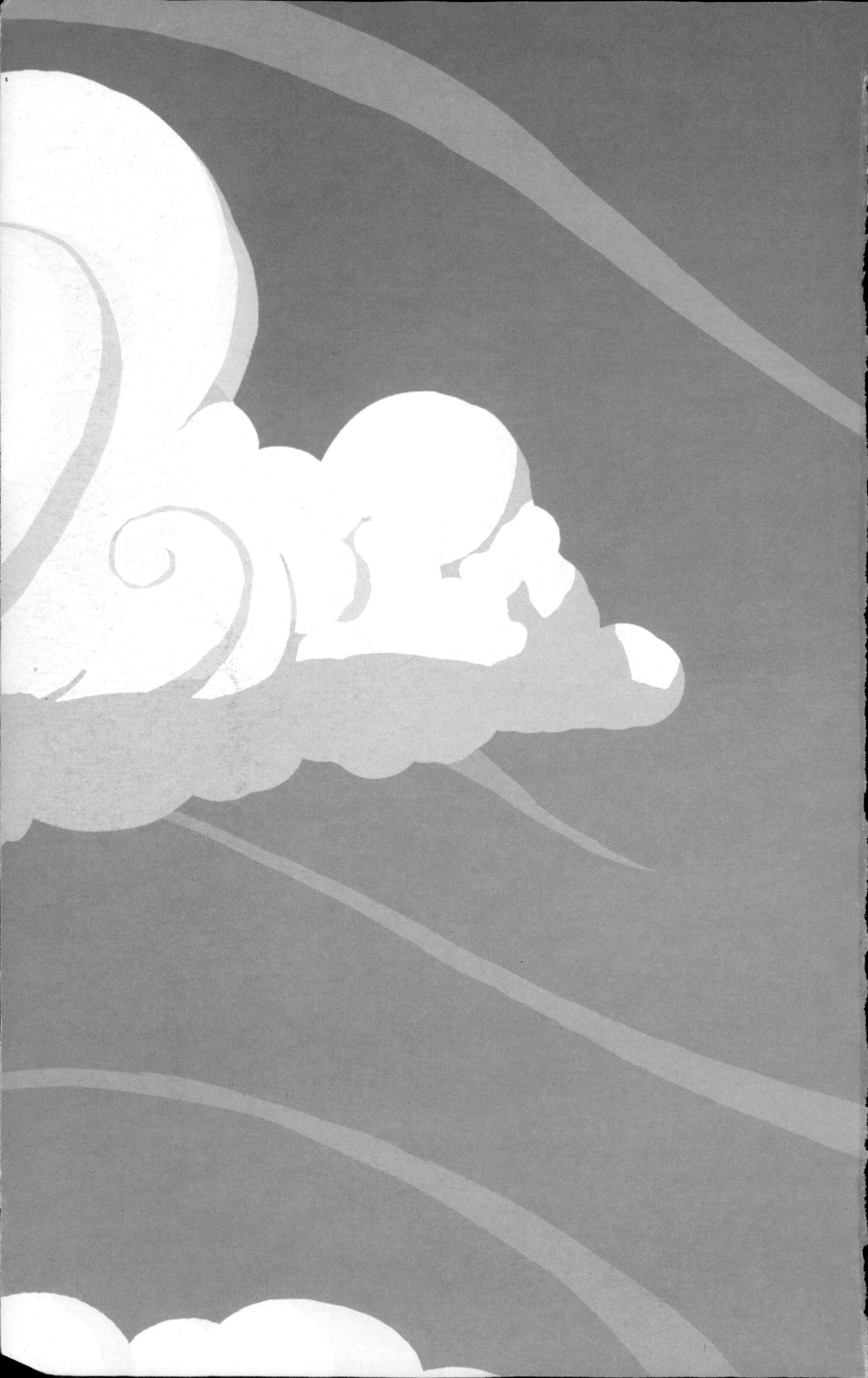

CONTENTS:

Air and Water

by
Enrico
Casarosa

poem
by
Kean
Soo

inspired
by
Antoine
de
Saint
Exupery

This quiet stillness
broken by a thundering storm
the roar of the engine
drowns everything out

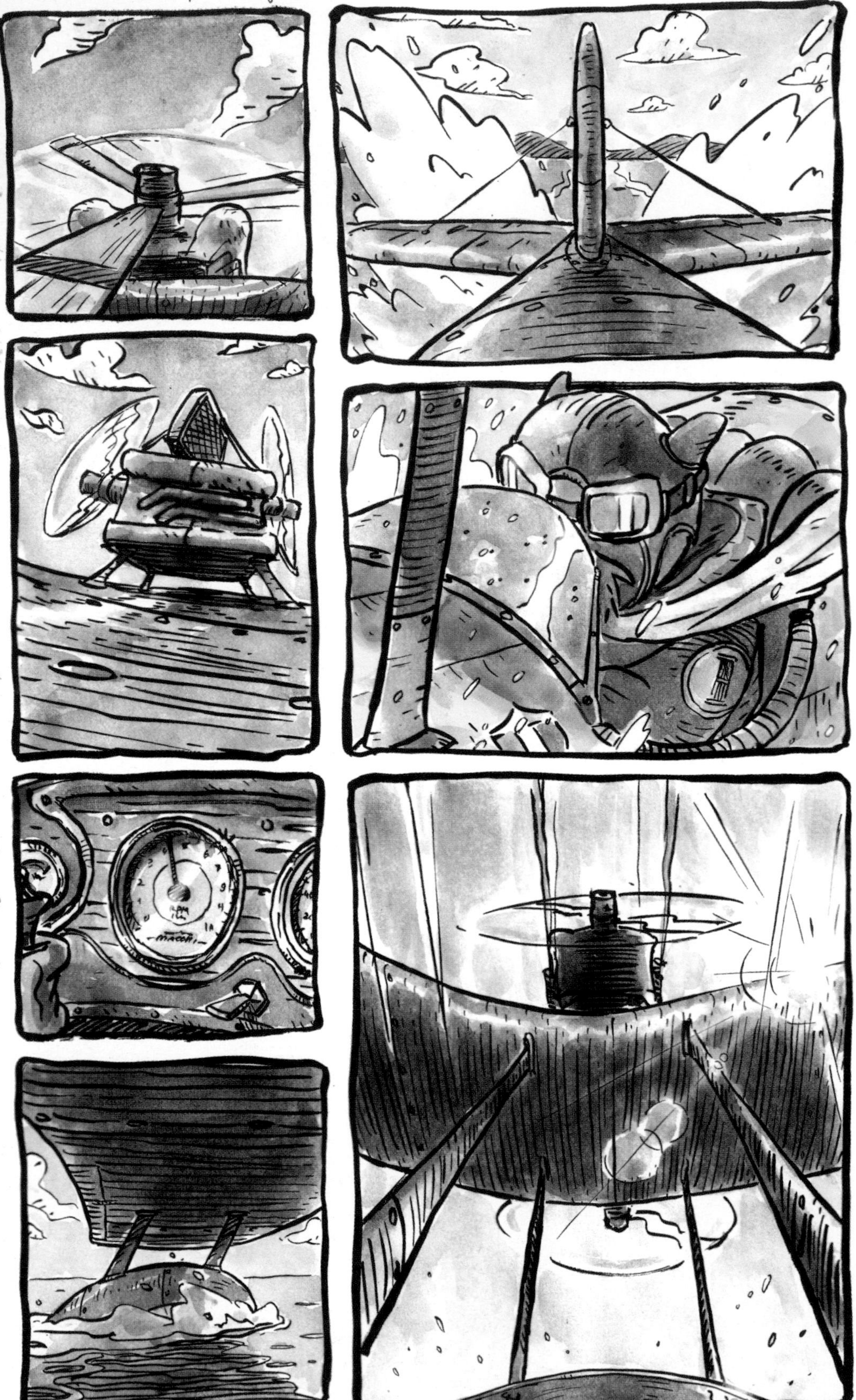

Slicing through the calm surface
the wind cuts into my skin
water arching across my vision

Heart in my throat
watching the needles rise
a shudder runs through me
the moment is ripe

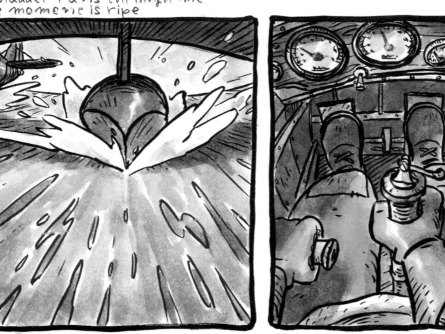

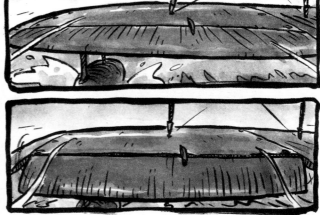

My grip tightens
steel feathers respond

and the sound fades
the world falls away ...

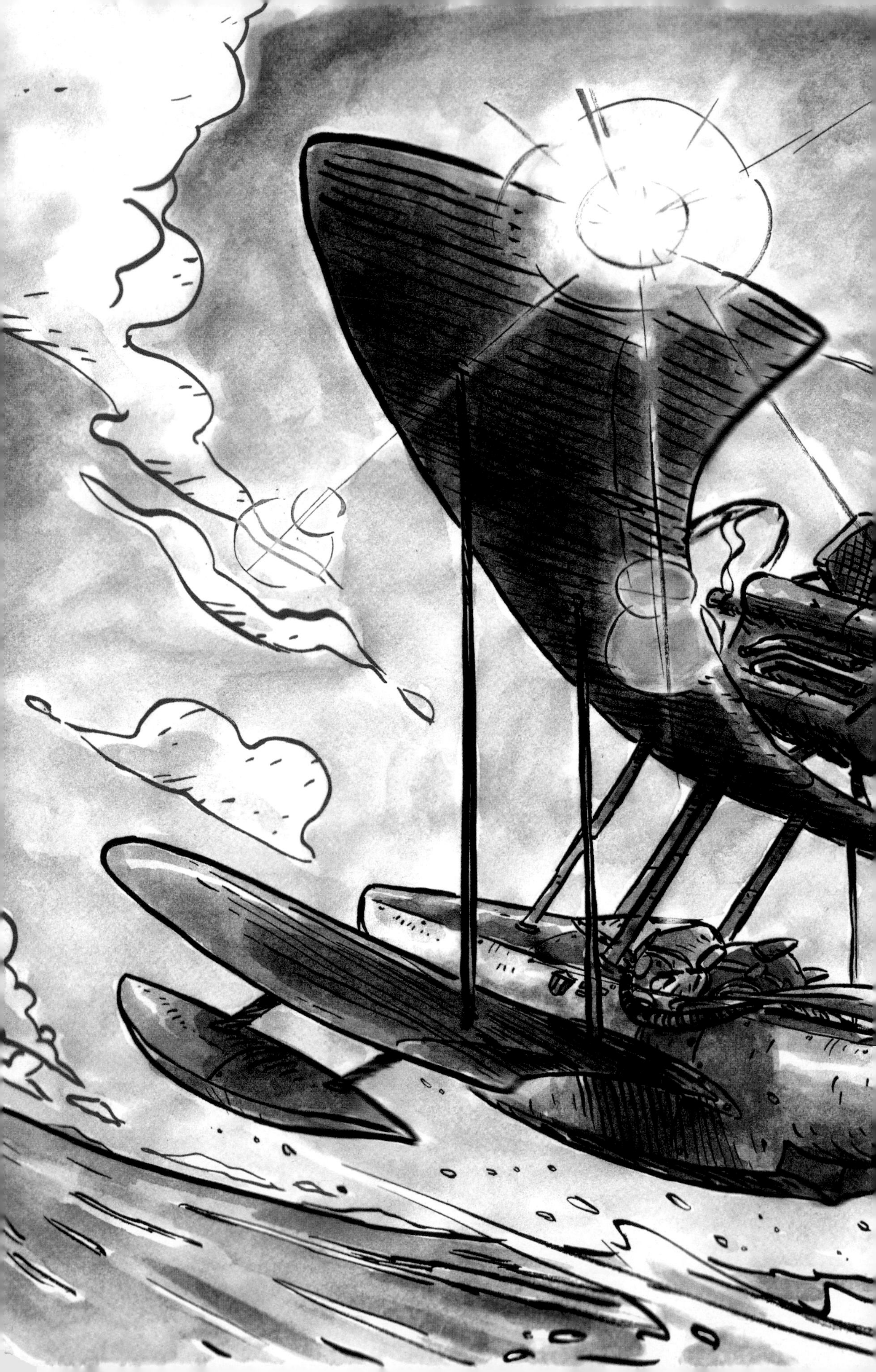

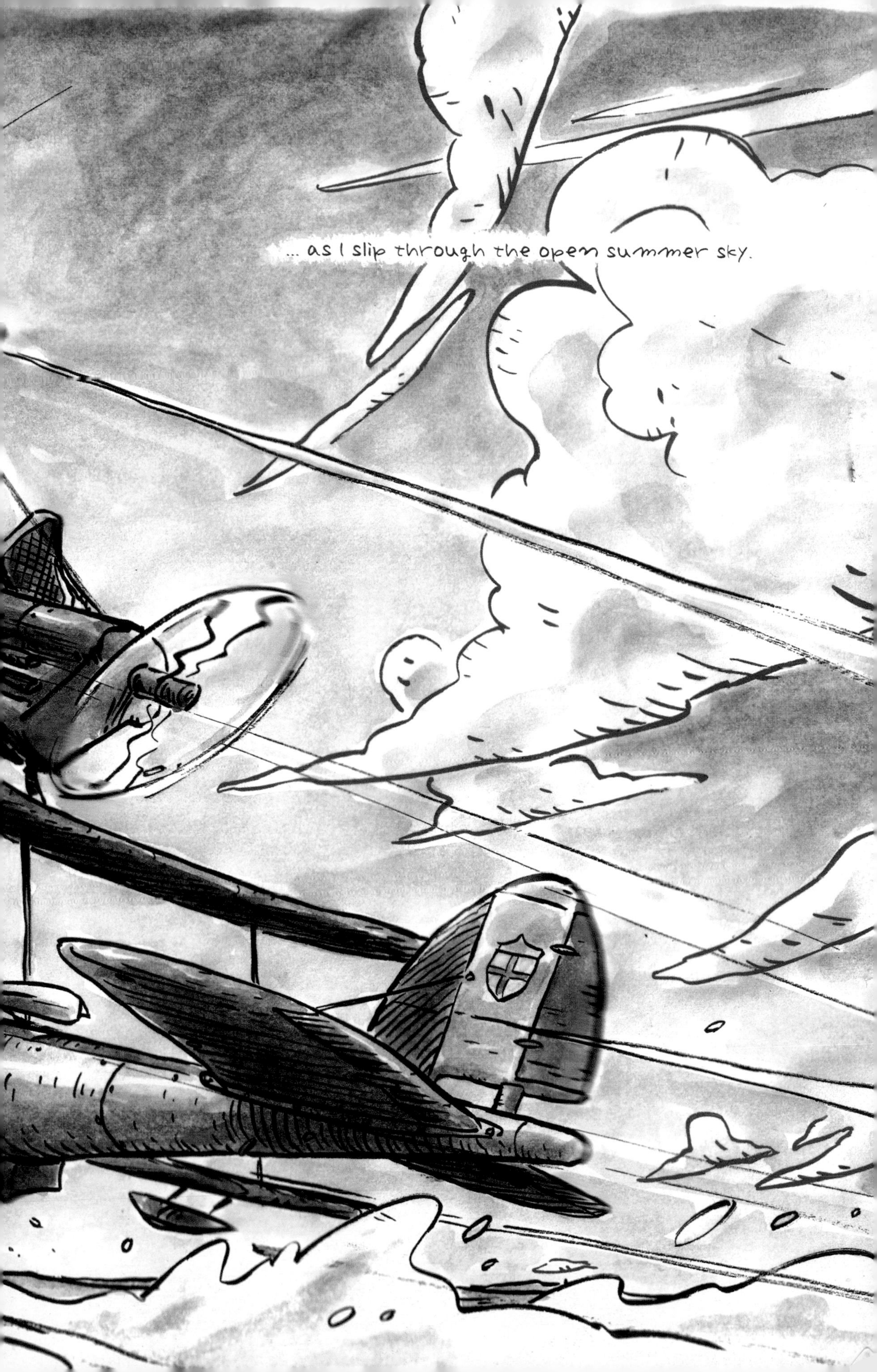
... as I slip through the open summer sky.

"Maiden Voyage" by Kazu Kibuishi

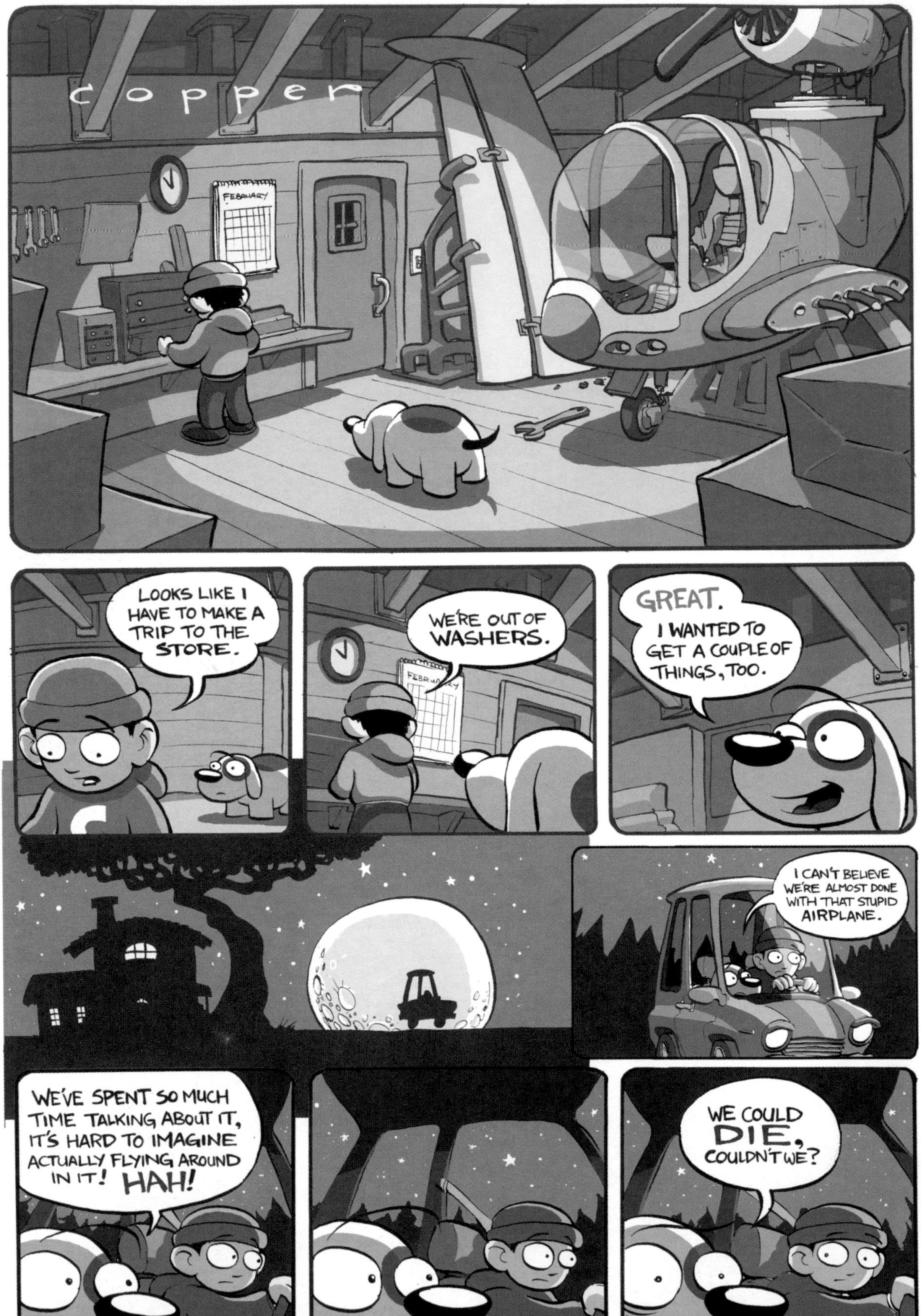
copper
FEBRUARY
LOOKS LIKE I HAVE TO MAKE A TRIP TO THE STORE.
WE'RE OUT OF WASHERS.
GREAT. I WANTED TO GET A COUPLE OF THINGS, TOO.
I CAN'T BELIEVE WE'RE ALMOST DONE WITH THAT STUPID AIRPLANE.
WE'VE SPENT SO MUCH TIME TALKING ABOUT IT, IT'S HARD TO IMAGINE ACTUALLY FLYING AROUND IN IT! HAH!
WE COULD DIE, COULDN'T WE?

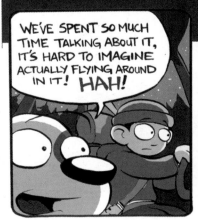

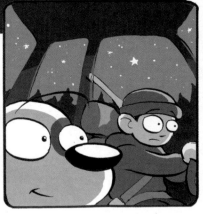

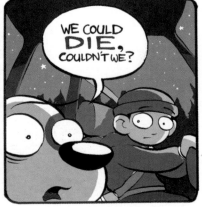

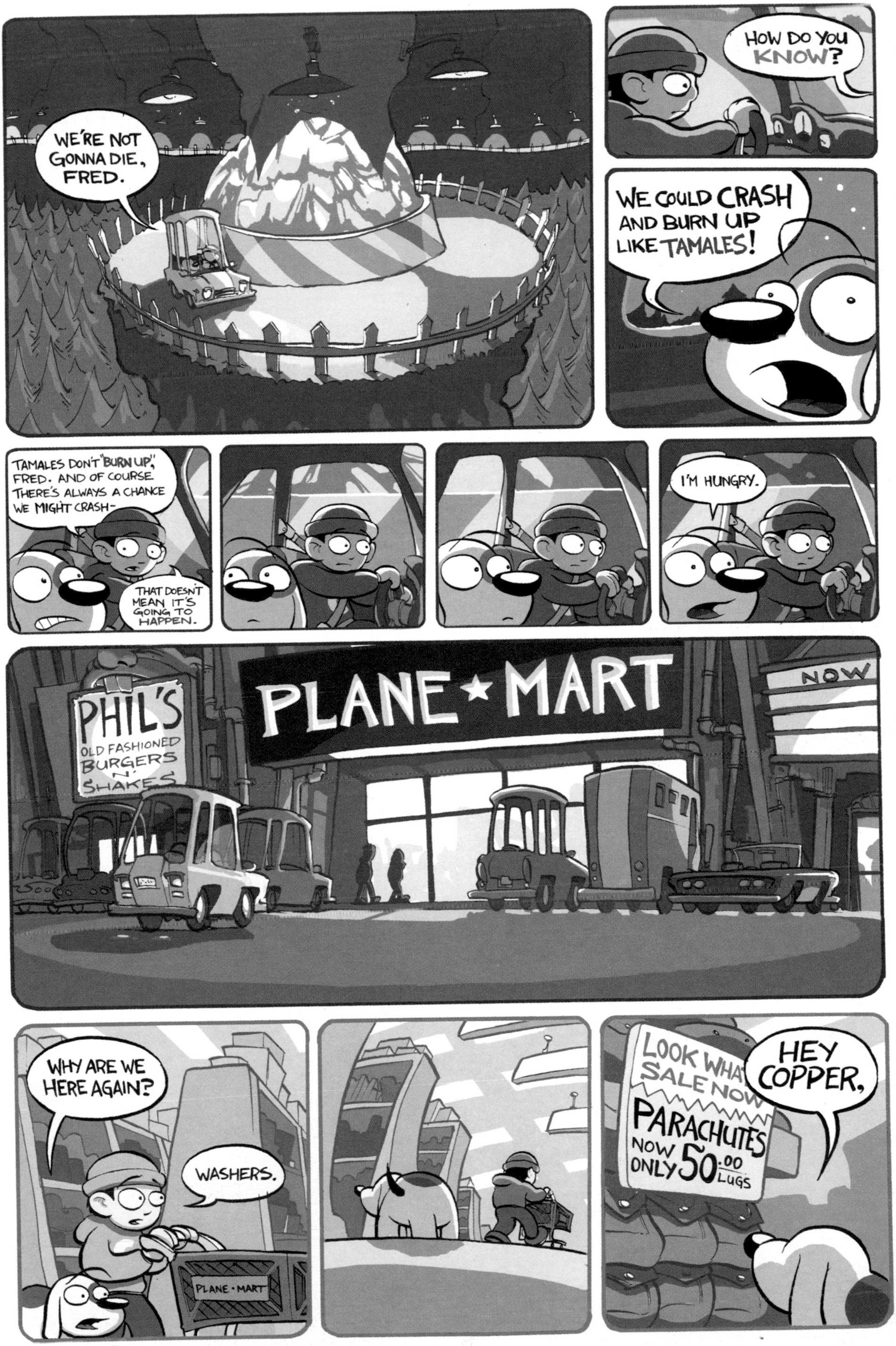
WE'RE NOT GONNA DIE, FRED.
HOW DO YOU KNOW?
WE COULD CRASH AND BURN UP LIKE TAMALES!
TAMALES DON'T "BURN UP", FRED. AND OF COURSE THERE'S ALWAYS A CHANCE WE MIGHT CRASH-
THAT DOESN'T MEAN IT'S GOING TO HAPPEN.
I'M HUNGRY.
PLANE ★ MART
PHIL'S OLD FASHIONED BURGERS N' SHAKES
NOW
WHY ARE WE HERE AGAIN?
WASHERS.
PLANE • MART
LOOK WHA SALE NOW
PARACHUTES NOW ONLY 50.00 LUGS
HEY COPPER,

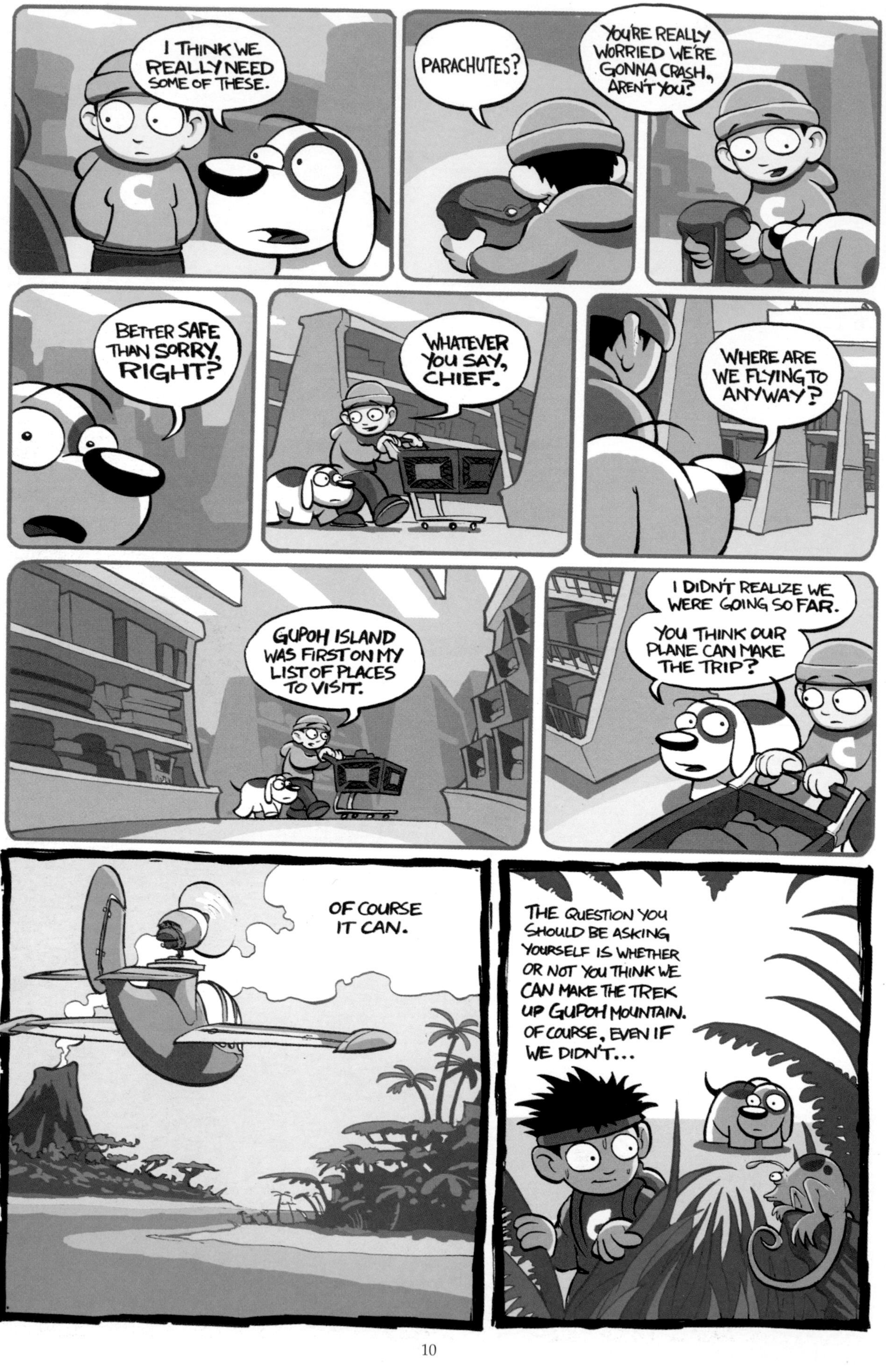
I THINK WE REALLY NEED SOME OF THESE.
PARACHUTES?
YOU'RE REALLY WORRIED WE'RE GONNA CRASH, AREN'T YOU?
BETTER SAFE THAN SORRY, RIGHT?
WHATEVER YOU SAY, CHIEF.
WHERE ARE WE FLYING TO ANYWAY?
GUPOH ISLAND WAS FIRST ON MY LIST OF PLACES TO VISIT.
I DIDN'T REALIZE WE WERE GOING SO FAR.
YOU THINK OUR PLANE CAN MAKE THE TRIP?
OF COURSE IT CAN.
THE QUESTION YOU SHOULD BE ASKING YOURSELF IS WHETHER OR NOT YOU THINK WE CAN MAKE THE TREK UP GUPOH MOUNTAIN. OF COURSE, EVEN IF WE DIDN'T...

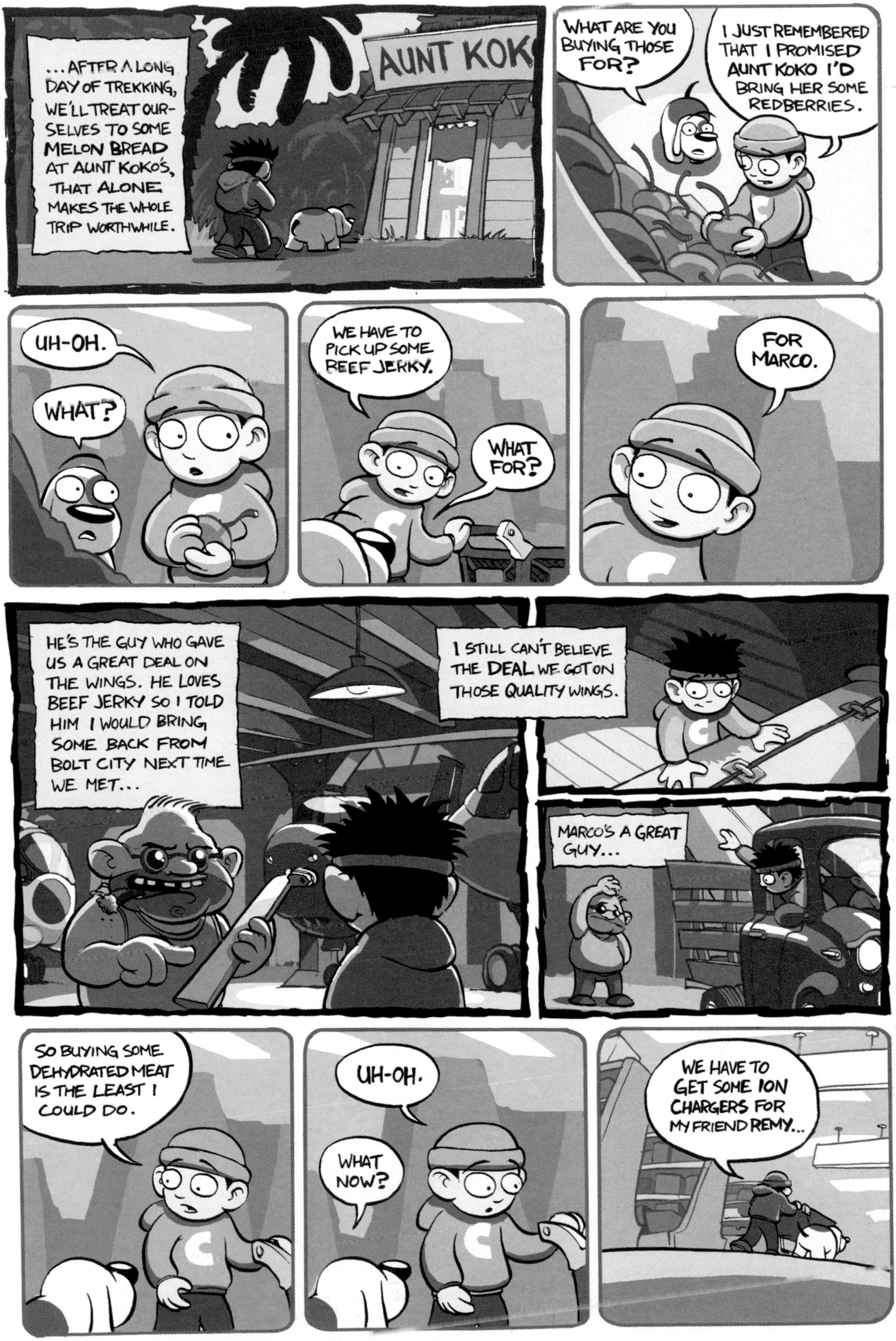
...AFTER A LONG DAY OF TREKKING, WE'LL TREAT OURSELVES TO SOME MELON BREAD AT AUNT KOKO'S, THAT ALONE MAKES THE WHOLE TRIP WORTHWHILE.
AUNT KOK
WHAT ARE YOU BUYING THOSE FOR?
I JUST REMEMBERED THAT I PROMISED AUNT KOKO I'D BRING HER SOME REDBERRIES.
UH-OH.
WHAT?
WE HAVE TO PICK UP SOME BEEF JERKY.
WHAT FOR?
FOR MARCO.
HE'S THE GUY WHO GAVE US A GREAT DEAL ON THE WINGS. HE LOVES BEEF JERKY SO I TOLD HIM I WOULD BRING SOME BACK FROM BOLT CITY NEXT TIME WE MET...
I STILL CAN'T BELIEVE THE DEAL WE GOT ON THOSE QUALITY WINGS.
MARCO'S A GREAT GUY...
SO BUYING SOME DEHYDRATED MEAT IS THE LEAST I COULD DO.
UH-OH.
WHAT NOW?
WE HAVE TO GET SOME ION CHARGERS FOR MY FRIEND REMY...

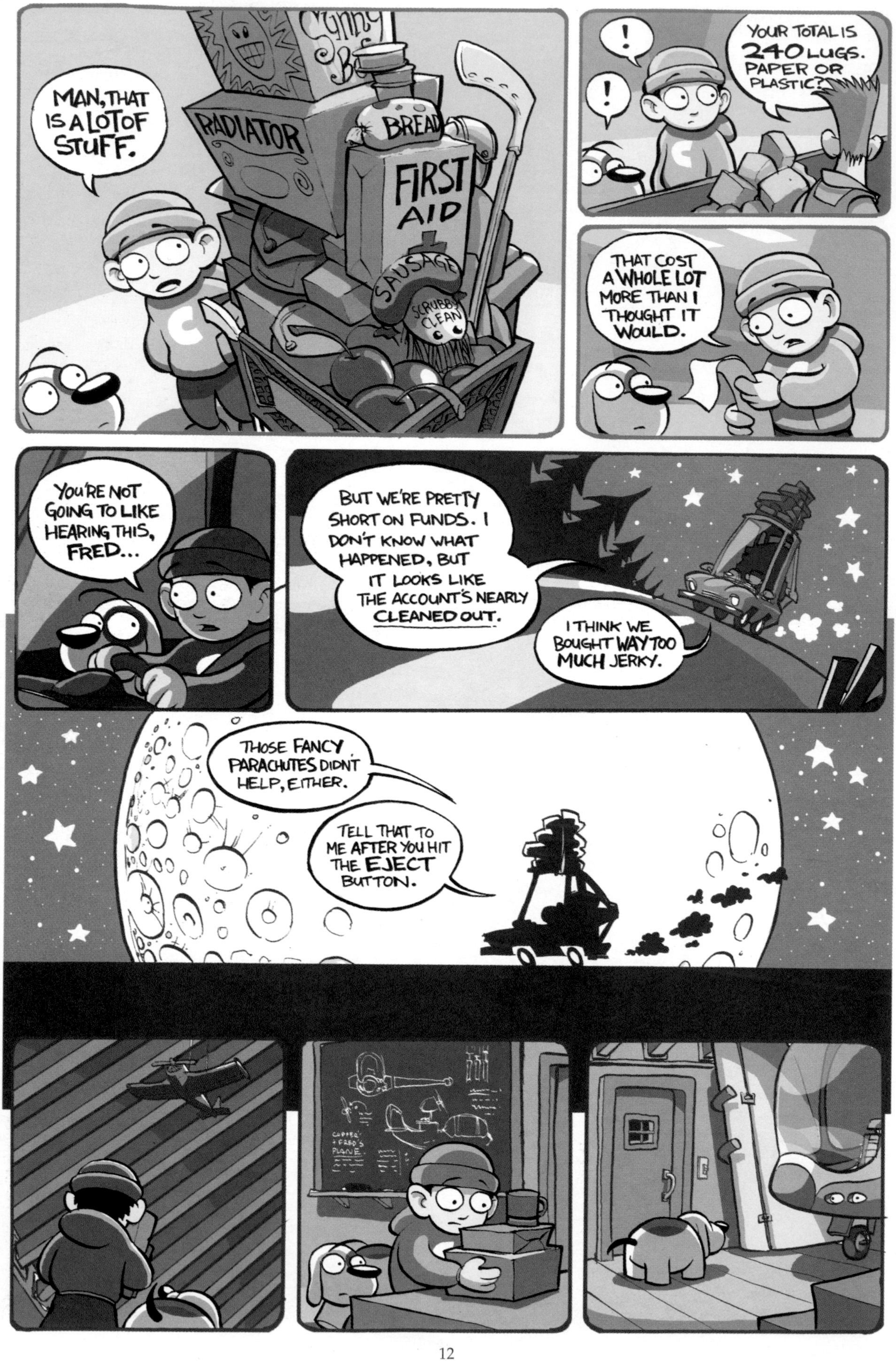
MAN, THAT IS A LOT OF STUFF.
RADIATOR
BREAD
FIRST AID
SAUSAGE
SCRUBBY CLEAN
!
!
YOUR TOTAL IS 240 LUGS. PAPER OR PLASTIC?
THAT COST A WHOLE LOT MORE THAN I THOUGHT IT WOULD.
YOU'RE NOT GOING TO LIKE HEARING THIS, FRED...
BUT WE'RE PRETTY SHORT ON FUNDS. I DON'T KNOW WHAT HAPPENED, BUT IT LOOKS LIKE THE ACCOUNT'S NEARLY CLEANED OUT.
I THINK WE BOUGHT WAY TOO MUCH JERKY.
THOSE FANCY PARACHUTES DIDN'T HELP, EITHER.
TELL THAT TO ME AFTER YOU HIT THE EJECT BUTTON.

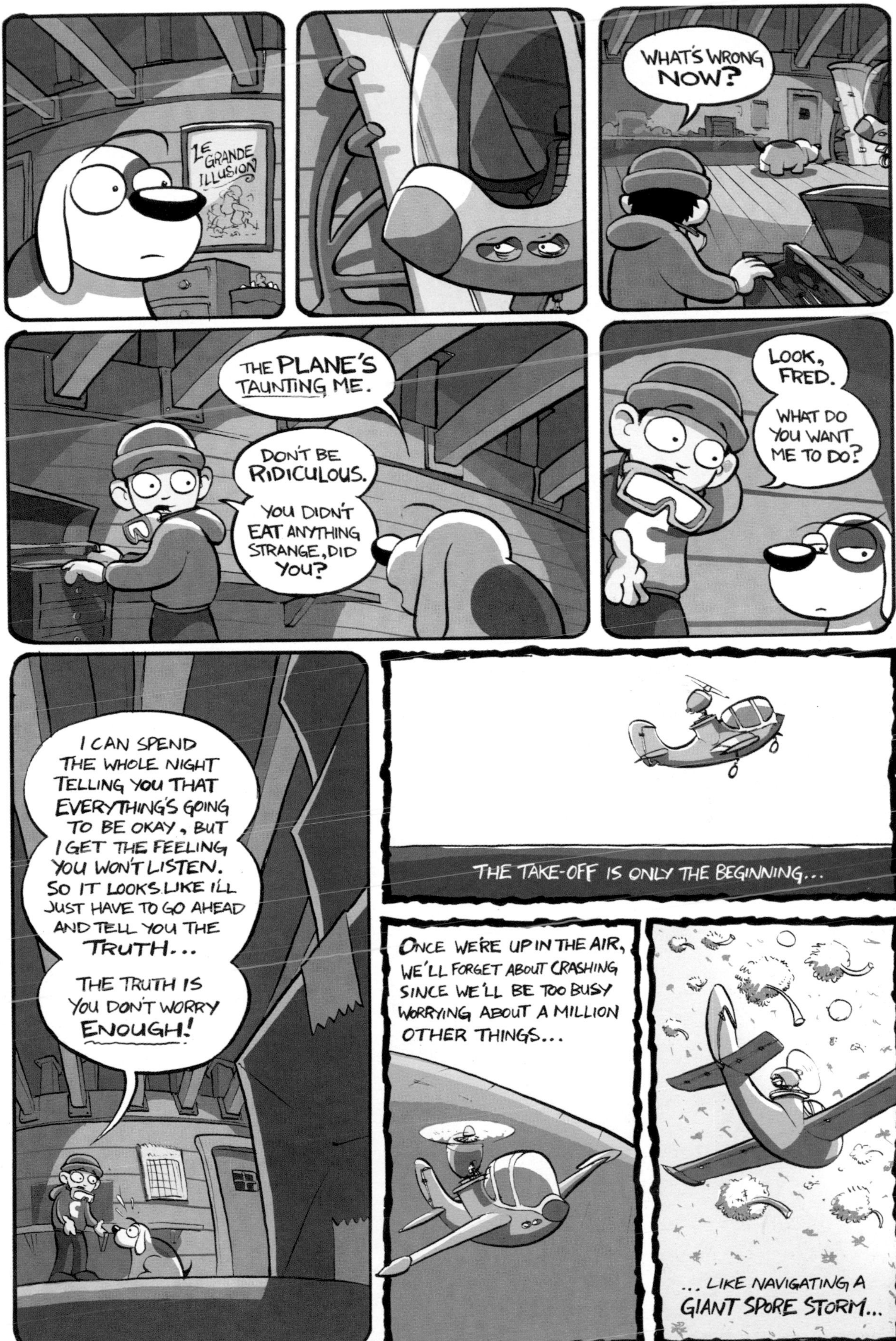
LE GRANDE ILLUSION
WHAT'S WRONG NOW?
THE PLANE'S TAUNTING ME.
DON'T BE RIDICULOUS.
YOU DIDN'T EAT ANYTHING STRANGE, DID YOU?
LOOK, FRED.
WHAT DO YOU WANT ME TO DO?
I CAN SPEND THE WHOLE NIGHT TELLING YOU THAT EVERYTHING'S GOING TO BE OKAY, BUT I GET THE FEELING YOU WON'T LISTEN. SO IT LOOKS LIKE I'LL JUST HAVE TO GO AHEAD AND TELL YOU THE TRUTH...
THE TRUTH IS YOU DON'T WORRY ENOUGH!
THE TAKE-OFF IS ONLY THE BEGINNING...
ONCE WE'RE UP IN THE AIR, WE'LL FORGET ABOUT CRASHING SINCE WE'LL BE TOO BUSY WORRYING ABOUT A MILLION OTHER THINGS...
...LIKE NAVIGATING A GIANT SPORE STORM...

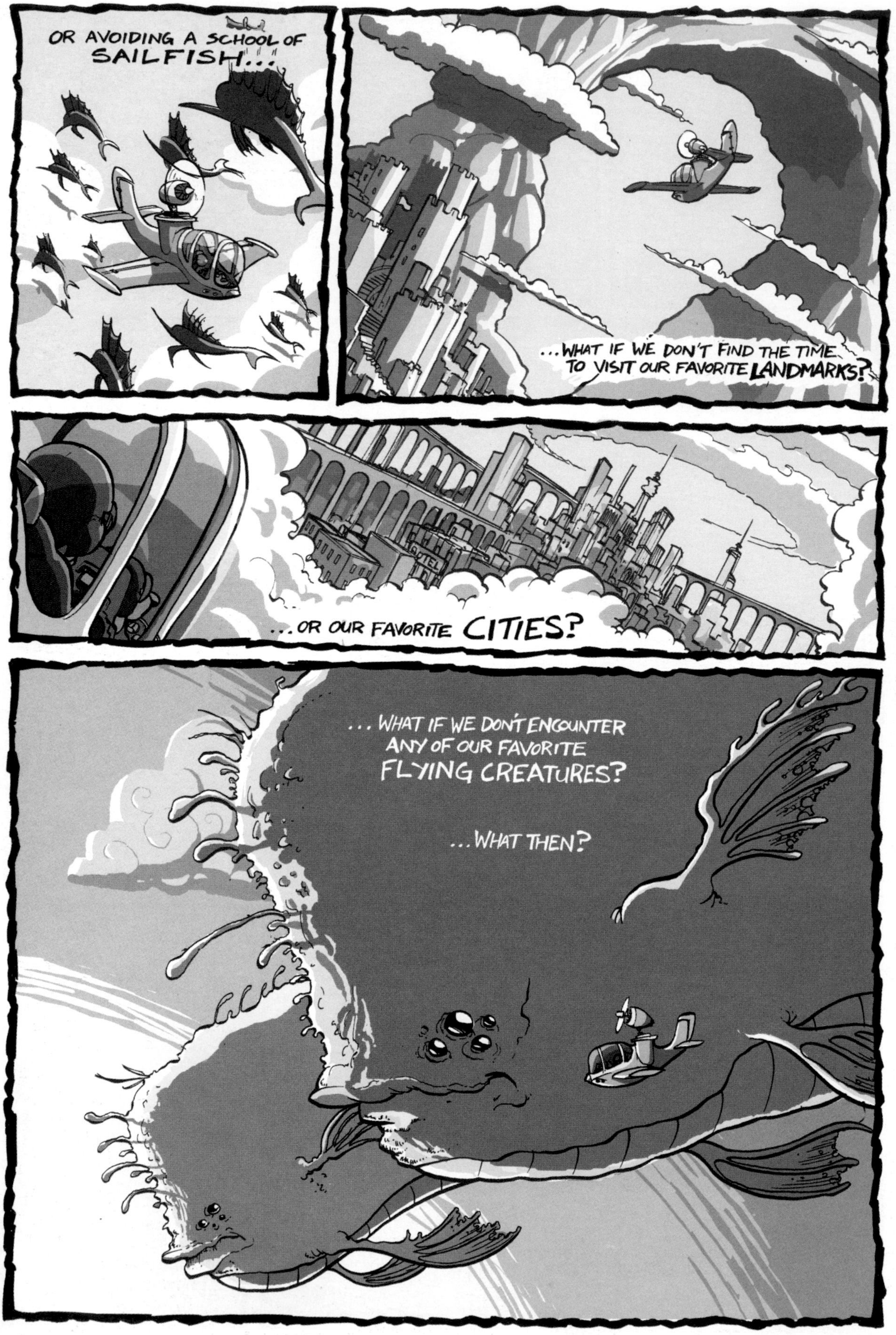
OR AVOIDING A SCHOOL OF SAILFISH...
...WHAT IF WE DON'T FIND THE TIME TO VISIT OUR FAVORITE LANDMARKS?
...OR OUR FAVORITE CITIES?
...WHAT IF WE DON'T ENCOUNTER ANY OF OUR FAVORITE FLYING CREATURES?
...WHAT THEN?

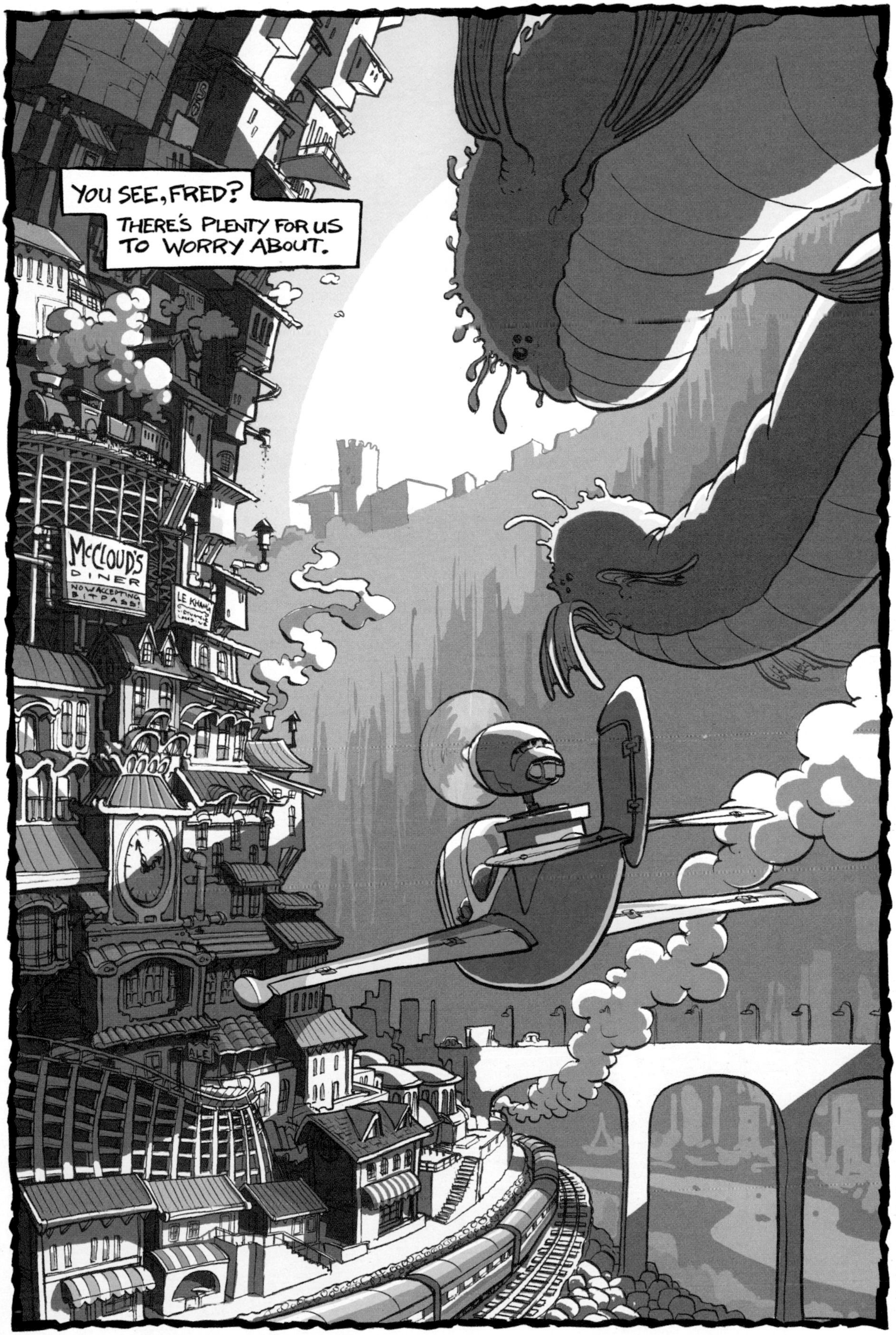
YOU SEE, FRED?
THERE'S PLENTY FOR US TO WORRY ABOUT.
McCLOUD'S DINER
NOW ACCEPTING BITPASS!
LE KHANA
ALE

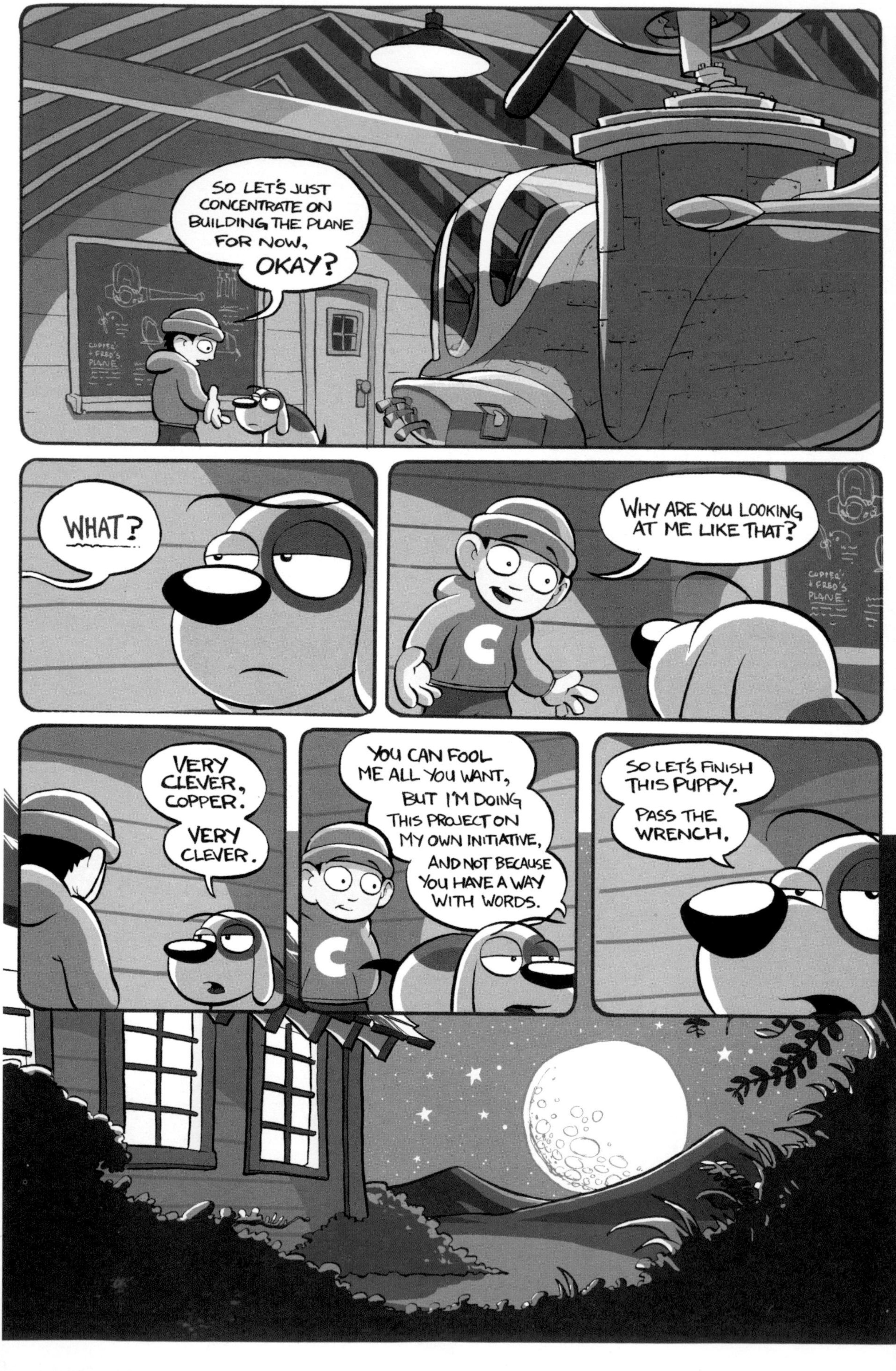
SO LET'S JUST CONCENTRATE ON BUILDING THE PLANE FOR NOW, OKAY?
COPPER + FRED'S PLANE
WHAT?
WHY ARE YOU LOOKING AT ME LIKE THAT?
COPPER + FRED'S PLANE
VERY CLEVER, COPPER.
VERY CLEVER.
YOU CAN FOOL ME ALL YOU WANT,
BUT I'M DOING THIS PROJECT ON MY OWN INITIATIVE,
AND NOT BECAUSE YOU HAVE A WAY WITH WORDS.
SO LET'S FINISH THIS PUPPY.
PASS THE WRENCH.

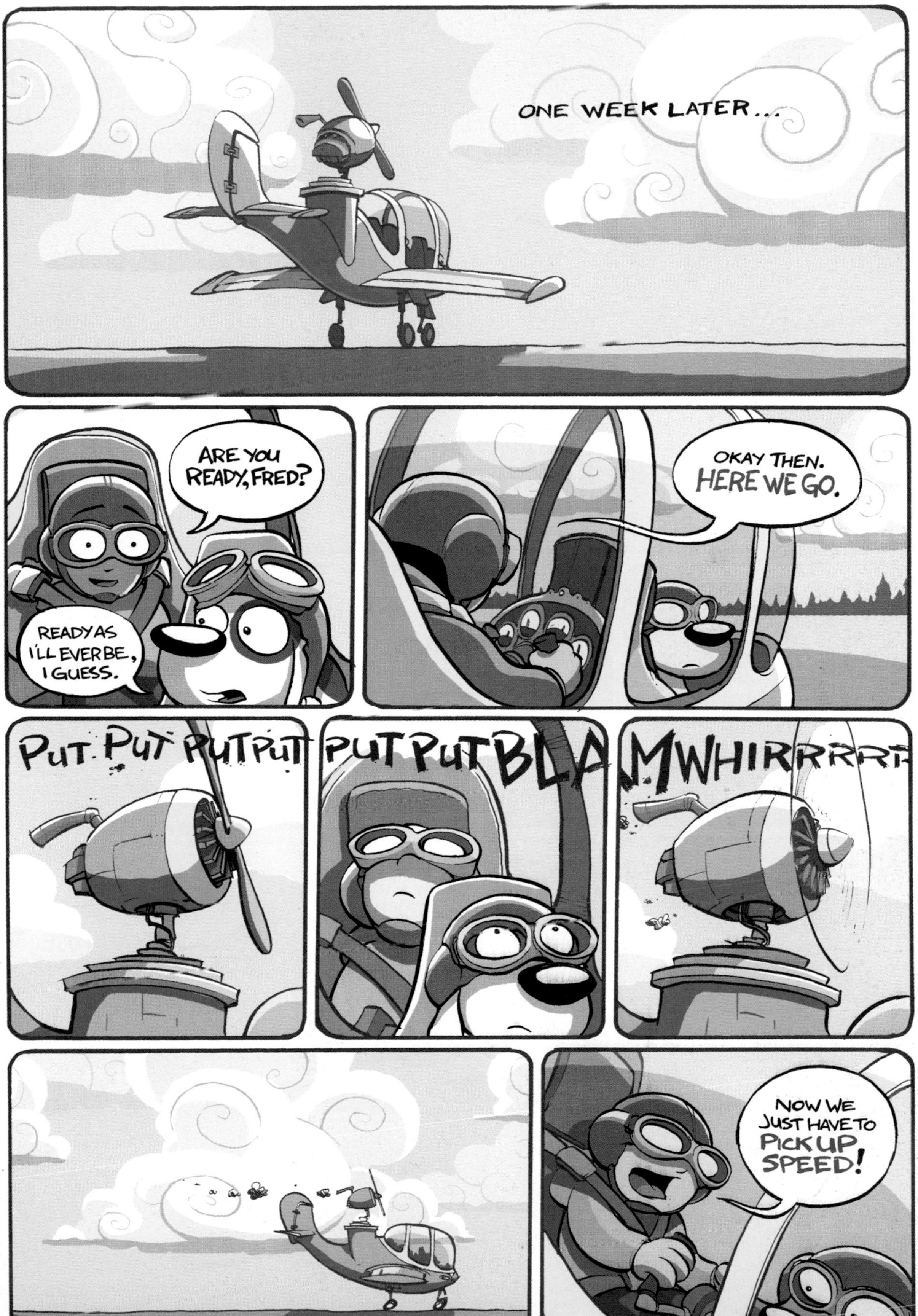
ONE WEEK LATER...
ARE YOU READY, FRED?
READY AS I'LL EVER BE, I GUESS.
OKAY THEN. HERE WE GO.
PUT PUT PUTPUT PUT PUT BLAM WHIRRRRR
NOW WE JUST HAVE TO PICK UP SPEED!

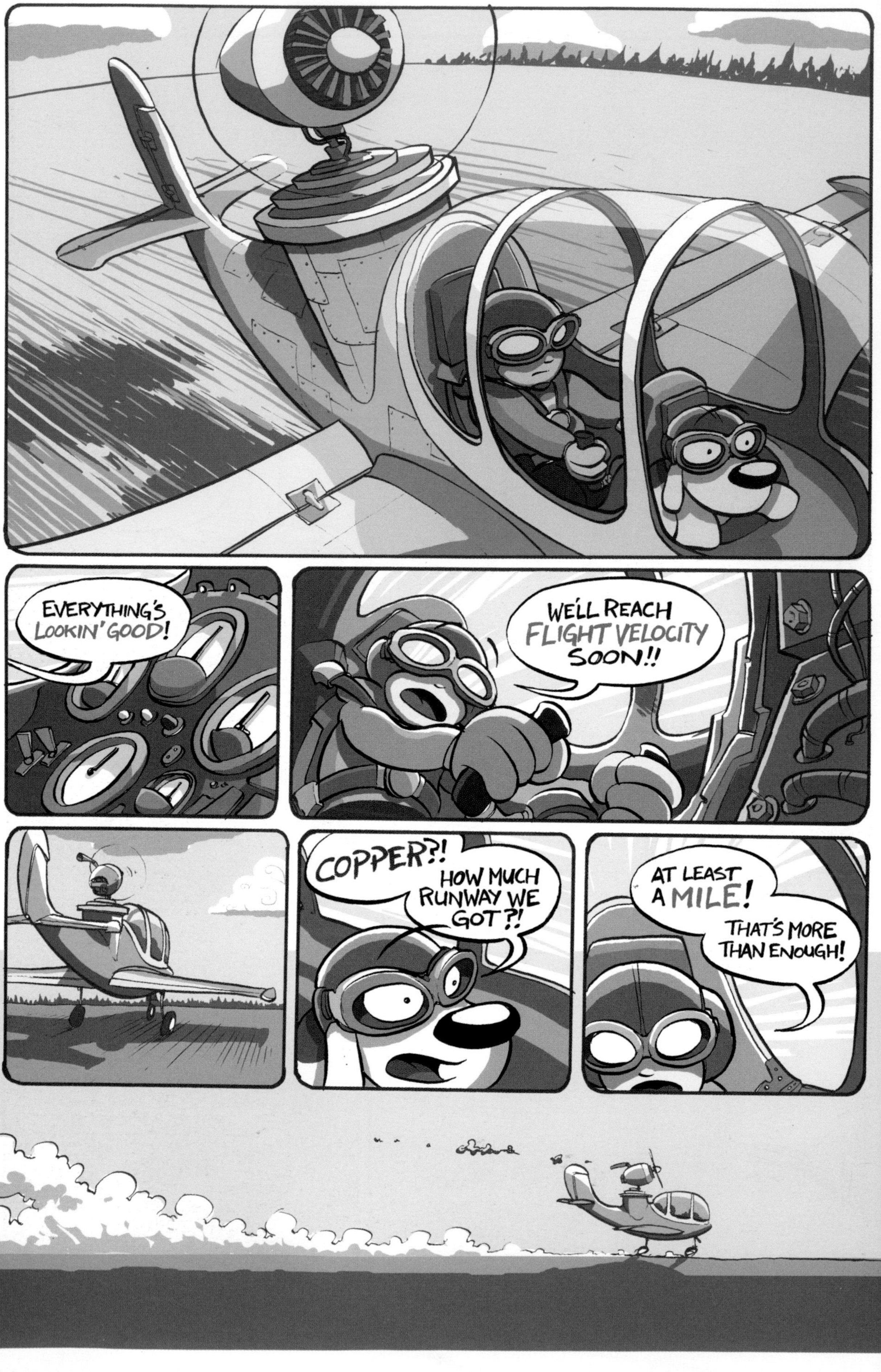
EVERYTHING'S LOOKIN' GOOD!
WE'LL REACH FLIGHT VELOCITY SOON!!
COPPER?!
HOW MUCH RUNWAY WE GOT?!
AT LEAST A MILE!
THAT'S MORE THAN ENOUGH!

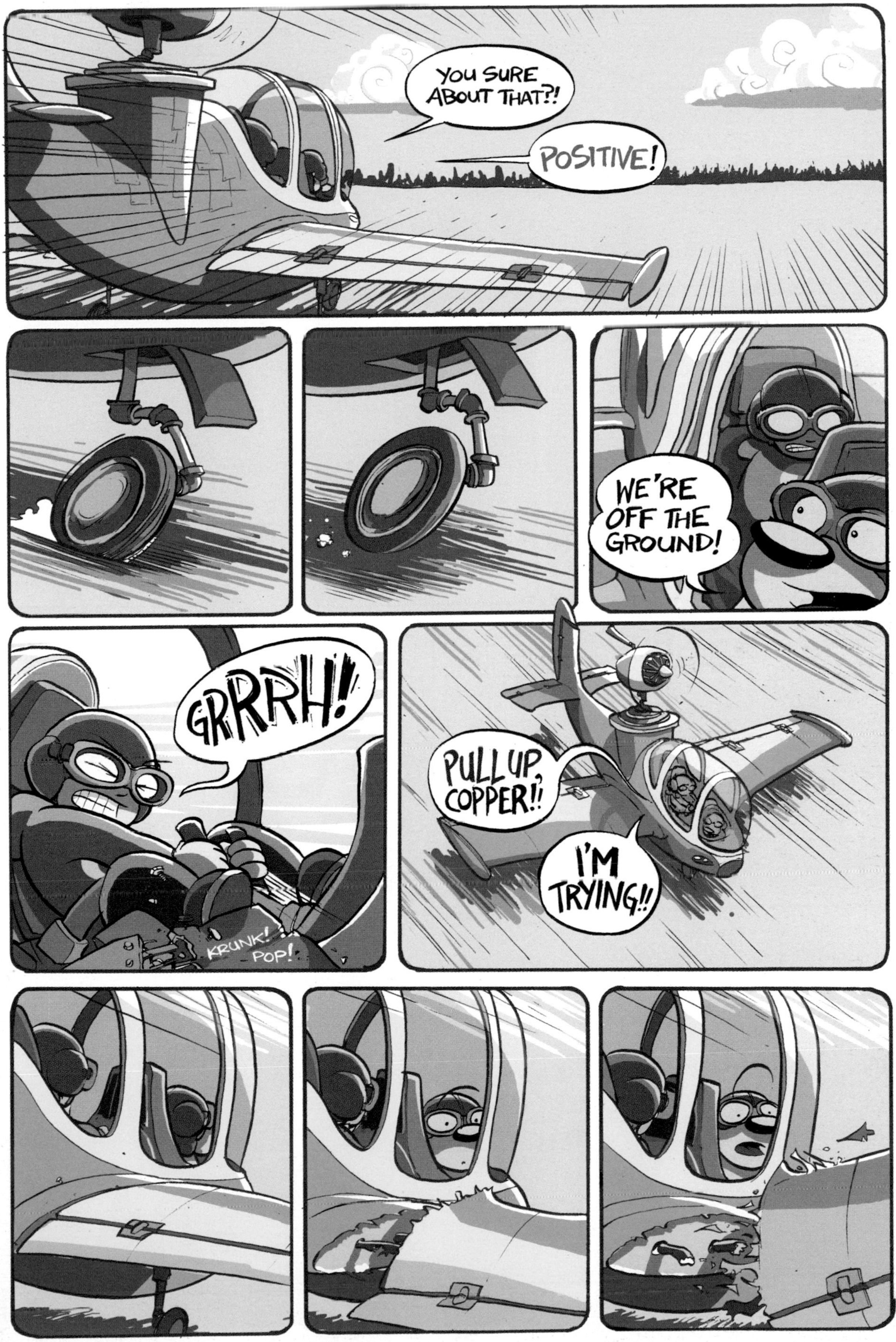
YOU SURE ABOUT THAT?!
POSITIVE!
WE'RE OFF THE GROUND!
GRRRH!
KRUNK!
POP!
PULL UP, COPPER!!
I'M TRYING!!

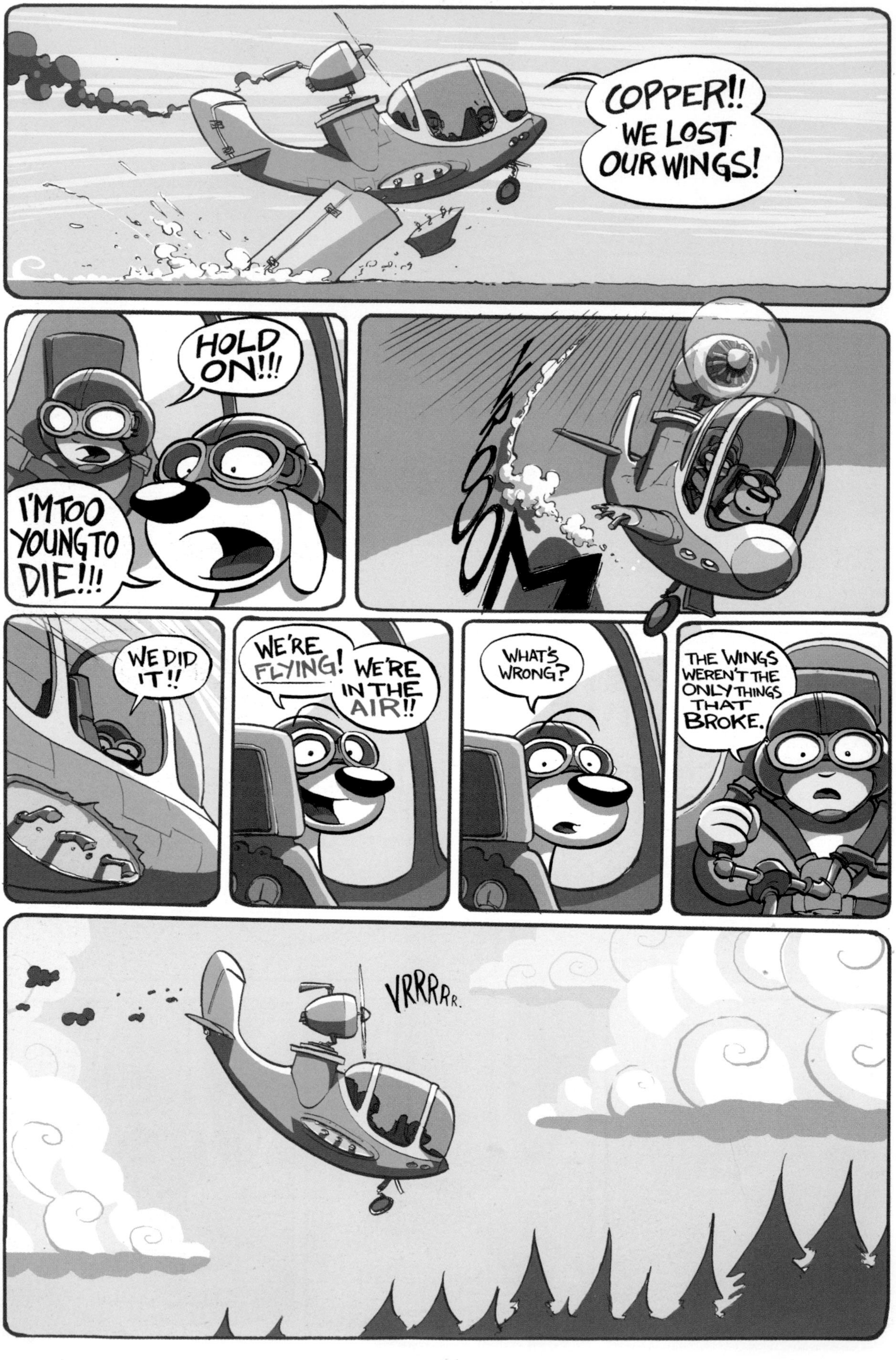
COPPER!! WE LOST OUR WINGS!
HOLD ON!!!
I'M TOO YOUNG TO DIE!!!
VROOOM
WE DID IT!!
WE'RE FLYING!
WE'RE IN THE AIR!!
WHAT'S WRONG?
THE WINGS WEREN'T THE ONLY THINGS THAT BROKE.
VRRRRR.

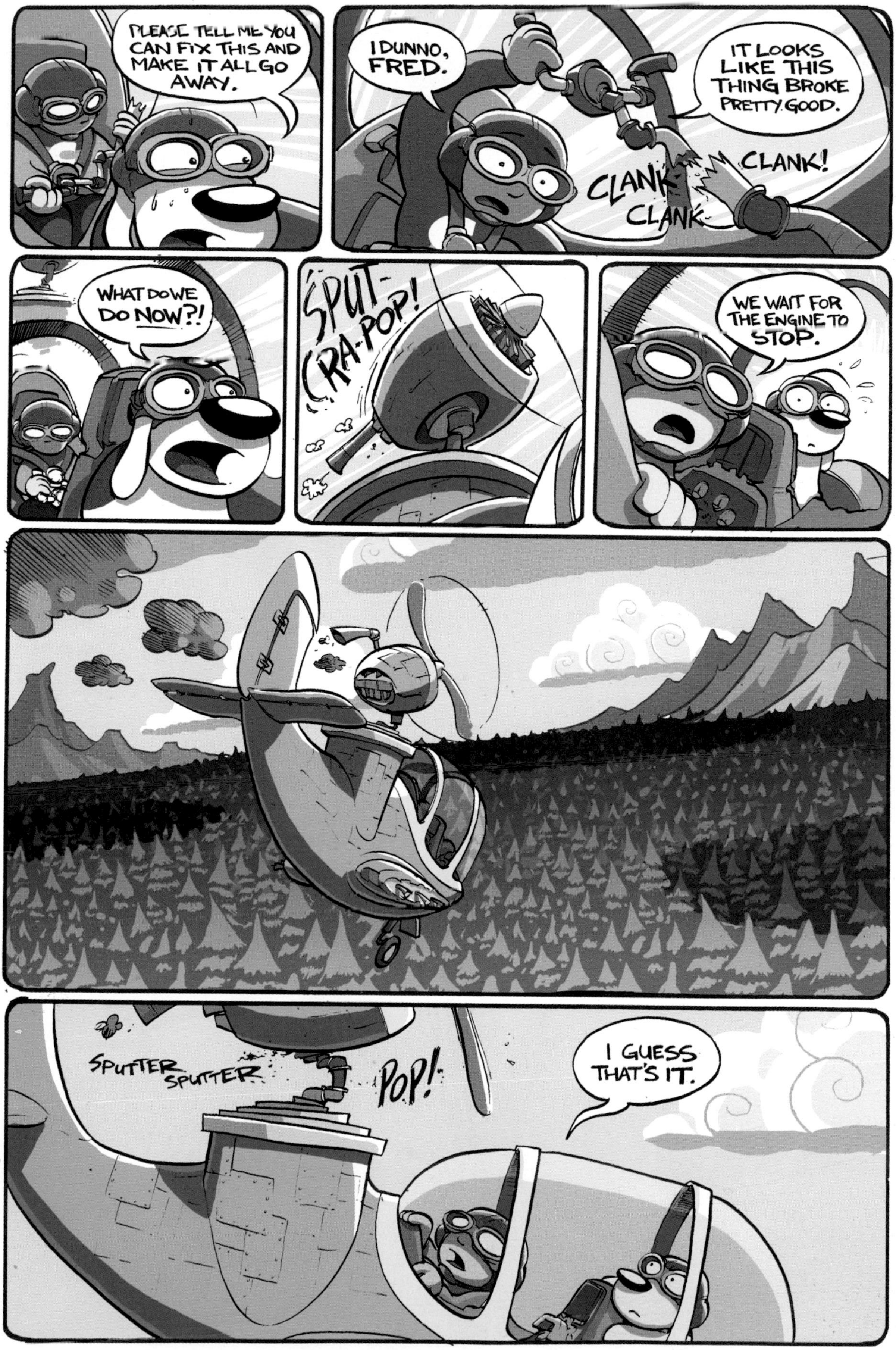
PLEASE TELL ME YOU CAN FIX THIS AND MAKE IT ALL GO AWAY.
I DUNNO, FRED.
IT LOOKS LIKE THIS THING BROKE PRETTY GOOD.
CLANK
CLANK
CLANK!
WHAT DO WE DO NOW?!
SPUT
CRA-POP!
WE WAIT FOR THE ENGINE TO STOP.
SPUTTER SPUTTER
POP!
I GUESS THAT'S IT.

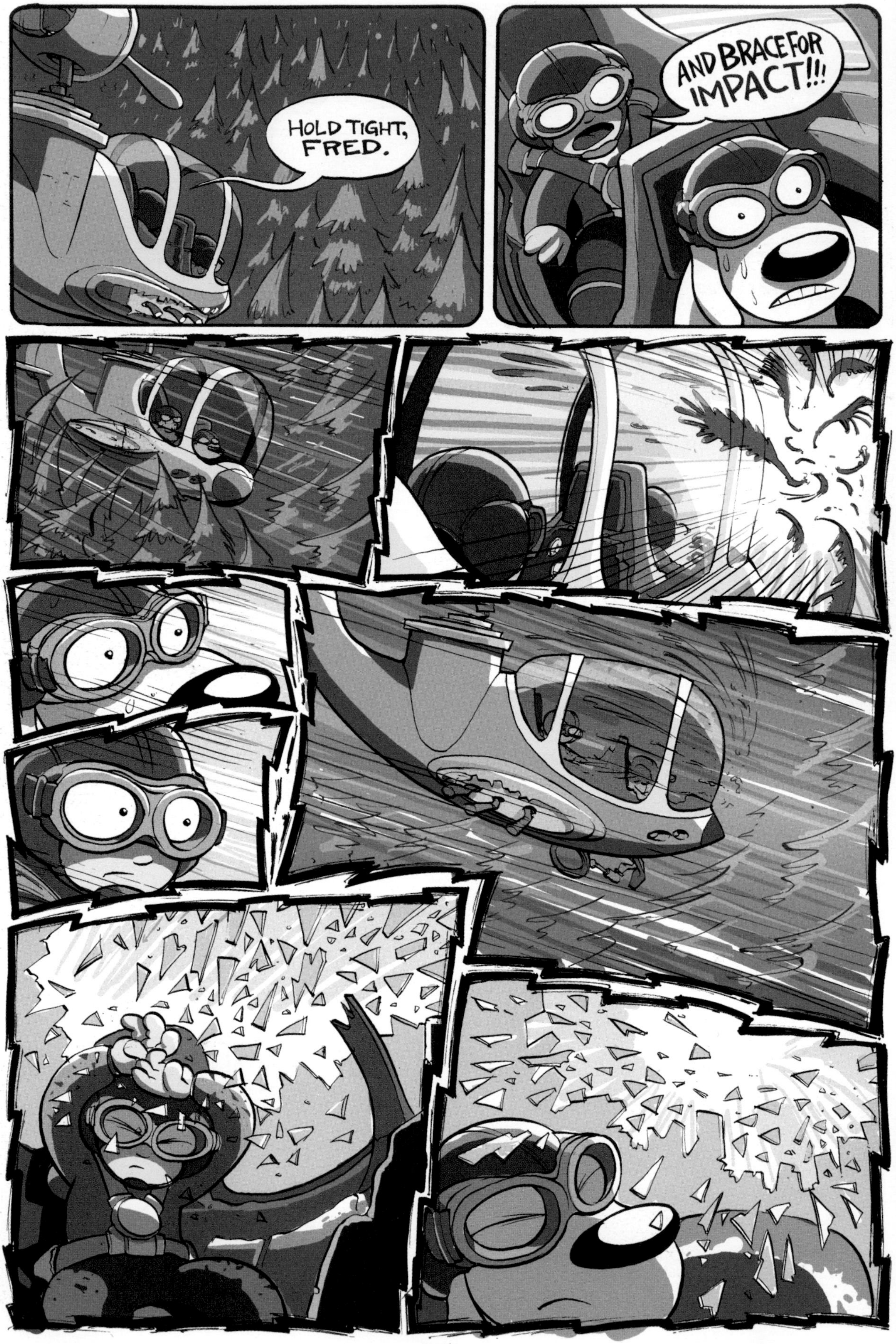
HOLD TIGHT, FRED.
AND BRACE FOR IMPACT!!!

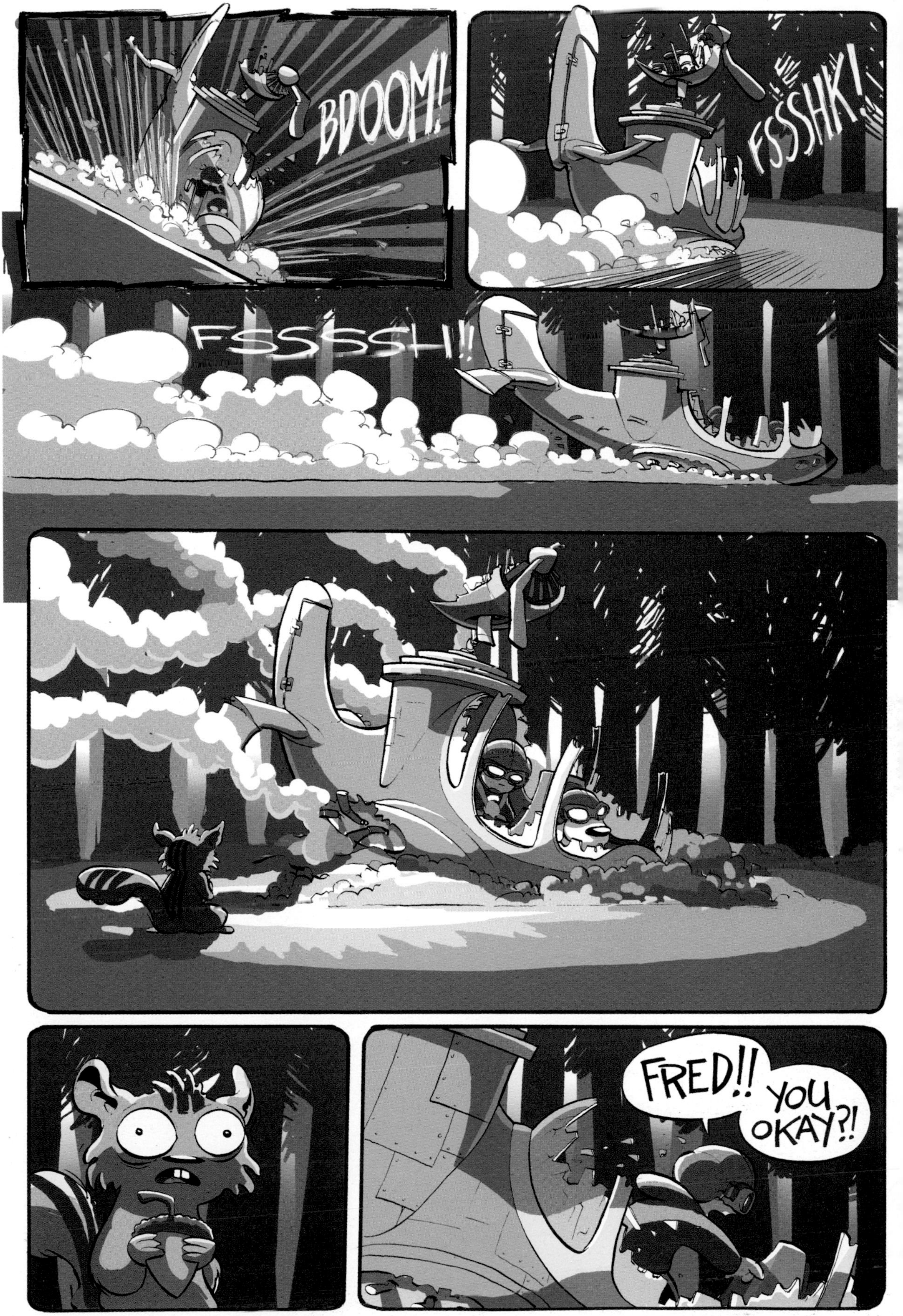
BDOOM!
FSSSHK!
FSSSSH!!
FRED!!
YOU OKAY?!

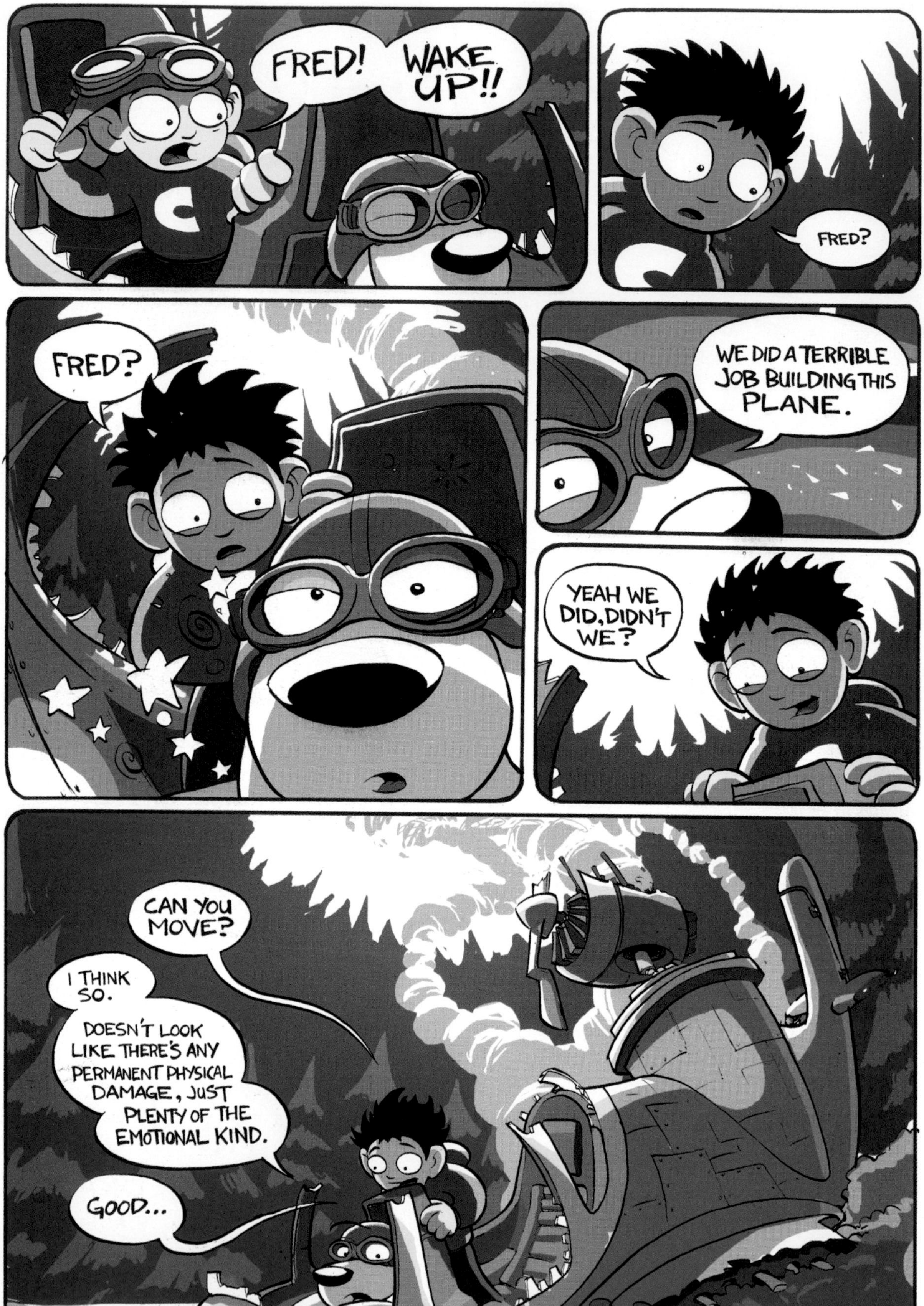
FRED!
WAKE UP!!
FRED?
FRED?
WE DID A TERRIBLE JOB BUILDING THIS PLANE.
YEAH WE DID, DIDN'T WE?
CAN YOU MOVE?
I THINK SO.
DOESN'T LOOK LIKE THERE'S ANY PERMANENT PHYSICAL DAMAGE, JUST PLENTY OF THE EMOTIONAL KIND.
GOOD...

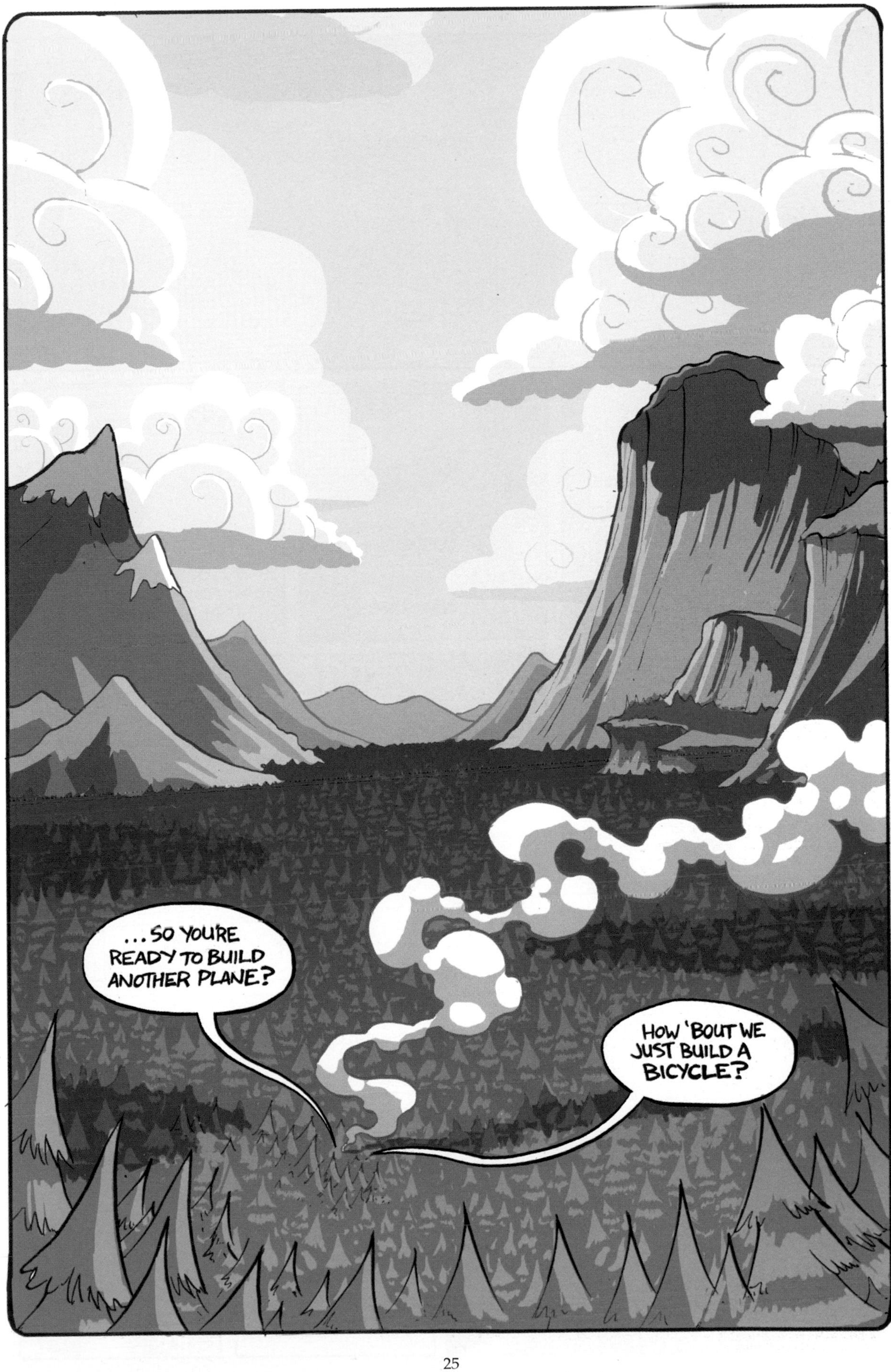
...SO YOU'RE READY TO BUILD ANOTHER PLANE?
HOW 'BOUT WE JUST BUILD A BICYCLE?

"Hugo Earheart" by Jake Parker

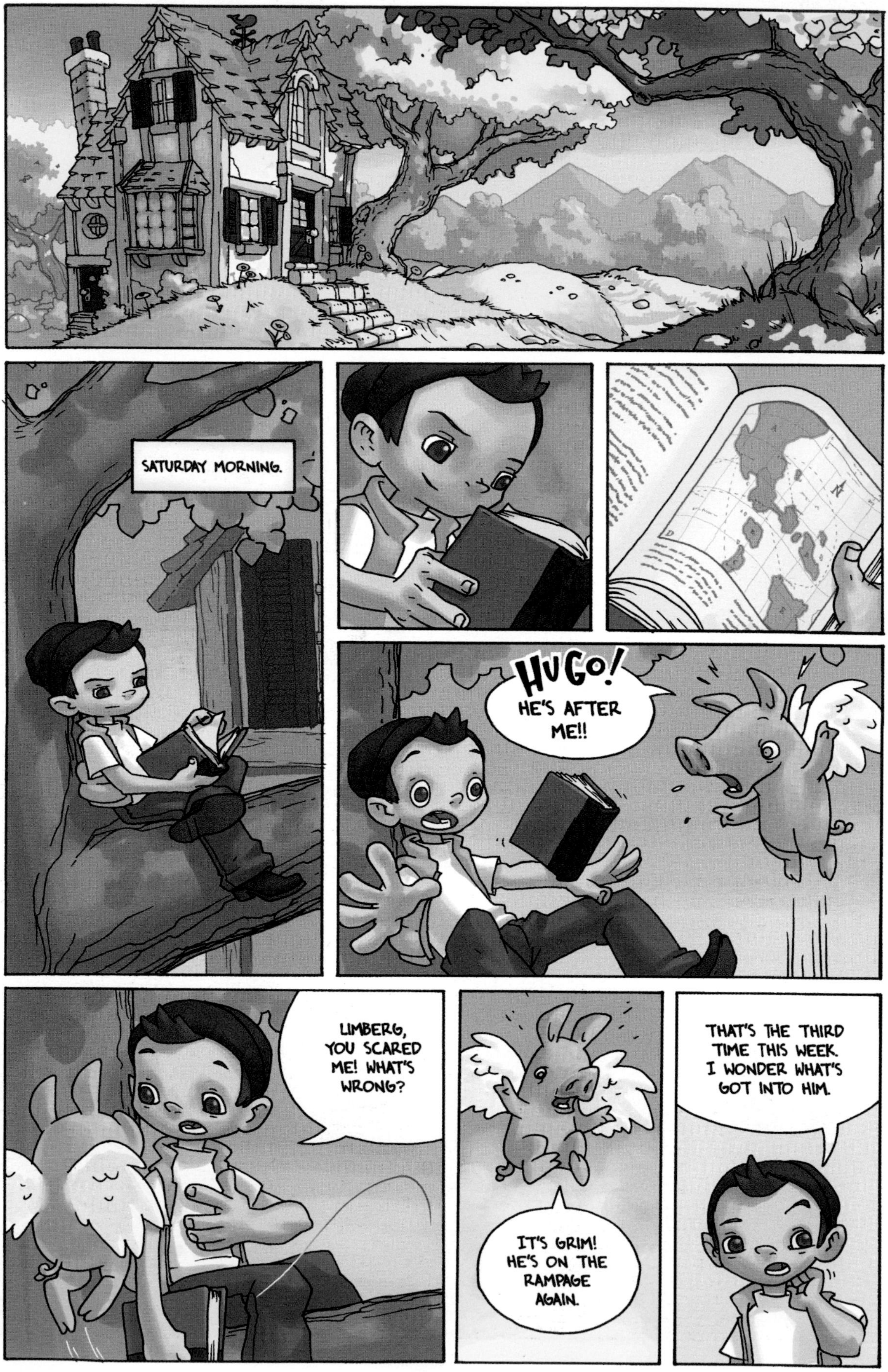

SATURDAY MORNING.
HUGO!
HE'S AFTER ME!!
LIMBERG, YOU SCARED ME! WHAT'S WRONG?
IT'S GRIM! HE'S ON THE RAMPAGE AGAIN.
THAT'S THE THIRD TIME THIS WEEK. I WONDER WHAT'S GOT INTO HIM.

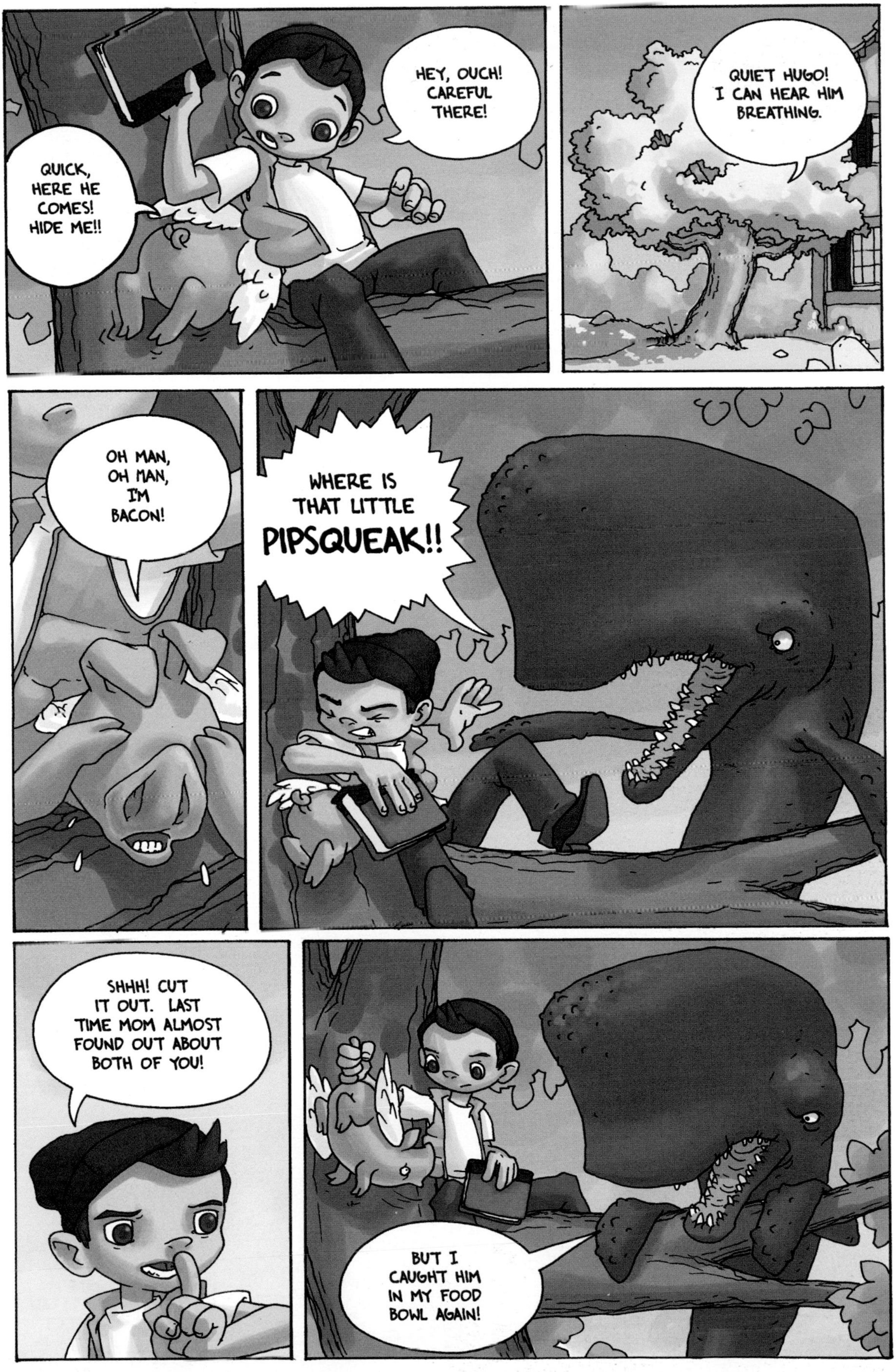
QUICK, HERE HE COMES! HIDE ME!!
HEY, OUCH! CAREFUL THERE!
QUIET HUGO! I CAN HEAR HIM BREATHING.
OH MAN, OH MAN, I'M BACON!
WHERE IS THAT LITTLE PIPSQUEAK!!
SHHH! CUT IT OUT. LAST TIME MOM ALMOST FOUND OUT ABOUT BOTH OF YOU!
BUT I CAUGHT HIM IN MY FOOD BOWL AGAIN!

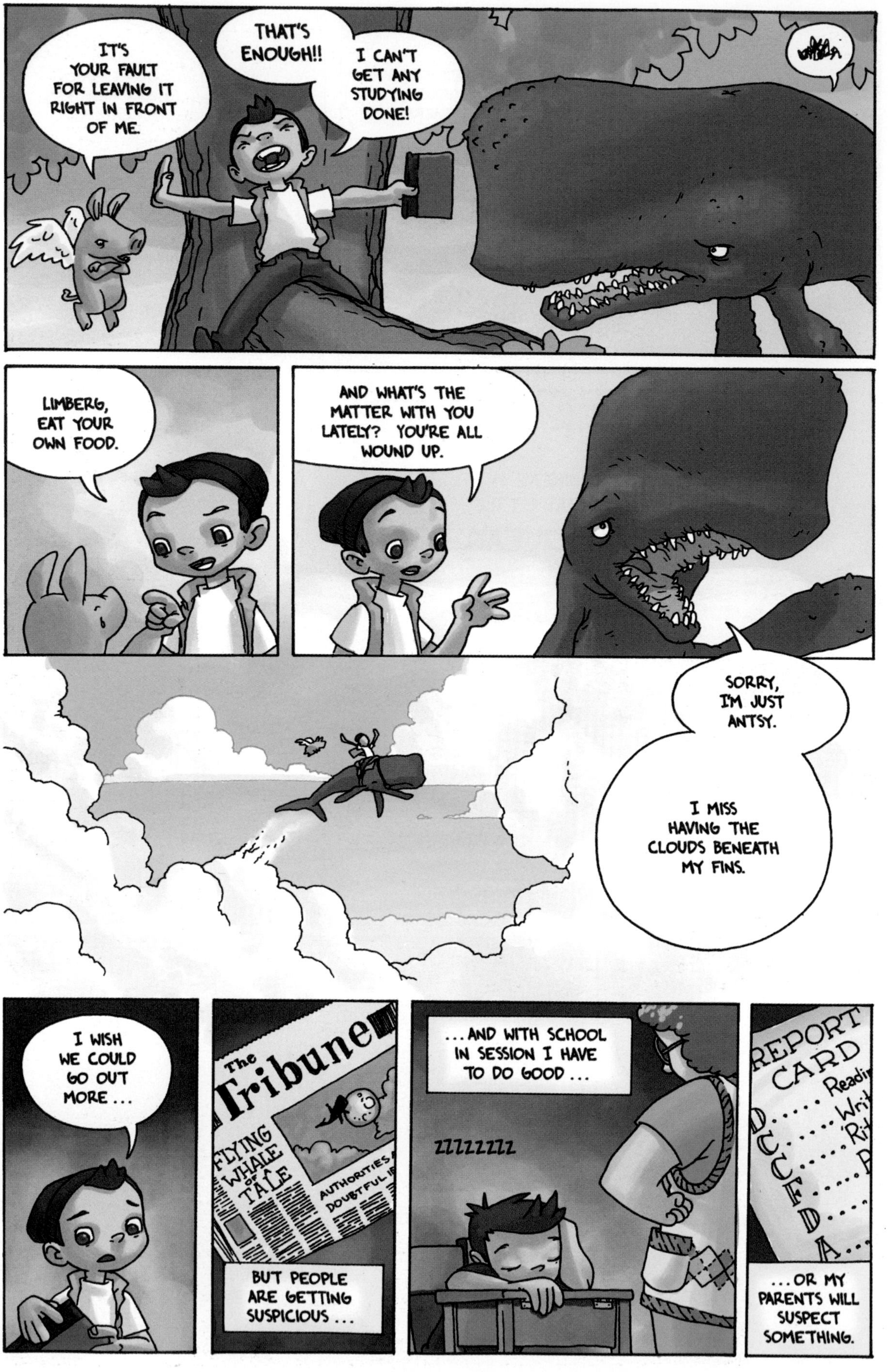
IT'S YOUR FAULT FOR LEAVING IT RIGHT IN FRONT OF ME.
THAT'S ENOUGH!!
I CAN'T GET ANY STUDYING DONE!
LIMBERG, EAT YOUR OWN FOOD.
AND WHAT'S THE MATTER WITH YOU LATELY? YOU'RE ALL WOUND UP.
SORRY, I'M JUST ANTSY.
I MISS HAVING THE CLOUDS BENEATH MY FINS.
I WISH WE COULD GO OUT MORE...
The Tribune
FLYING WHALE OF A TALE
AUTHORITIES DOUBTFUL
BUT PEOPLE ARE GETTING SUSPICIOUS...
...AND WITH SCHOOL IN SESSION I HAVE TO DO GOOD...
ZZZZZZZ
REPORT CARD
...OR MY PARENTS WILL SUSPECT SOMETHING.

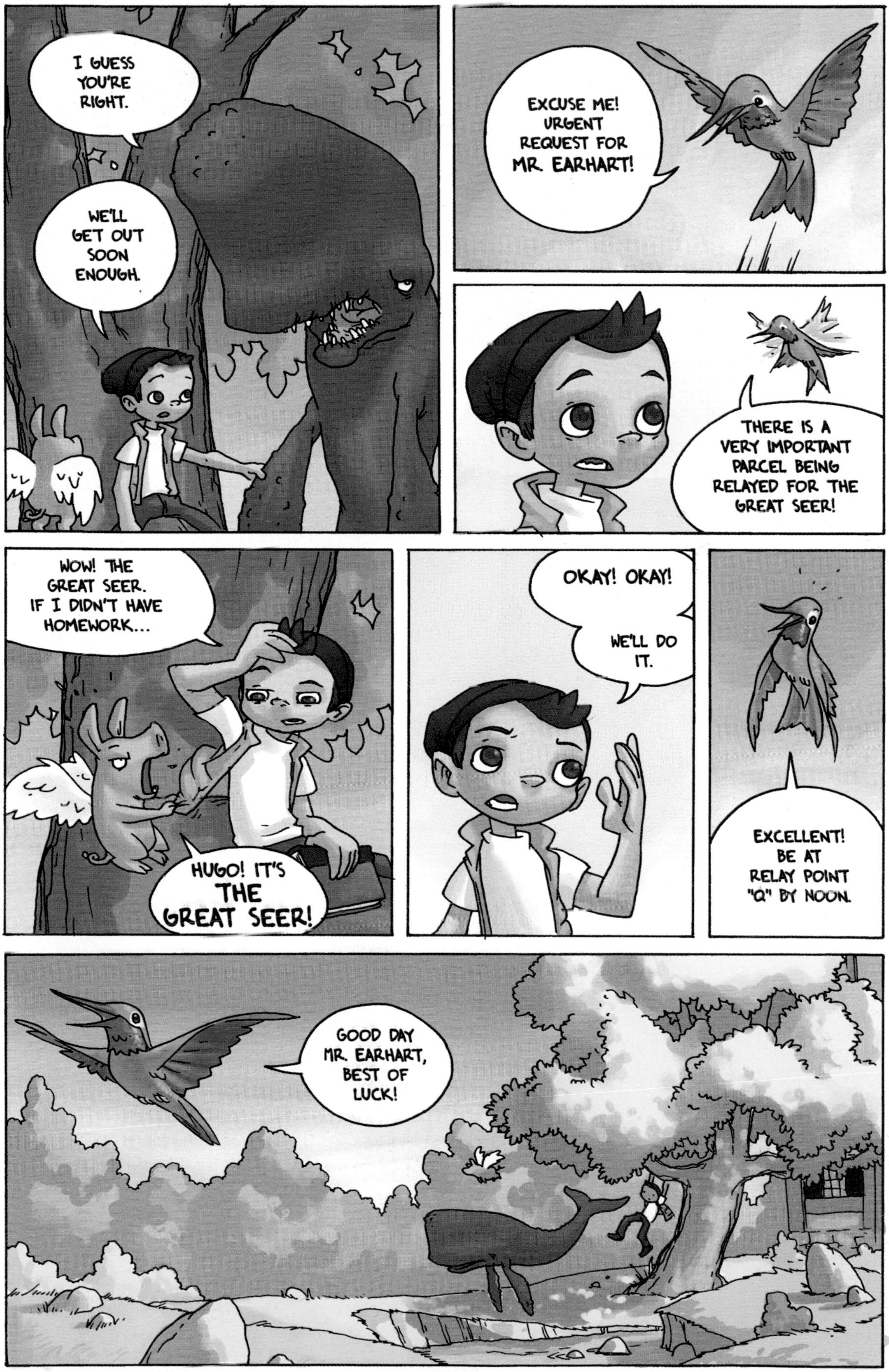
I GUESS YOU'RE RIGHT.
WE'LL GET OUT SOON ENOUGH.
EXCUSE ME! URGENT REQUEST FOR MR. EARHART!
THERE IS A VERY IMPORTANT PARCEL BEING RELAYED FOR THE GREAT SEER!
WOW! THE GREAT SEER. IF I DIDN'T HAVE HOMEWORK...
HUGO! IT'S THE GREAT SEER!
OKAY! OKAY!
WE'LL DO IT.
EXCELLENT! BE AT RELAY POINT "Q" BY NOON.
GOOD DAY MR. EARHART, BEST OF LUCK!

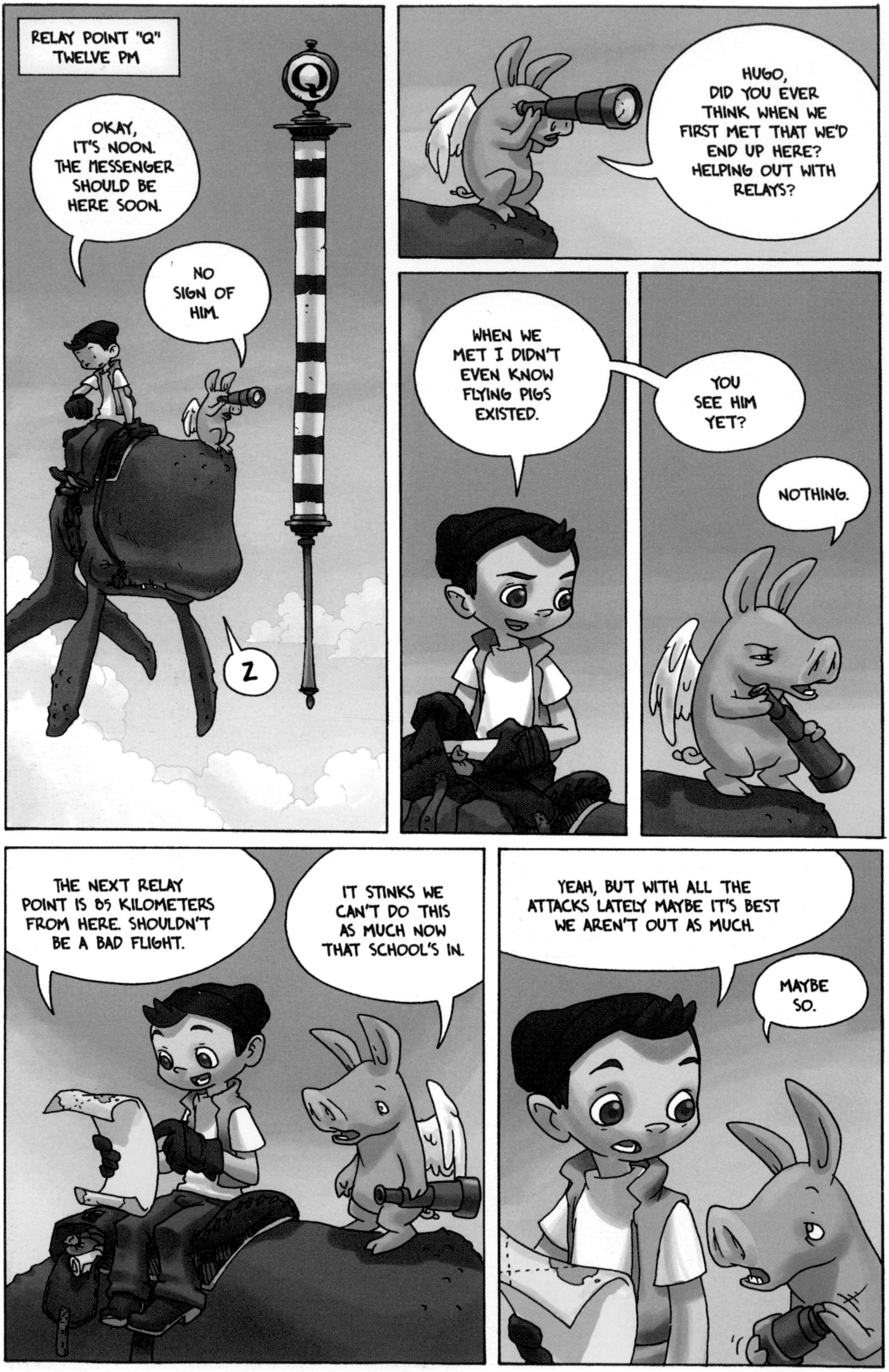
RELAY POINT "Q" TWELVE PM
OKAY, IT'S NOON. THE MESSENGER SHOULD BE HERE SOON.
NO SIGN OF HIM.
Z
HUGO, DID YOU EVER THINK WHEN WE FIRST MET THAT WE'D END UP HERE? HELPING OUT WITH RELAYS?
WHEN WE MET I DIDN'T EVEN KNOW FLYING PIGS EXISTED.
YOU SEE HIM YET?
NOTHING.
THE NEXT RELAY POINT IS 85 KILOMETERS FROM HERE. SHOULDN'T BE A BAD FLIGHT.
IT STINKS WE CAN'T DO THIS AS MUCH NOW THAT SCHOOL'S IN.
YEAH, BUT WITH ALL THE ATTACKS LATELY MAYBE IT'S BEST WE AREN'T OUT AS MUCH.
MAYBE SO.

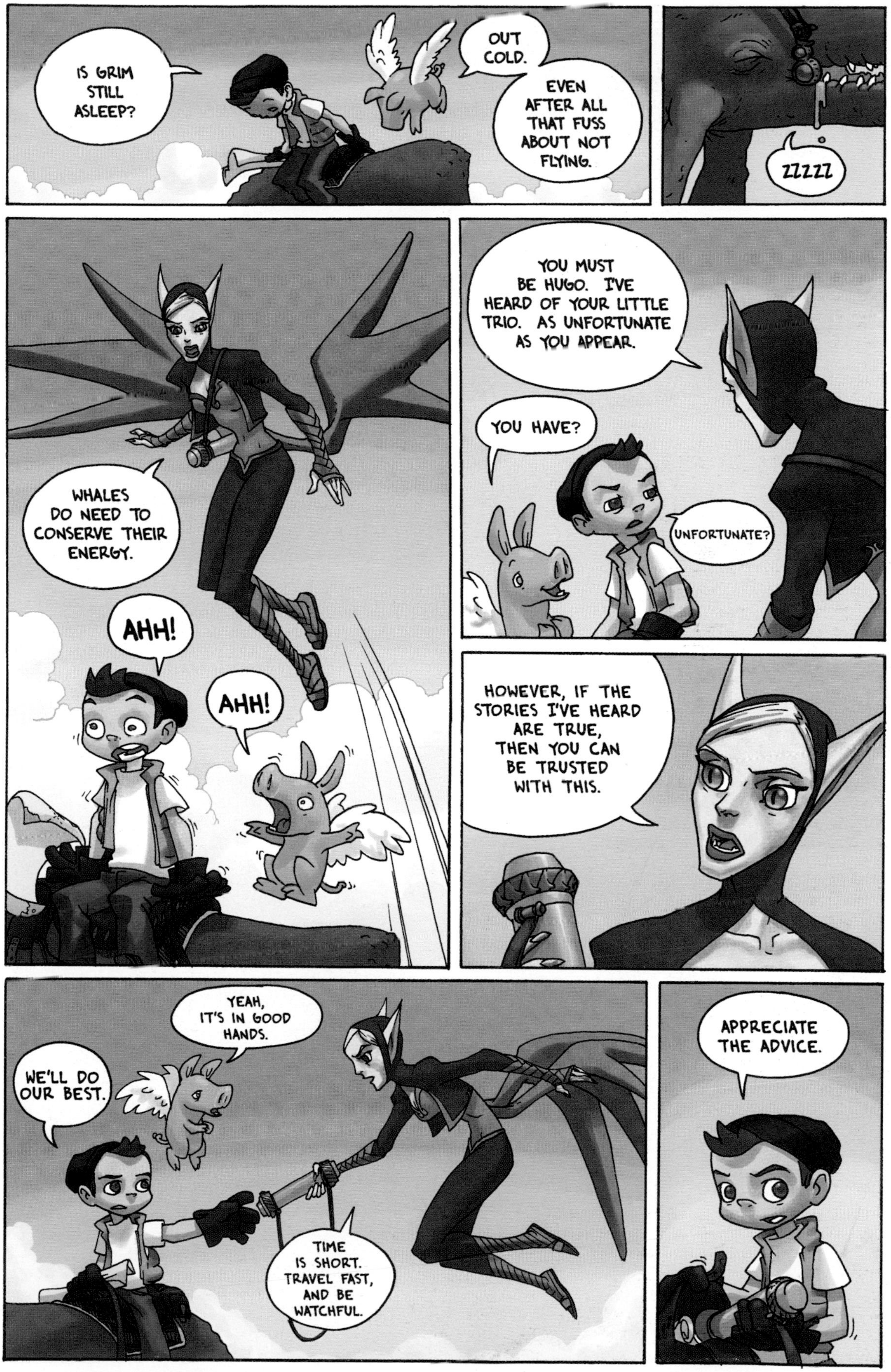
IS GRIM STILL ASLEEP?
OUT COLD.
EVEN AFTER ALL THAT FUSS ABOUT NOT FLYING.
ZZZZZ
WHALES DO NEED TO CONSERVE THEIR ENERGY.
AHH!
AHH!
YOU MUST BE HUGO. I'VE HEARD OF YOUR LITTLE TRIO. AS UNFORTUNATE AS YOU APPEAR.
YOU HAVE?
UNFORTUNATE?
HOWEVER, IF THE STORIES I'VE HEARD ARE TRUE, THEN YOU CAN BE TRUSTED WITH THIS.
WE'LL DO OUR BEST.
YEAH, IT'S IN GOOD HANDS.
TIME IS SHORT. TRAVEL FAST, AND BE WATCHFUL.
APPRECIATE THE ADVICE.

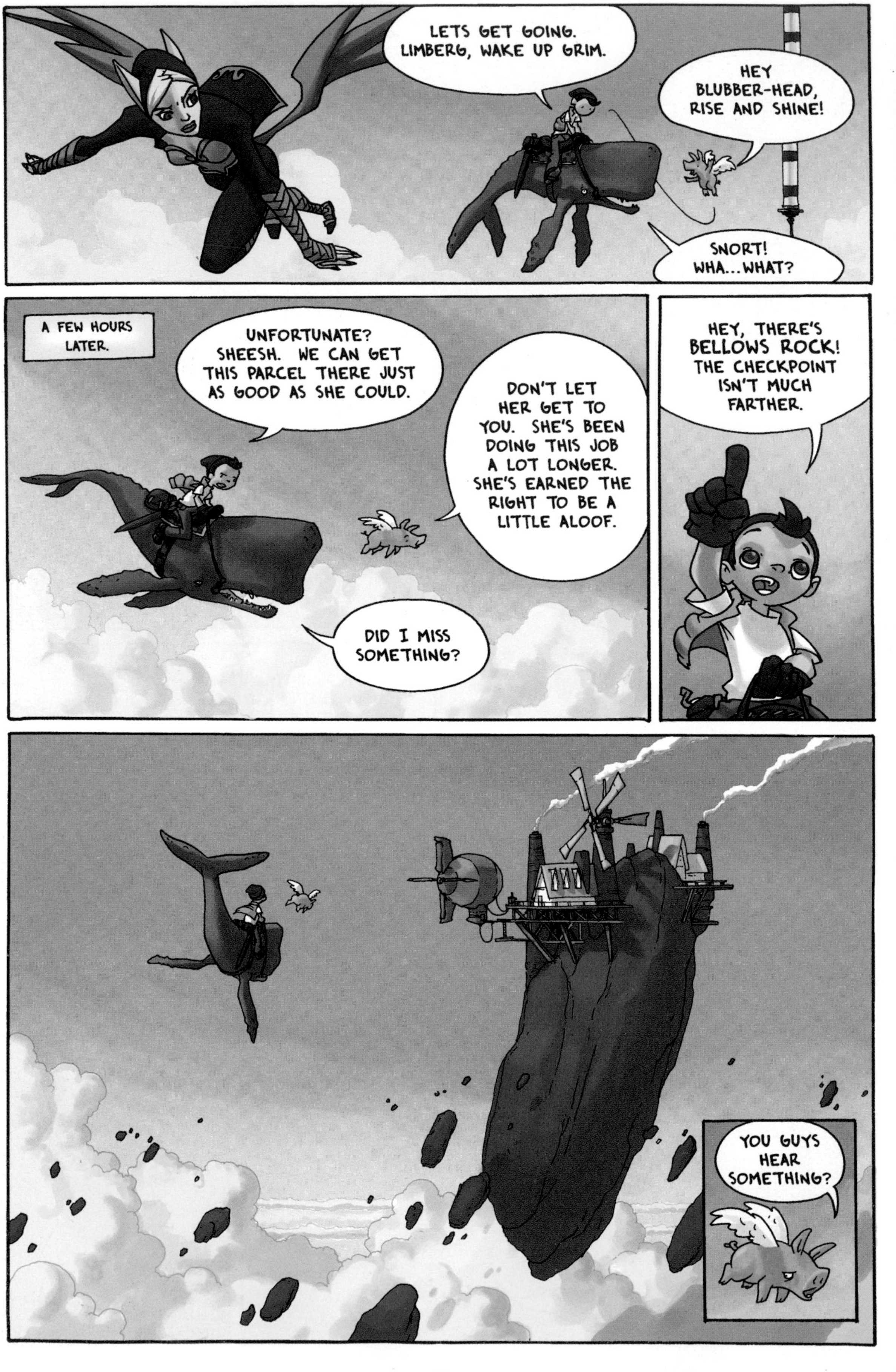
LETS GET GOING. LIMBERG, WAKE UP GRIM.
HEY BLUBBER-HEAD, RISE AND SHINE!
SNORT! WHA... WHAT?
A FEW HOURS LATER.
UNFORTUNATE? SHEESH. WE CAN GET THIS PARCEL THERE JUST AS GOOD AS SHE COULD.
DON'T LET HER GET TO YOU. SHE'S BEEN DOING THIS JOB A LOT LONGER. SHE'S EARNED THE RIGHT TO BE A LITTLE ALOOF.
DID I MISS SOMETHING?
HEY, THERE'S BELLOWS ROCK! THE CHECKPOINT ISN'T MUCH FARTHER.
YOU GUYS HEAR SOMETHING?

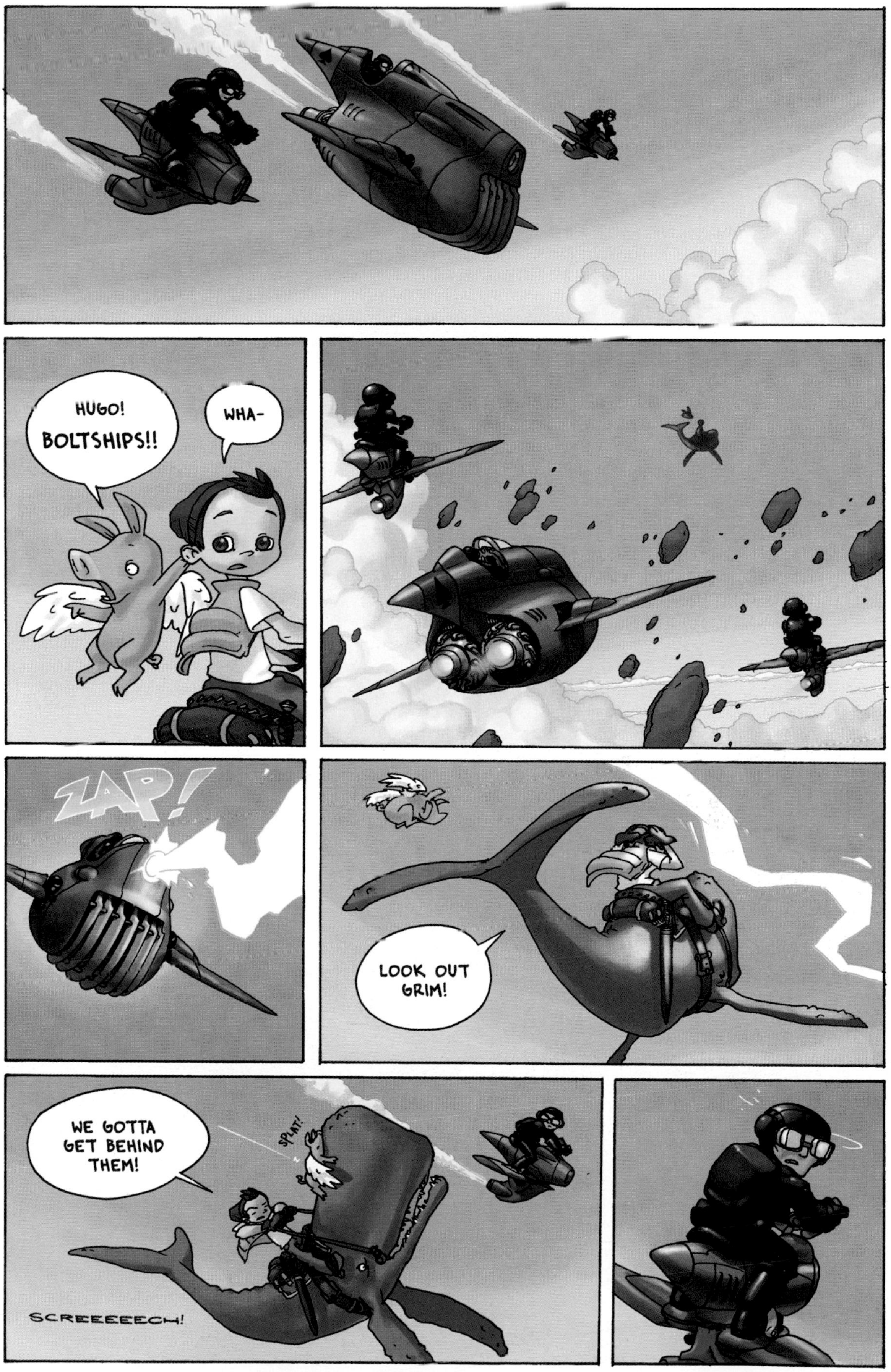
HUGO! BOLTSHIPS!!
WHA-
ZAP!
LOOK OUT GRIM!
WE GOTTA GET BEHIND THEM!
SPLAT!
SCREEEEEECH!

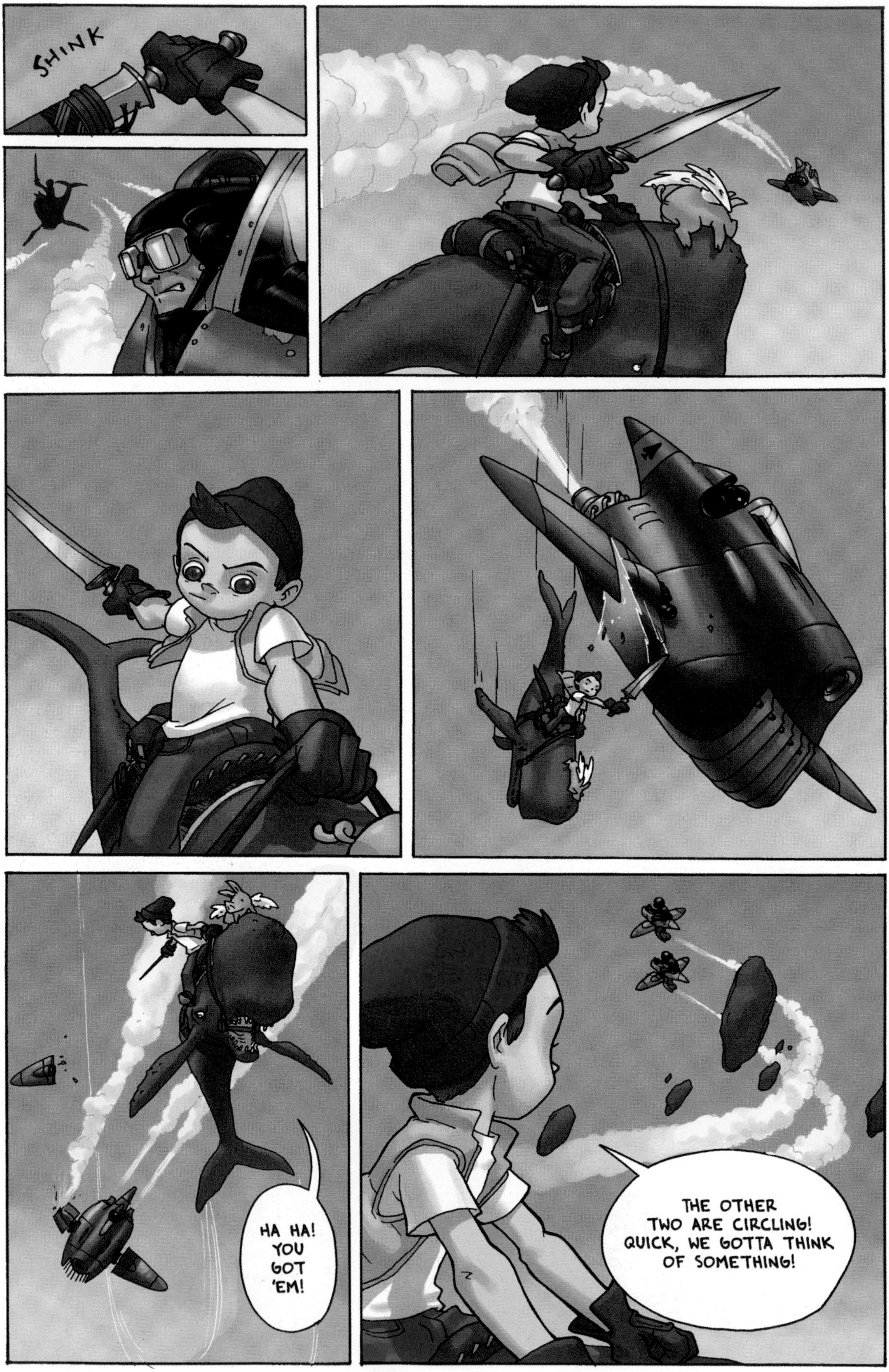
SHINK
HA HA! YOU GOT 'EM!
THE OTHER TWO ARE CIRCLING! QUICK, WE GOTTA THINK OF SOMETHING!

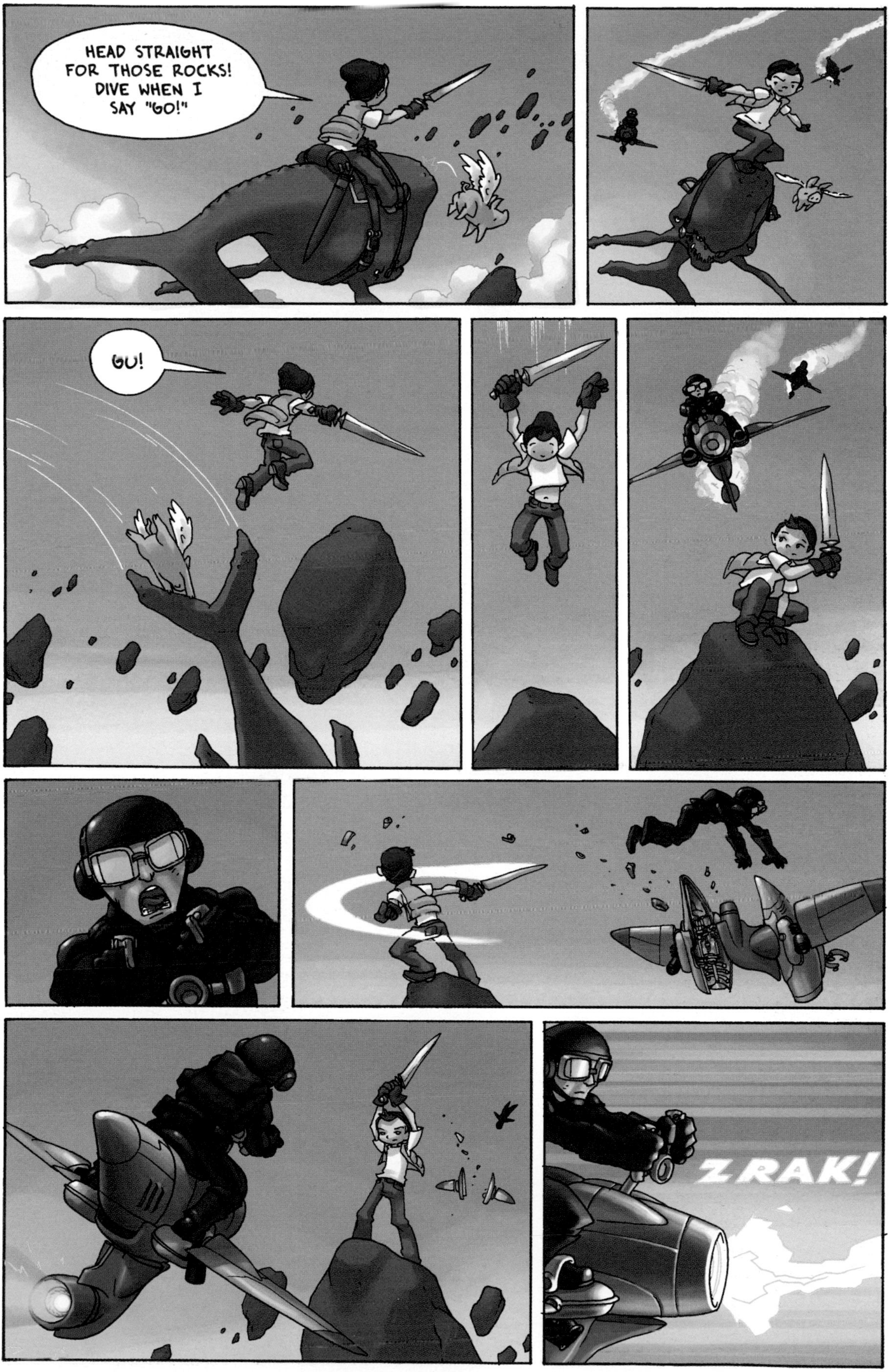
HEAD STRAIGHT FOR THOSE ROCKS! DIVE WHEN I SAY "GO!"
GO!
ZRAK!

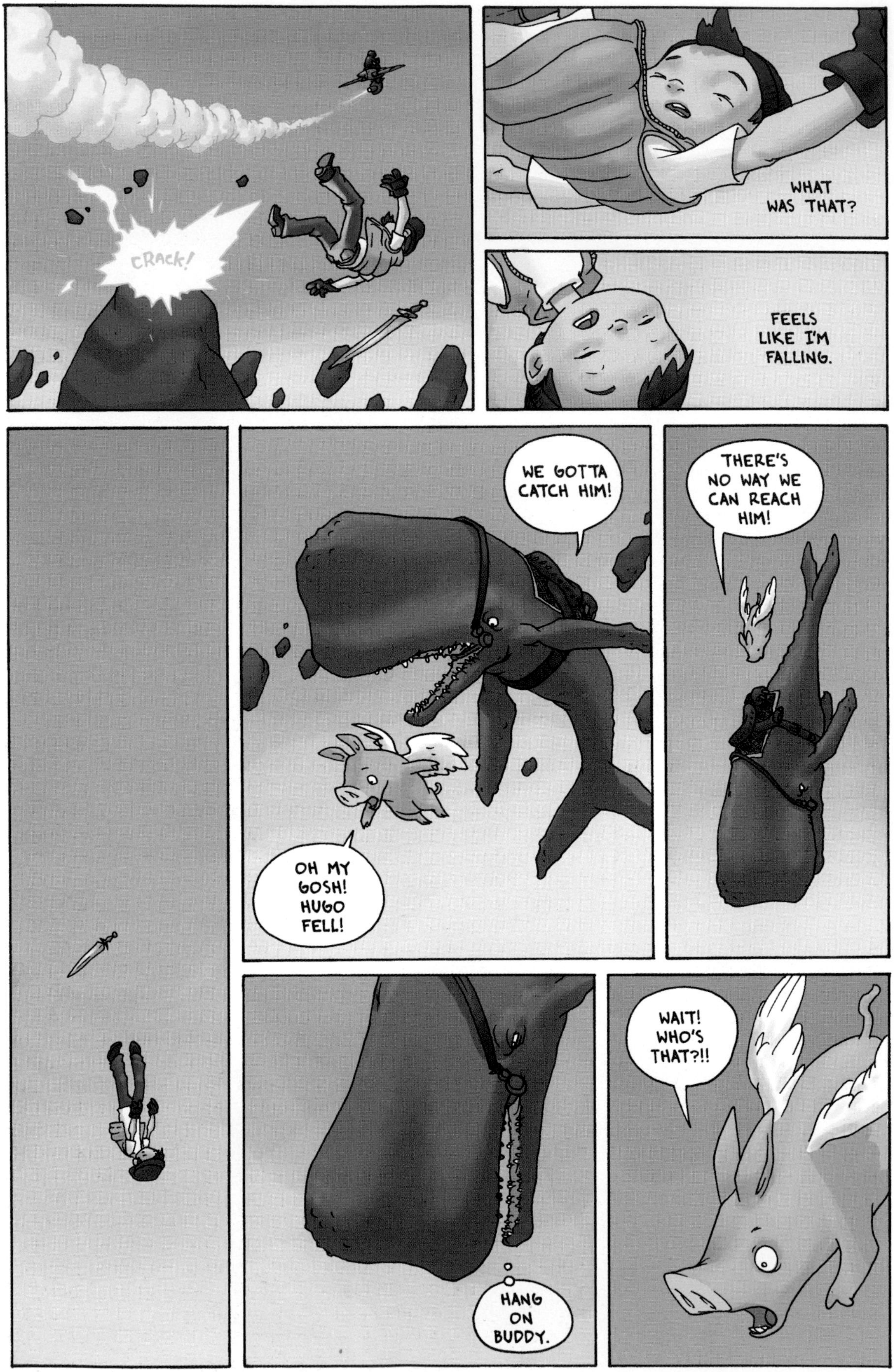
CRACK!
WHAT WAS THAT?
FEELS LIKE I'M FALLING.
WE GOTTA CATCH HIM!
OH MY GOSH! HUGO FELL!
THERE'S NO WAY WE CAN REACH HIM!
HANG ON BUDDY.
WAIT! WHO'S THAT?!!

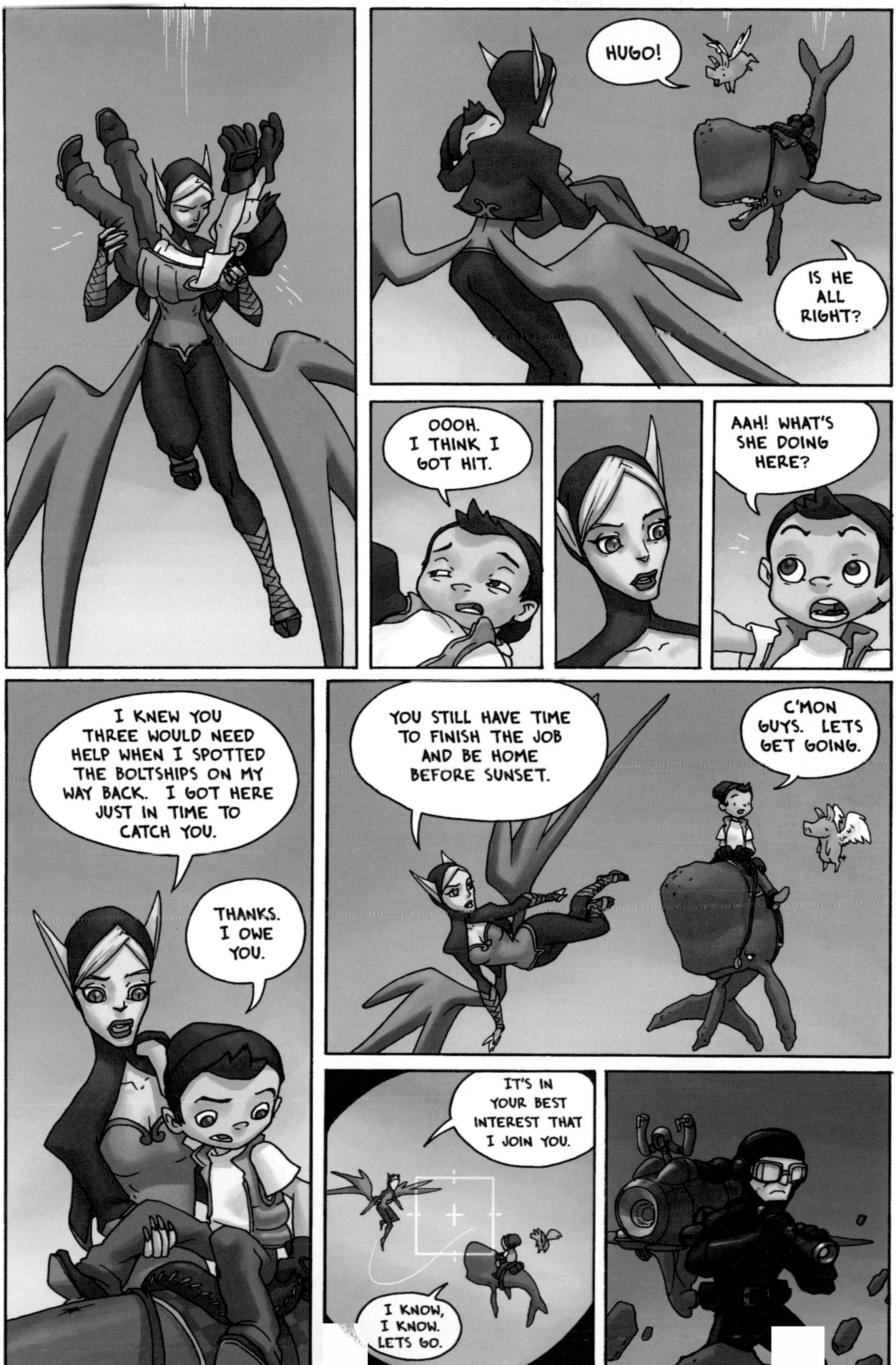
HUGO!
IS HE ALL RIGHT?
OOOH. I THINK I GOT HIT.
AAH! WHAT'S SHE DOING HERE?
I KNEW YOU THREE WOULD NEED HELP WHEN I SPOTTED THE BOLTSHIPS ON MY WAY BACK. I GOT HERE JUST IN TIME TO CATCH YOU.
THANKS. I OWE YOU.
YOU STILL HAVE TIME TO FINISH THE JOB AND BE HOME BEFORE SUNSET.
C'MON GUYS. LETS GET GOING.
IT'S IN YOUR BEST INTEREST THAT I JOIN YOU.
I KNOW, I KNOW. LETS GO.

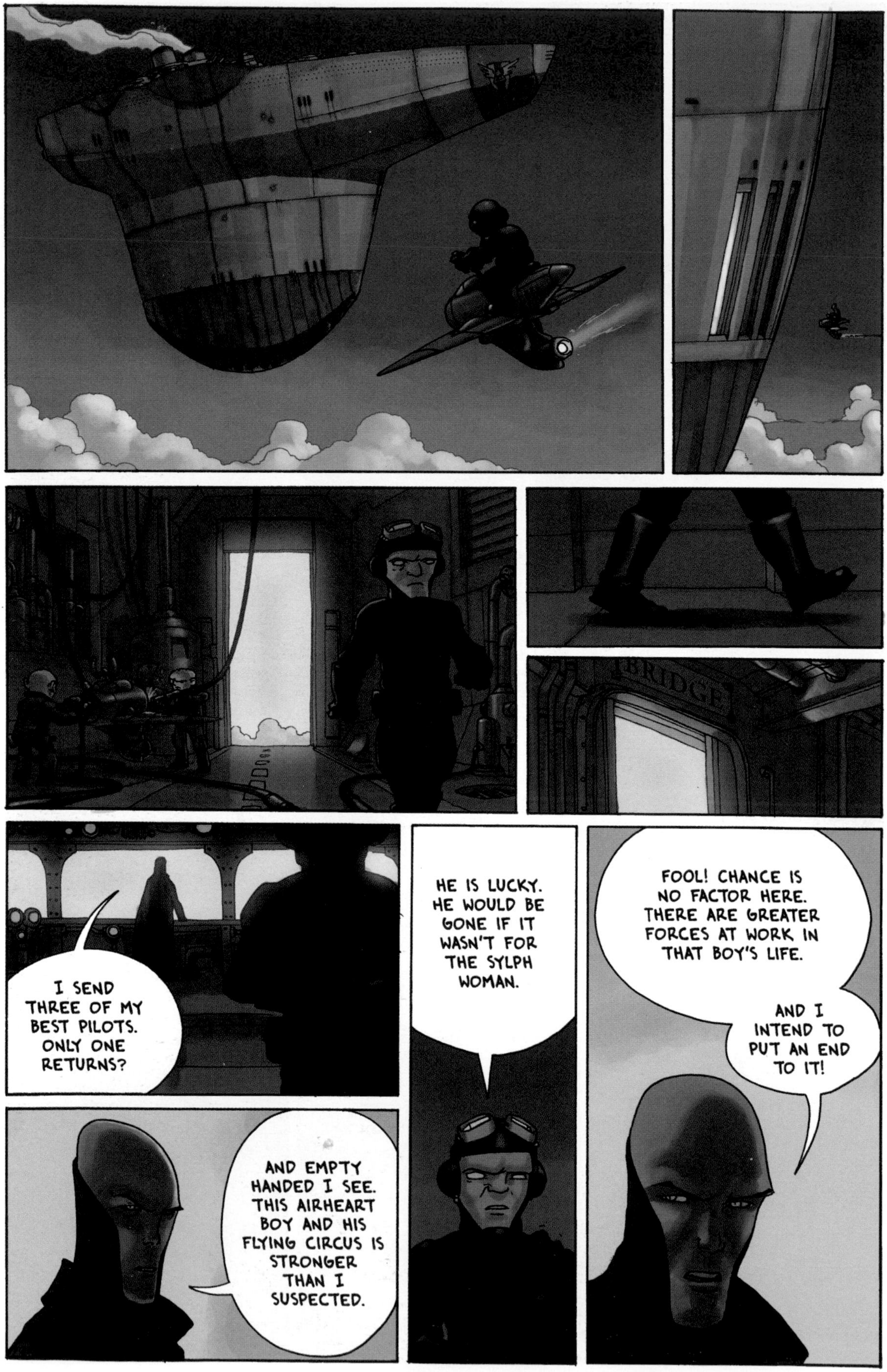
BRIDGE
I SEND THREE OF MY BEST PILOTS. ONLY ONE RETURNS?
HE IS LUCKY. HE WOULD BE GONE IF IT WASN'T FOR THE SYLPH WOMAN.
FOOL! CHANCE IS NO FACTOR HERE. THERE ARE GREATER FORCES AT WORK IN THAT BOY'S LIFE.
AND I INTEND TO PUT AN END TO IT!
AND EMPTY HANDED I SEE. THIS AIRHEART BOY AND HIS FLYING CIRCUS IS STRONGER THAN I SUSPECTED.

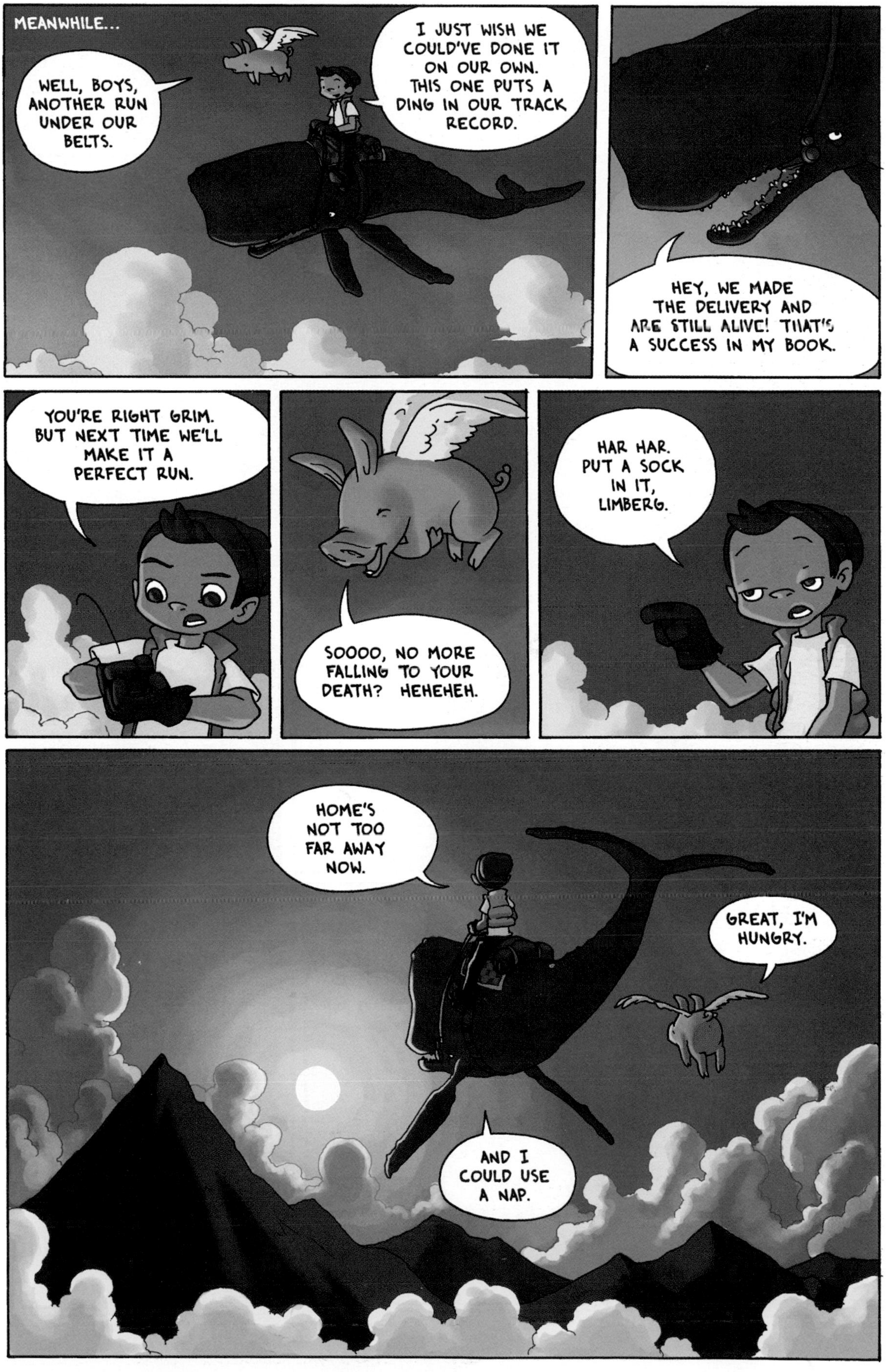
MEANWHILE...
WELL, BOYS, ANOTHER RUN UNDER OUR BELTS.
I JUST WISH WE COULD'VE DONE IT ON OUR OWN. THIS ONE PUTS A DING IN OUR TRACK RECORD.
HEY, WE MADE THE DELIVERY AND ARE STILL ALIVE! THAT'S A SUCCESS IN MY BOOK.
YOU'RE RIGHT GRIM. BUT NEXT TIME WE'LL MAKE IT A PERFECT RUN.
SOOOO, NO MORE FALLING TO YOUR DEATH? HEHEHEH.
HAR HAR. PUT A SOCK IN IT, LIMBERG.
HOME'S NOT TOO FAR AWAY NOW.
GREAT, I'M HUNGRY.
AND I COULD USE A NAP.

I wish...

by vera brosgol

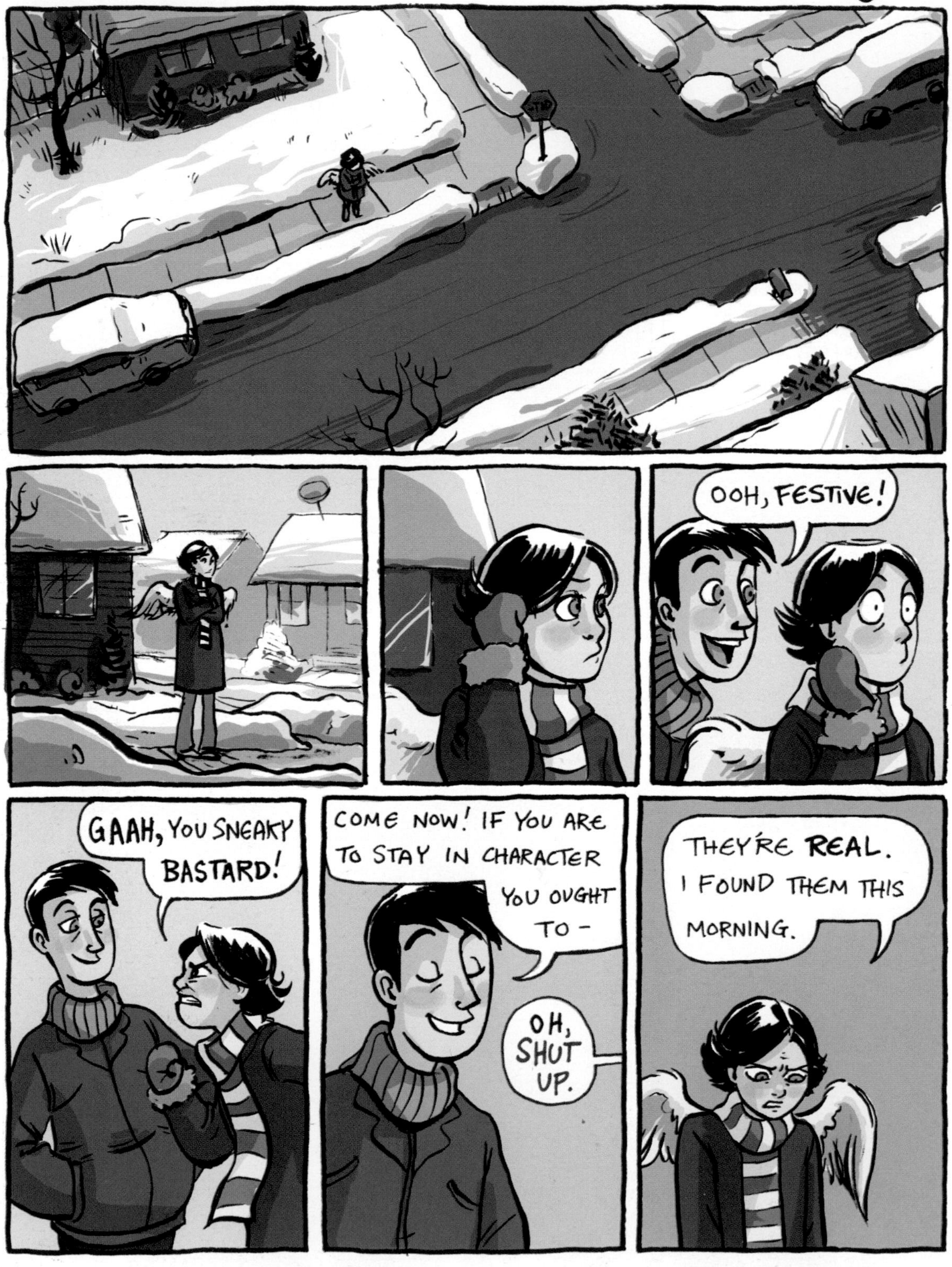
STOP
OOH, FESTIVE!
GAAH, YOU SNEAKY BASTARD!
COME NOW! IF YOU ARE TO STAY IN CHARACTER YOU OUGHT TO -
OH, SHUT UP.
THEY'RE **REAL**. I FOUND THEM THIS MORNING.

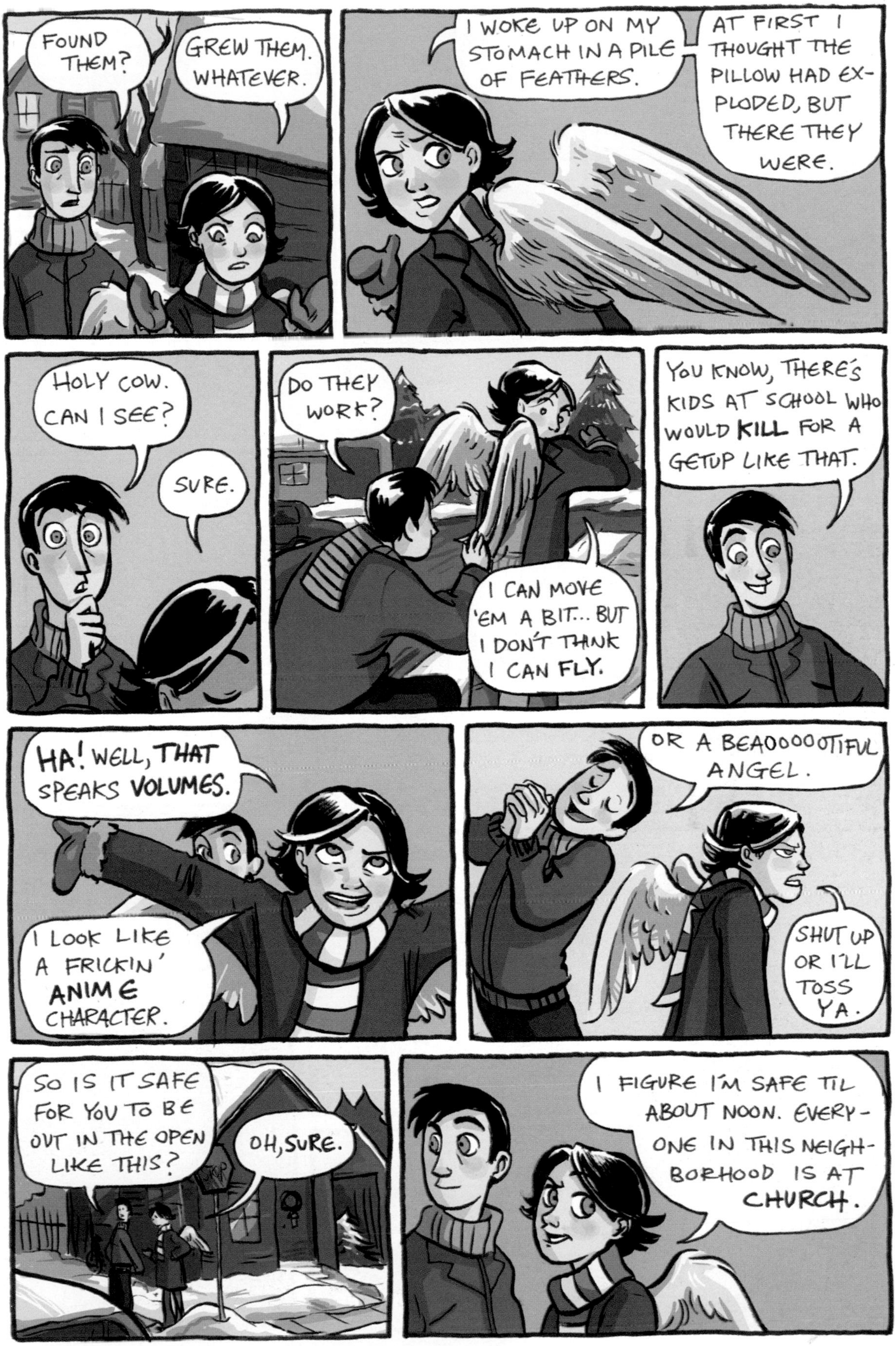
FOUND THEM?
GREW THEM. WHATEVER.
I WOKE UP ON MY STOMACH IN A PILE OF FEATHERS.
AT FIRST I THOUGHT THE PILLOW HAD EXPLODED, BUT THERE THEY WERE.
HOLY COW. CAN I SEE?
SURE.
DO THEY WORK?
I CAN MOVE 'EM A BIT... BUT I DON'T THINK I CAN FLY.
YOU KNOW, THERE'S KIDS AT SCHOOL WHO WOULD KILL FOR A GETUP LIKE THAT.
HA! WELL, THAT SPEAKS VOLUMES.
I LOOK LIKE A FRICKIN' ANIME CHARACTER.
OR A BEAOOOOOTIFUL ANGEL.
SHUT UP OR I'LL TOSS YA.
SO IS IT SAFE FOR YOU TO BE OUT IN THE OPEN LIKE THIS?
OH, SURE.
I FIGURE I'M SAFE TIL ABOUT NOON. EVERYONE IN THIS NEIGHBORHOOD IS AT CHURCH.

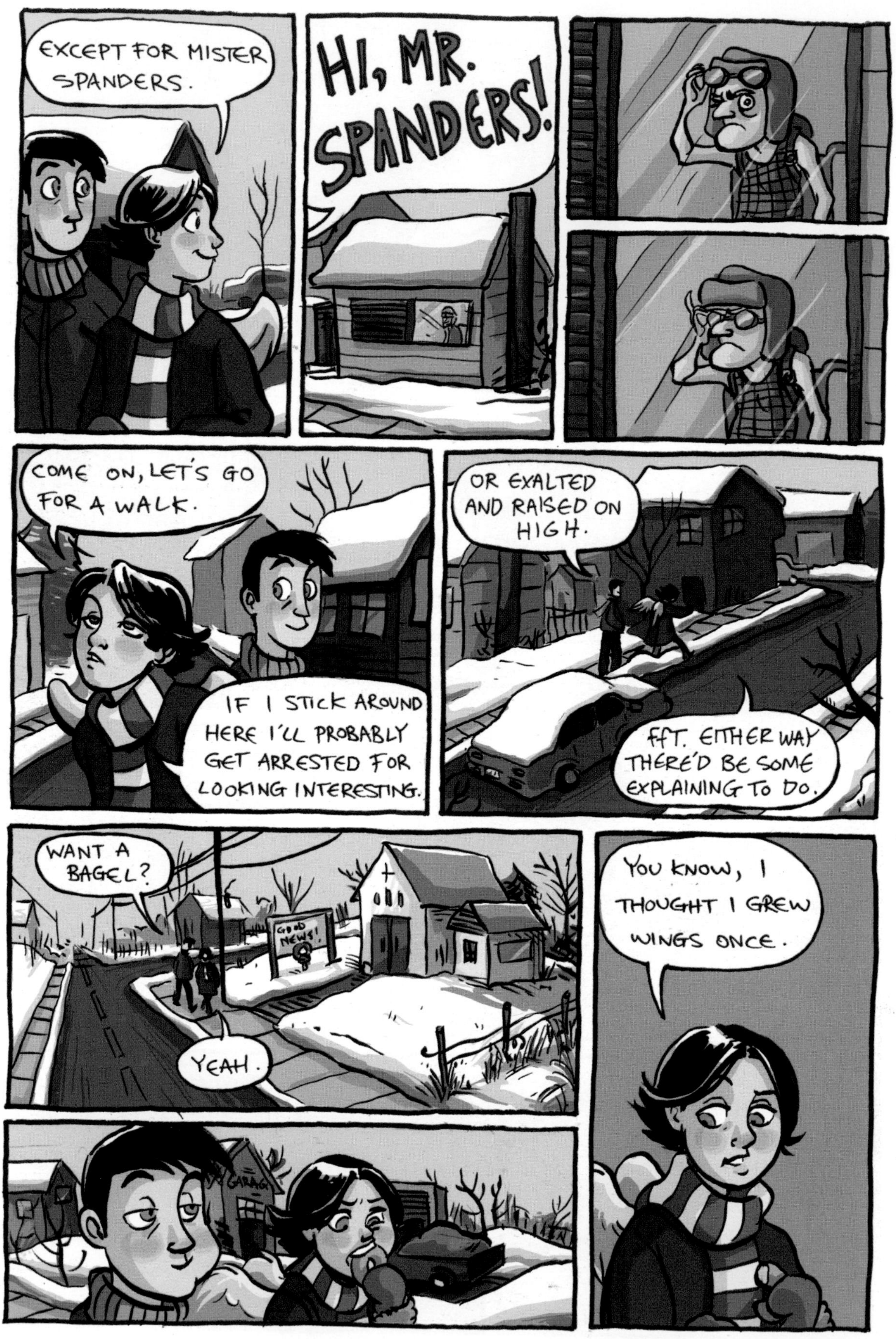
EXCEPT FOR MISTER SPANDERS.
HI, MR. SPANDERS!
COME ON, LET'S GO FOR A WALK.
IF I STICK AROUND HERE I'LL PROBABLY GET ARRESTED FOR LOOKING INTERESTING.
OR EXALTED AND RAISED ON HIGH.
FFT. EITHER WAY THERE'D BE SOME EXPLAINING TO DO.
WANT A BAGEL?
GOOD NEWS!
YEAH.
YOU KNOW, I THOUGHT I GREW WINGS ONCE.

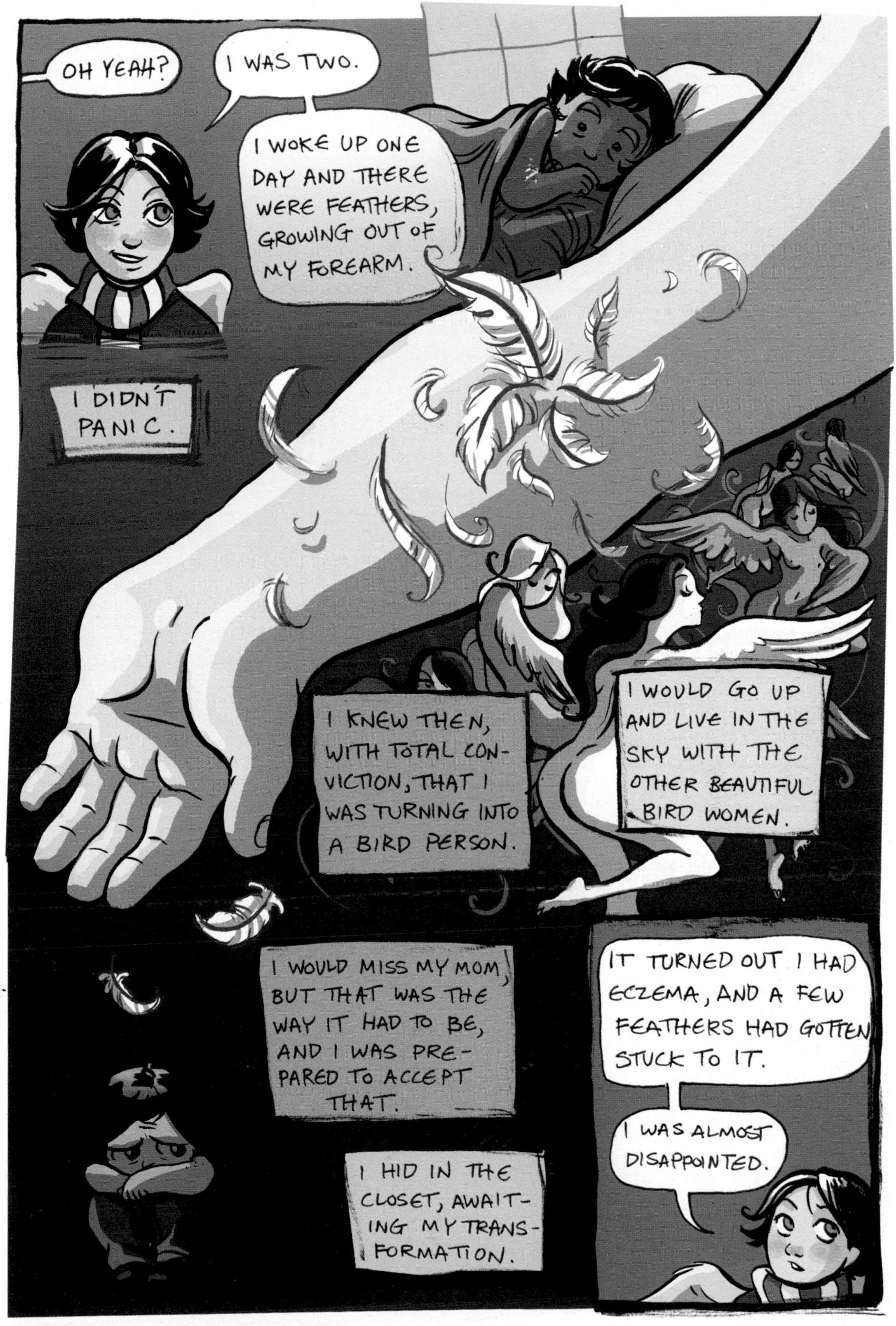
OH YEAH?
I WAS TWO.
I WOKE UP ONE DAY AND THERE WERE FEATHERS, GROWING OUT OF MY FOREARM.
I DIDN'T PANIC.
I KNEW THEN, WITH TOTAL CON-VICTION, THAT I WAS TURNING INTO A BIRD PERSON.
I WOULD GO UP AND LIVE IN THE SKY WITH THE OTHER BEAUTIFUL BIRD WOMEN.
I WOULD MISS MY MOM, BUT THAT WAS THE WAY IT HAD TO BE, AND I WAS PRE-PARED TO ACCEPT THAT.
I HID IN THE CLOSET, AWAIT-ING MY TRANS-FORMATION.
IT TURNED OUT I HAD ECZEMA, AND A FEW FEATHERS HAD GOTTEN STUCK TO IT.
I WAS ALMOST DISAPPOINTED.

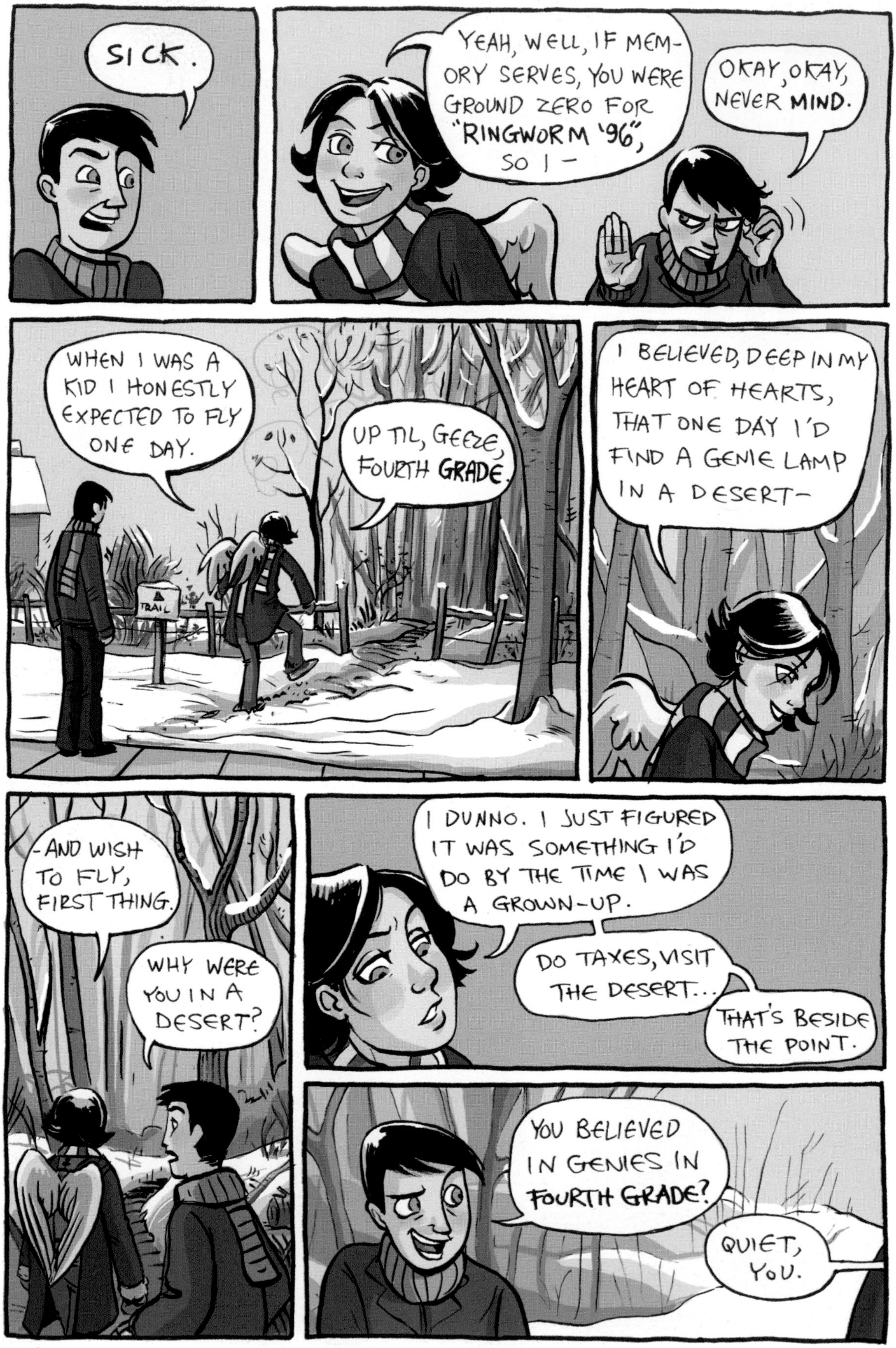
SICK.
YEAH, WELL, IF MEMORY SERVES, YOU WERE GROUND ZERO FOR "RINGWORM '96", SO I -
OKAY, OKAY, NEVER MIND.
WHEN I WAS A KID I HONESTLY EXPECTED TO FLY ONE DAY.
UP TIL, GEEZE, FOURTH GRADE.
TRAIL
I BELIEVED, DEEP IN MY HEART OF HEARTS, THAT ONE DAY I'D FIND A GENIE LAMP IN A DESERT-
-AND WISH TO FLY, FIRST THING.
WHY WERE YOU IN A DESERT?
I DUNNO. I JUST FIGURED IT WAS SOMETHING I'D DO BY THE TIME I WAS A GROWN-UP.
DO TAXES, VISIT THE DESERT...
THAT'S BESIDE THE POINT.
YOU BELIEVED IN GENIES IN FOURTH GRADE?
QUIET, YOU.

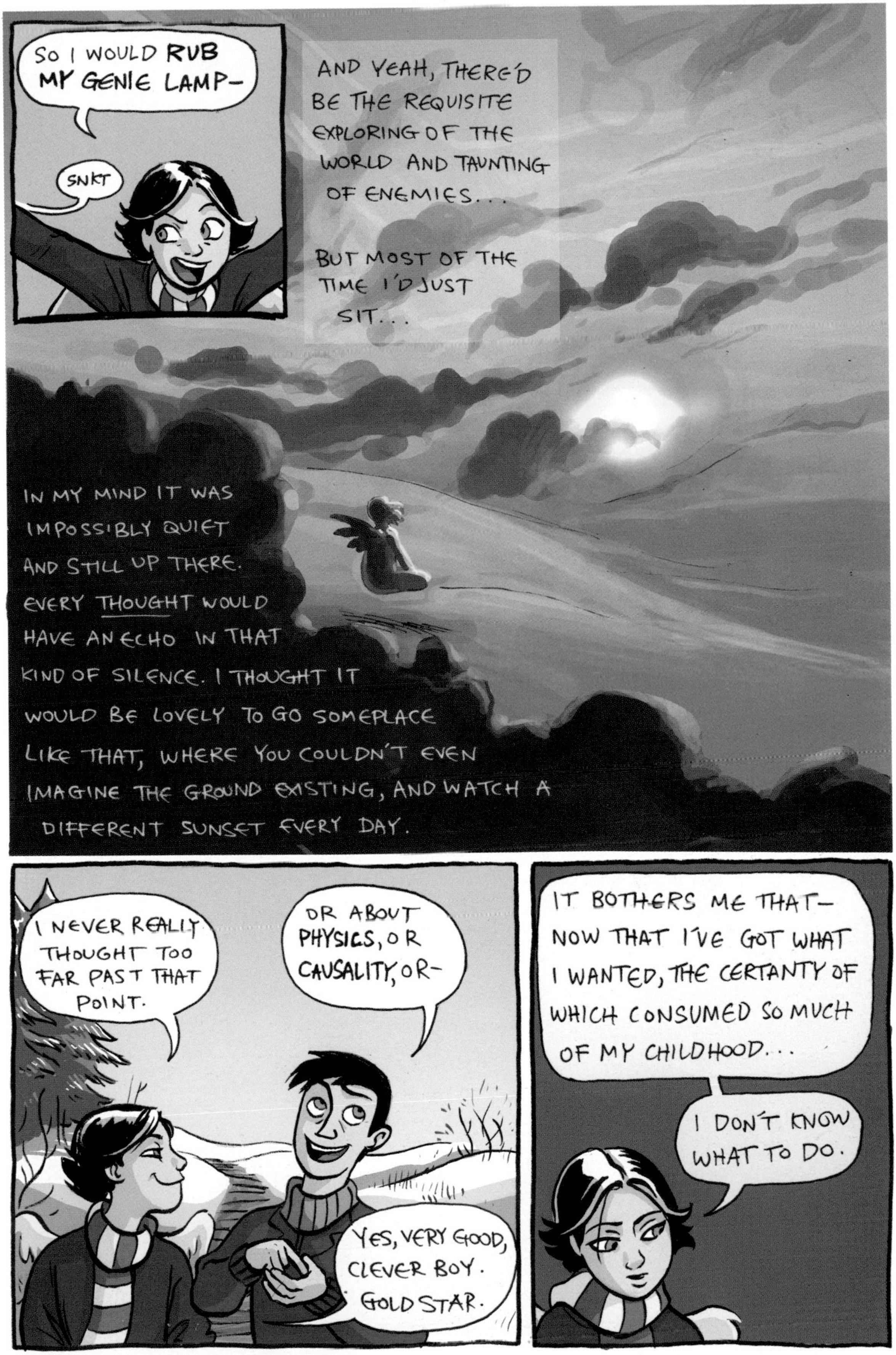
So I would RUB MY GENIE LAMP–
SNKT
AND YEAH, THERE'D BE THE REQUISITE EXPLORING OF THE WORLD AND TAUNTING OF ENEMIES...
BUT MOST OF THE TIME I'D JUST SIT...
IN MY MIND IT WAS IMPOSSIBLY QUIET AND STILL UP THERE. EVERY THOUGHT WOULD HAVE AN ECHO IN THAT KIND OF SILENCE. I THOUGHT IT WOULD BE LOVELY TO GO SOMEPLACE LIKE THAT, WHERE YOU COULDN'T EVEN IMAGINE THE GROUND EXISTING, AND WATCH A DIFFERENT SUNSET EVERY DAY.
I NEVER REALLY THOUGHT TOO FAR PAST THAT POINT.
OR ABOUT PHYSICS, OR CAUSALITY, OR–
YES, VERY GOOD, CLEVER BOY. GOLD STAR.
IT BOTHERS ME THAT– NOW THAT I'VE GOT WHAT I WANTED, THE CERTANTY OF WHICH CONSUMED SO MUCH OF MY CHILDHOOD...
I DON'T KNOW WHAT TO DO.

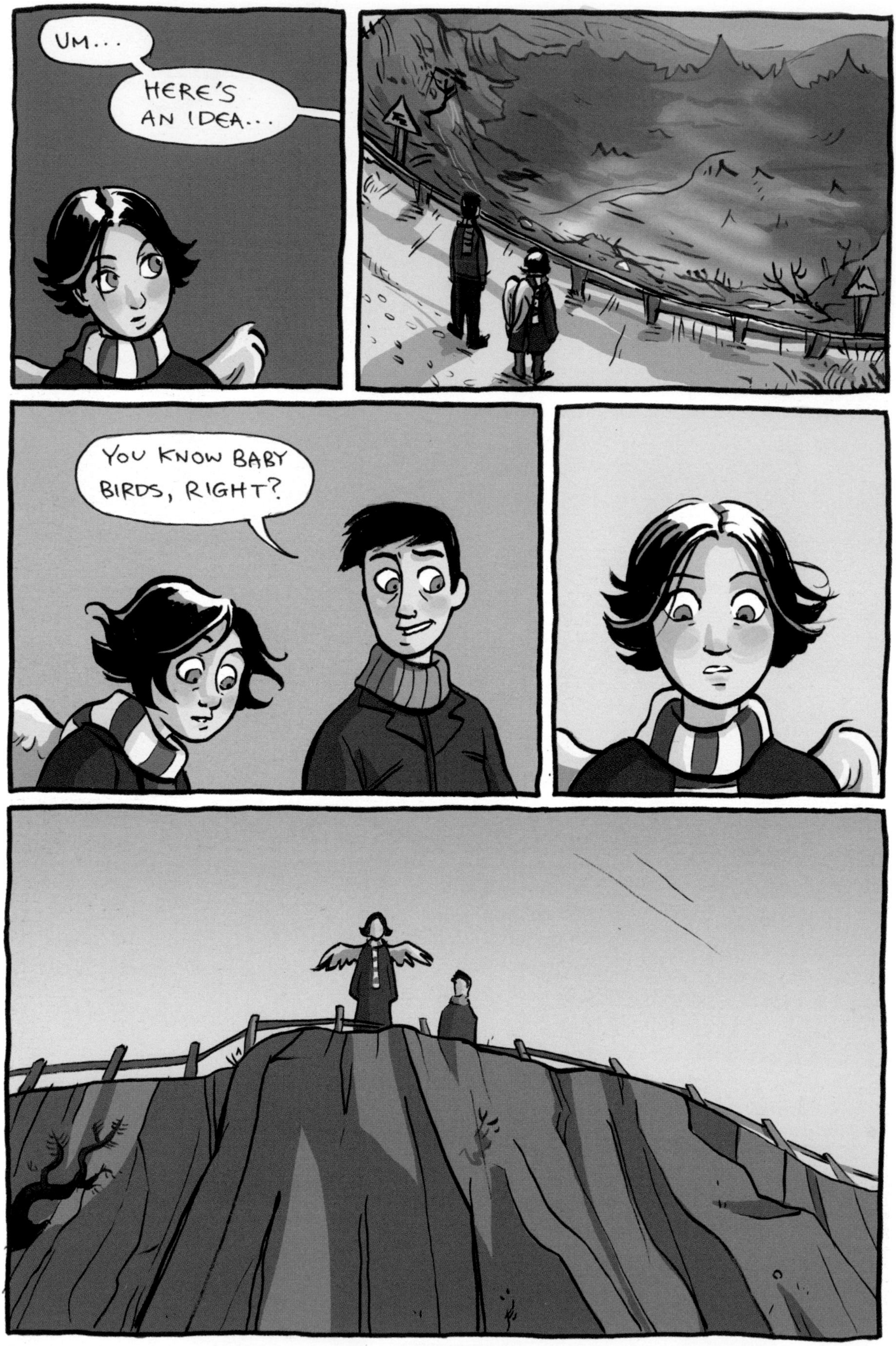
UM...
HERE'S AN IDEA...
YOU KNOW BABY BIRDS, RIGHT?

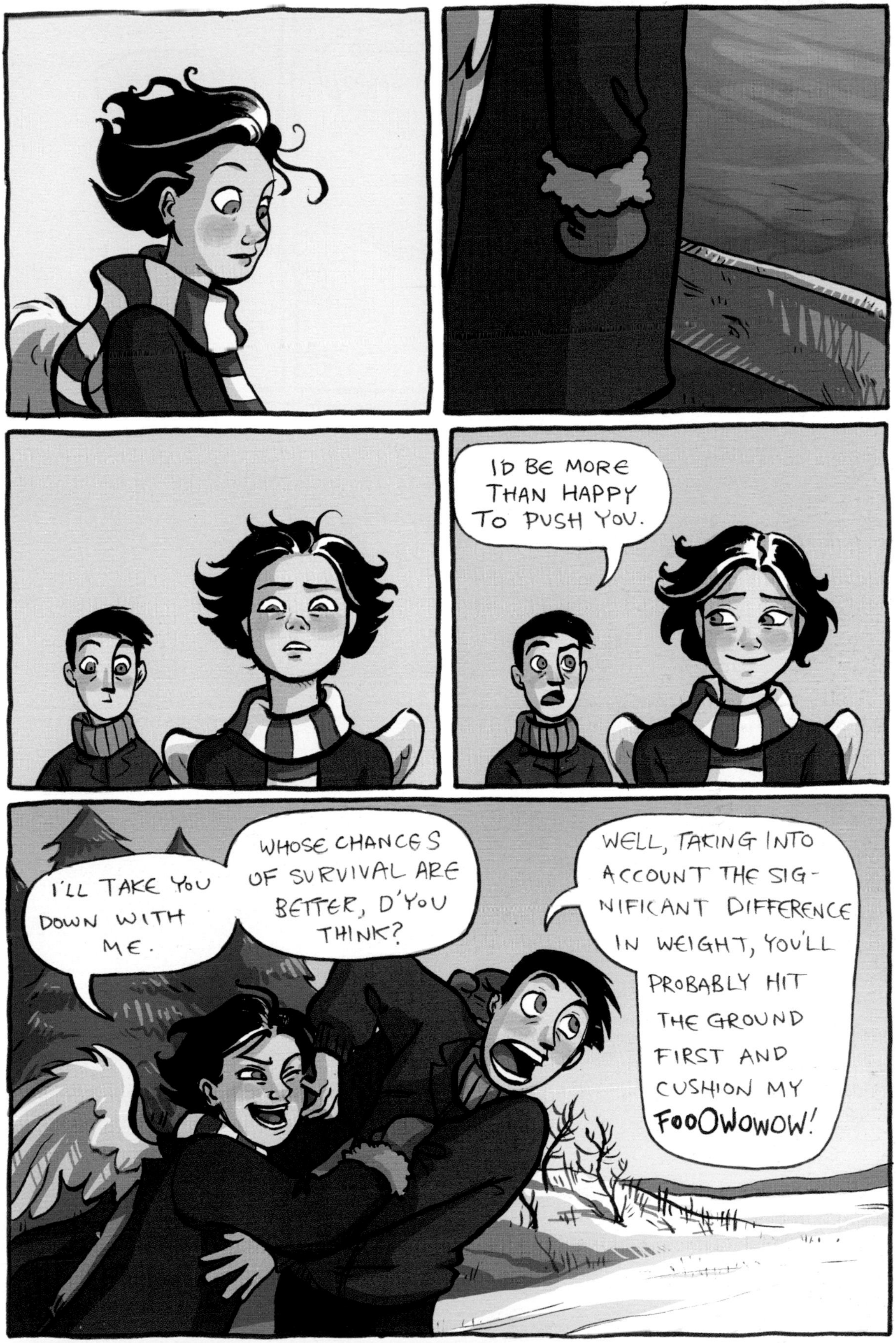
ID BE MORE THAN HAPPY TO PUSH YOU.
I'LL TAKE YOU DOWN WITH ME.
WHOSE CHANCES OF SURVIVAL ARE BETTER, D'YOU THINK?
WELL, TAKING INTO ACCOUNT THE SIG-NIFICANT DIFFERENCE IN WEIGHT, YOU'LL PROBABLY HIT THE GROUND FIRST AND CUSHION MY FOOOWOWOW!

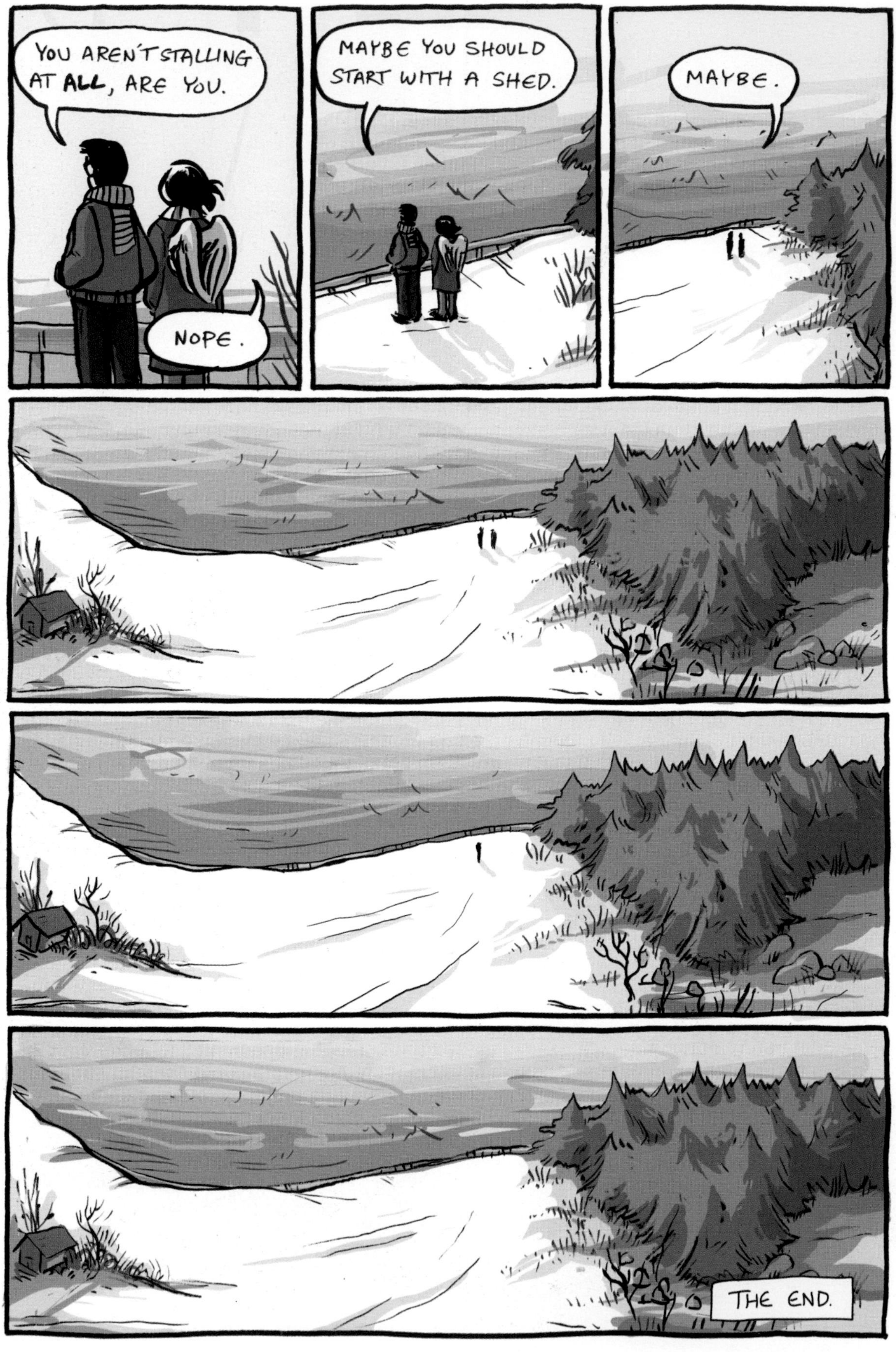
YOU AREN'T STALLING AT **ALL**, ARE YOU.
NOPE.
MAYBE YOU SHOULD START WITH A SHED.
MAYBE.
THE END.

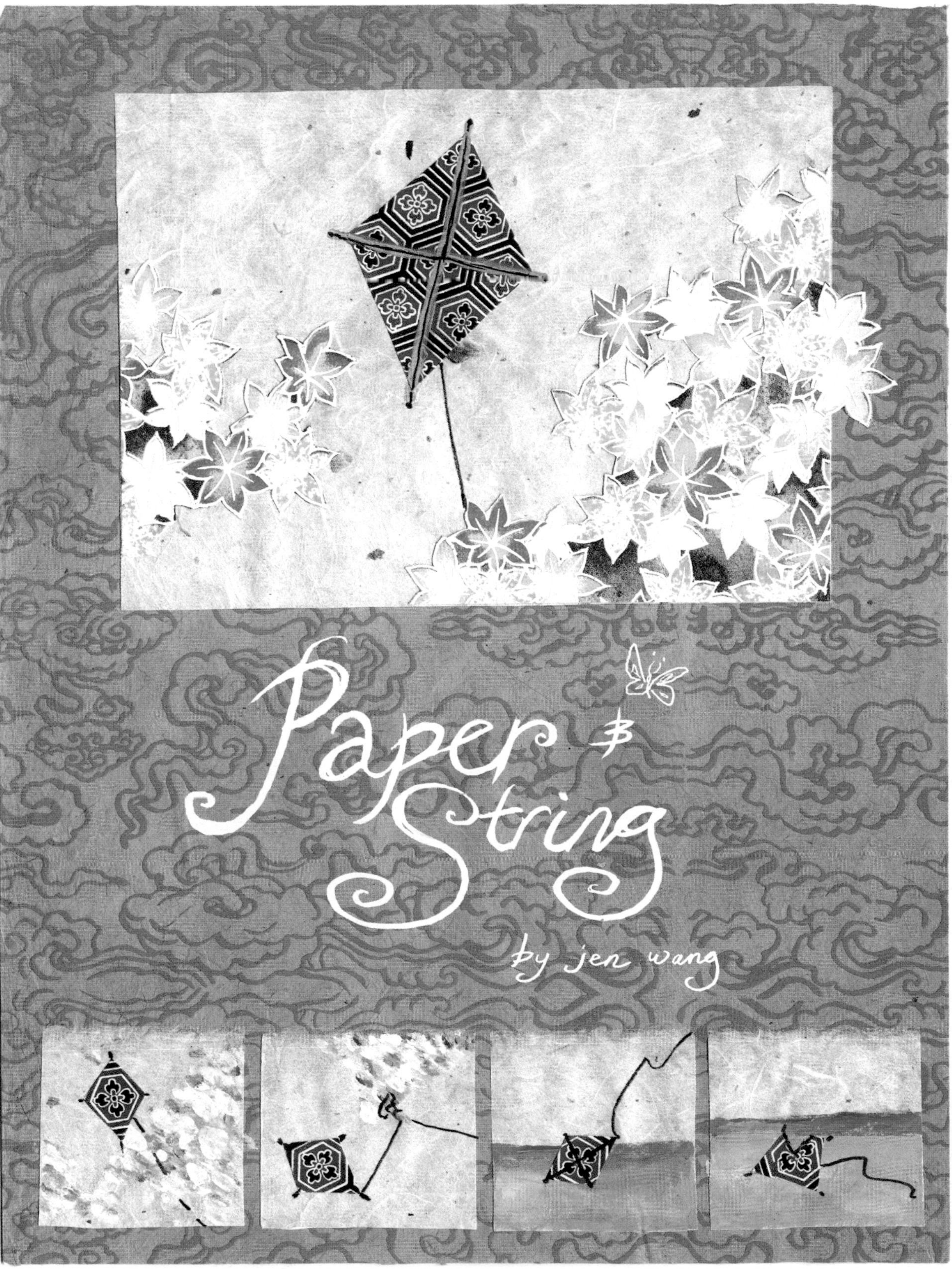
Paper & String
by jen wang

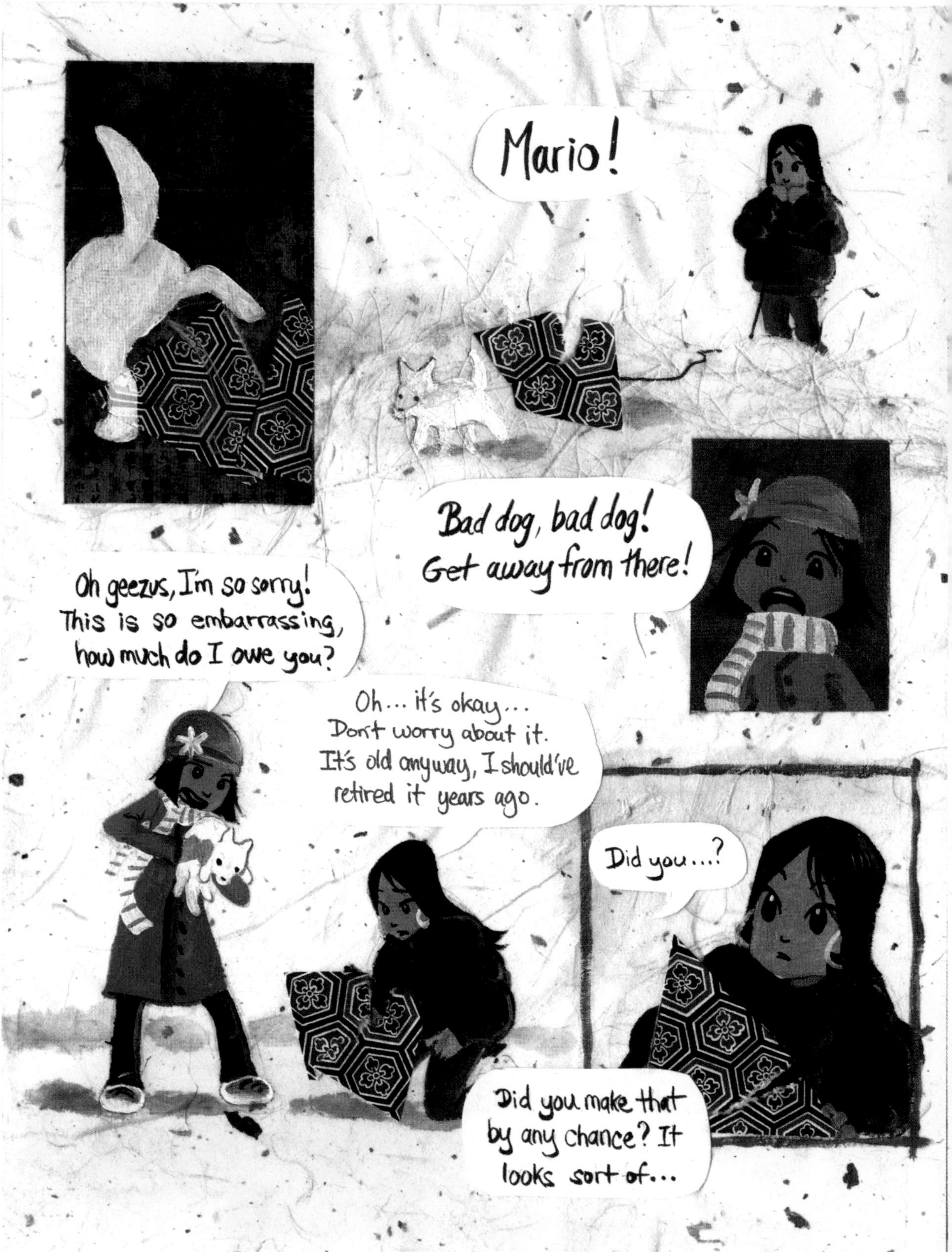
Mario!
Bad dog, bad dog! Get away from there!
Oh geezus, I'm so sorry! This is so embarrassing, how much do I owe you?
Oh... it's okay... Don't worry about it. It's old anyway, I should've retired it years ago.
Did you...?
Did you make that by any chance? It looks sort of...

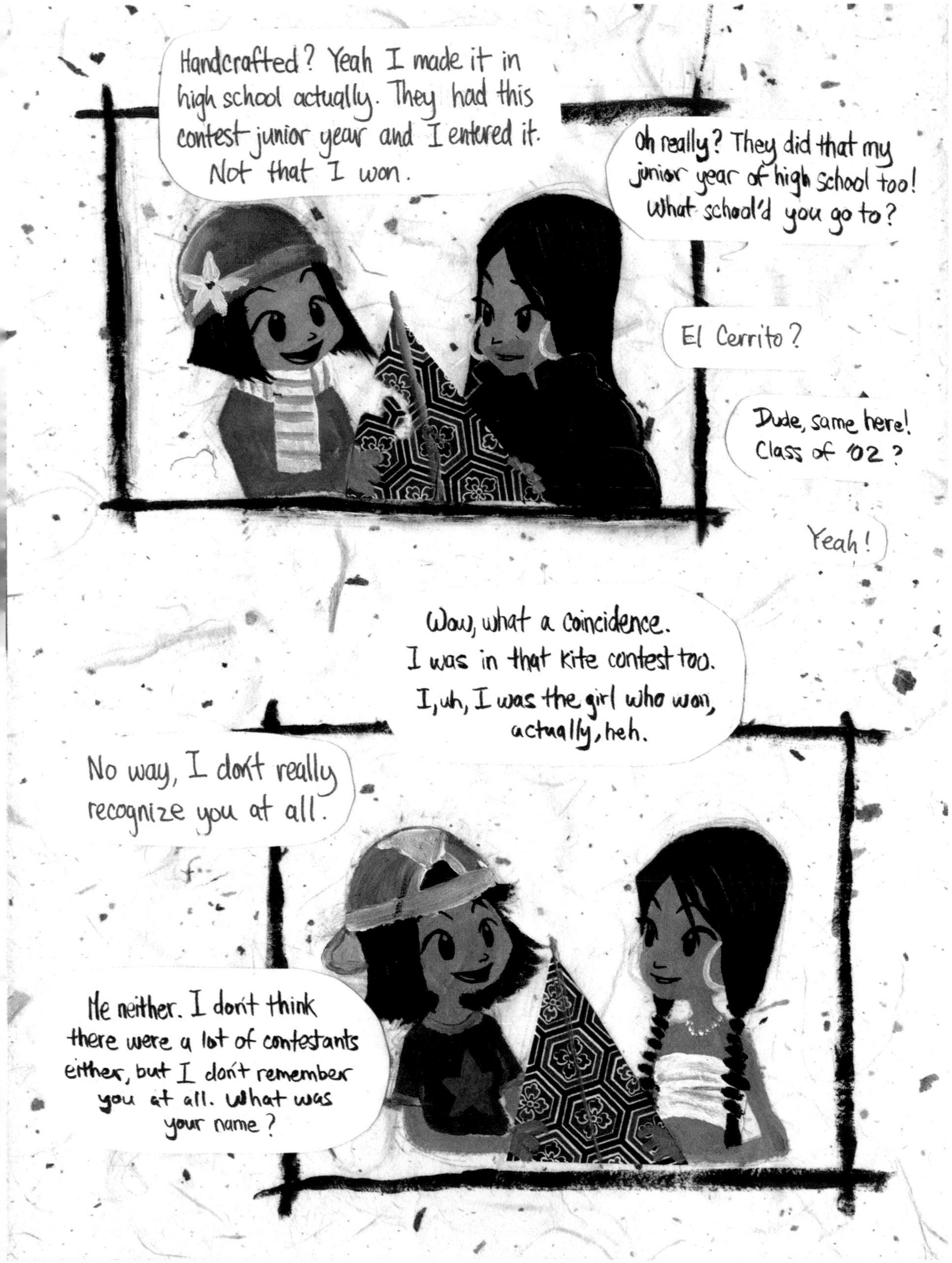

Handcrafted? Yeah I made it in high school actually. They had this contest junior year and I entered it. Not that I won.
Oh really? They did that my junior year of high school too! What school'd you go to?
El Cerrito?
Dude, same here! Class of '02?
Yeah!
Wow, what a coincidence. I was in that kite contest too. I, uh, I was the girl who won, actually, heh.
No way, I don't really recognize you at all.
Me neither. I don't think there were a lot of contestants either, but I don't remember you at all. What was your name?

Hesa. Hesa Lee. I don't think we hung out in the same crowd. I didn't participate in a lot of school activities so you probably didn't see me much.

Really, huh? Yeah you know I never really paid attention to other crowds anyway.

I was somewhere between the preppy kids and the kids in limbo that didn't really fit in any particular social clique.

Nobody ever feels like they belong in high school.

"I dunno, you'd think a lot of our classmates did.
But yeah, I never really paid much attention to your crowd. Not that I had anything against you guys. I guess you just all seemed the same. Although you could probably say the same about me."

—Jilleen Yep

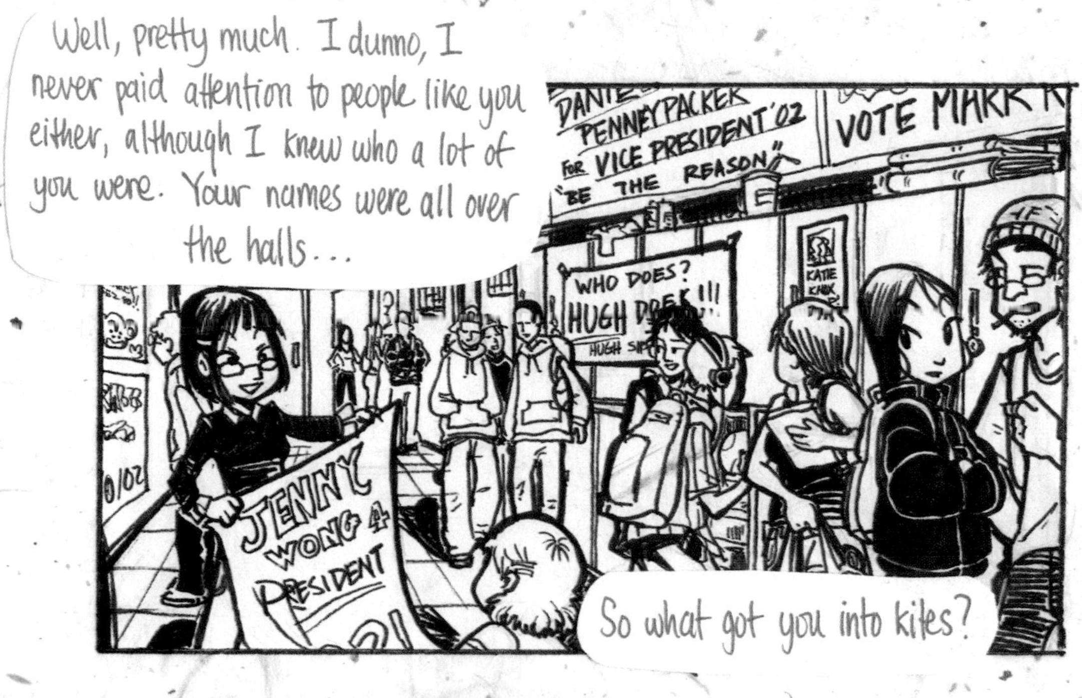
Well, pretty much. I dunno, I never paid attention to people like you either, although I knew who a lot of you were. Your names were all over the halls...
PENNEYPACKER
FOR VICE PRESIDENT '02
"BE THE REASON"
VOTE
WHO DOES?
KATIE KNOX
JENNY WONG 4 PRESIDENT
So what got you into kites?

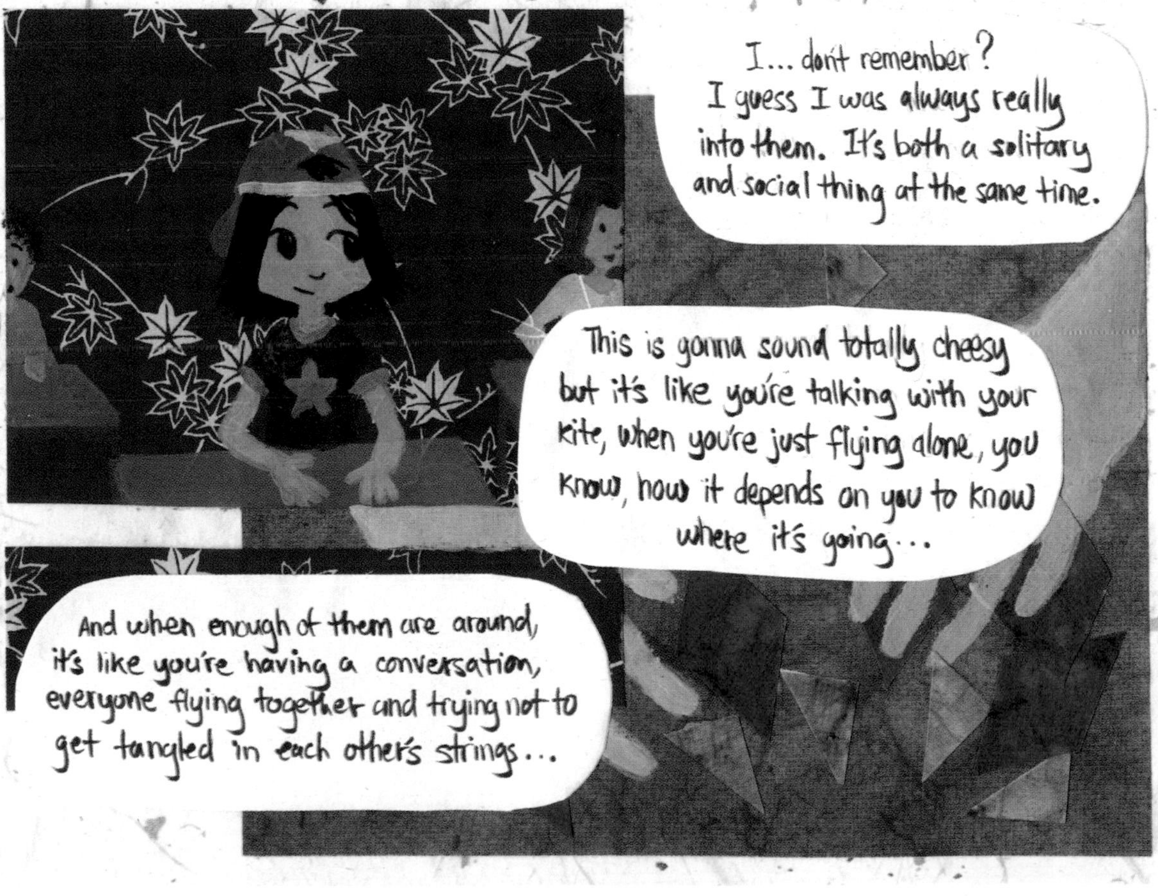
I... don't remember? I guess I was always really into them. It's both a solitary and social thing at the same time.
This is gonna sound totally cheesy but it's like you're talking with your kite, when you're just flying alone, you know, how it depends on you to know where it's going...
And when enough of them are around, it's like you're having a conversation, everyone flying together and trying not to get tangled in each other's strings...

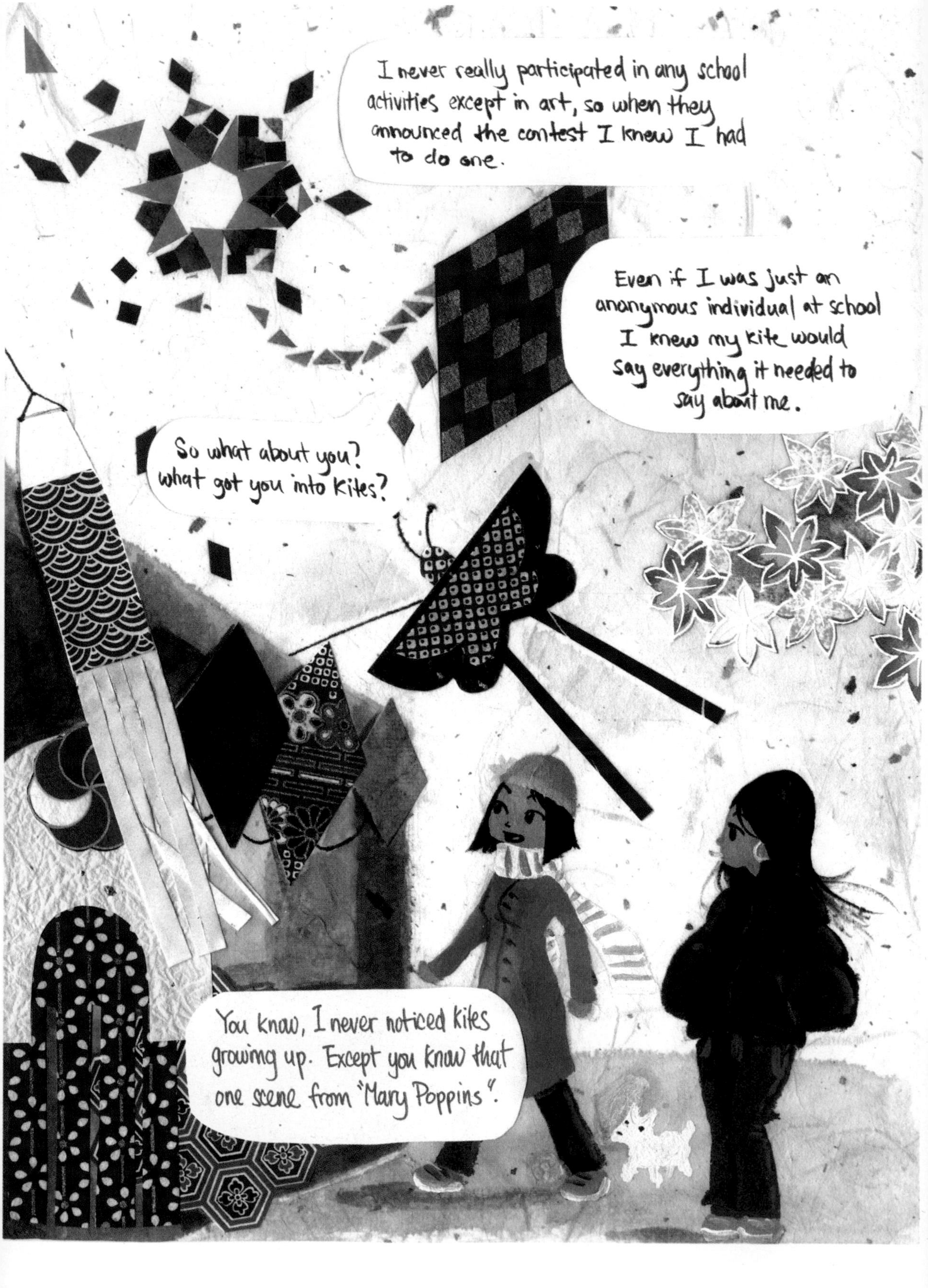
I never really participated in any school activities except in art, so when they announced the contest I knew I had to do one.
Even if I was just an anonymous individual at school I knew my kite would say everything it needed to say about me.
So what about you? what got you into kites?
You know, I never noticed kites growing up. Except you know that one scene from "Mary Poppins".

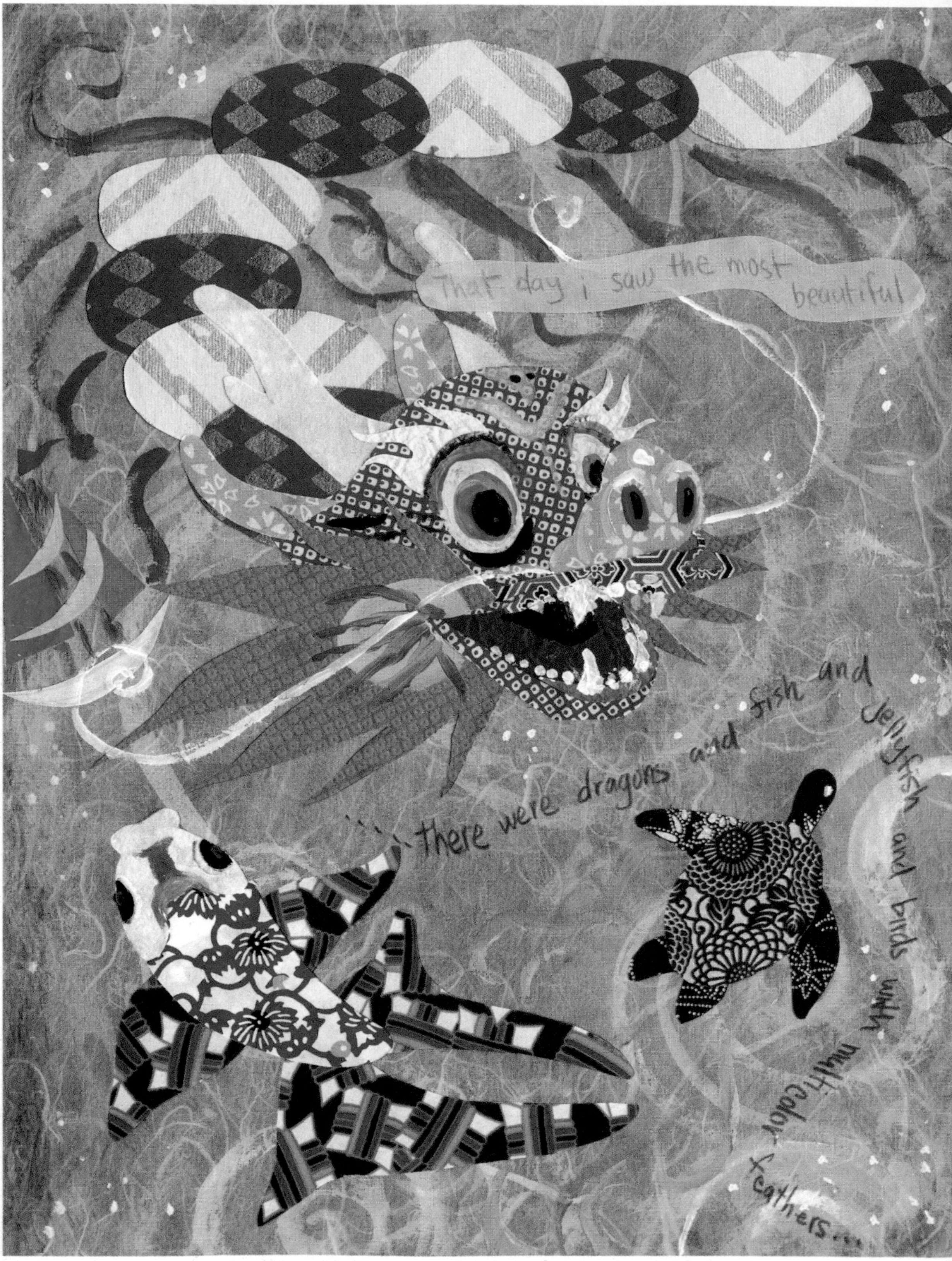
That day i saw the most beautiful
... there were dragons and fish and jellyfish and birds with multicolor feathers...

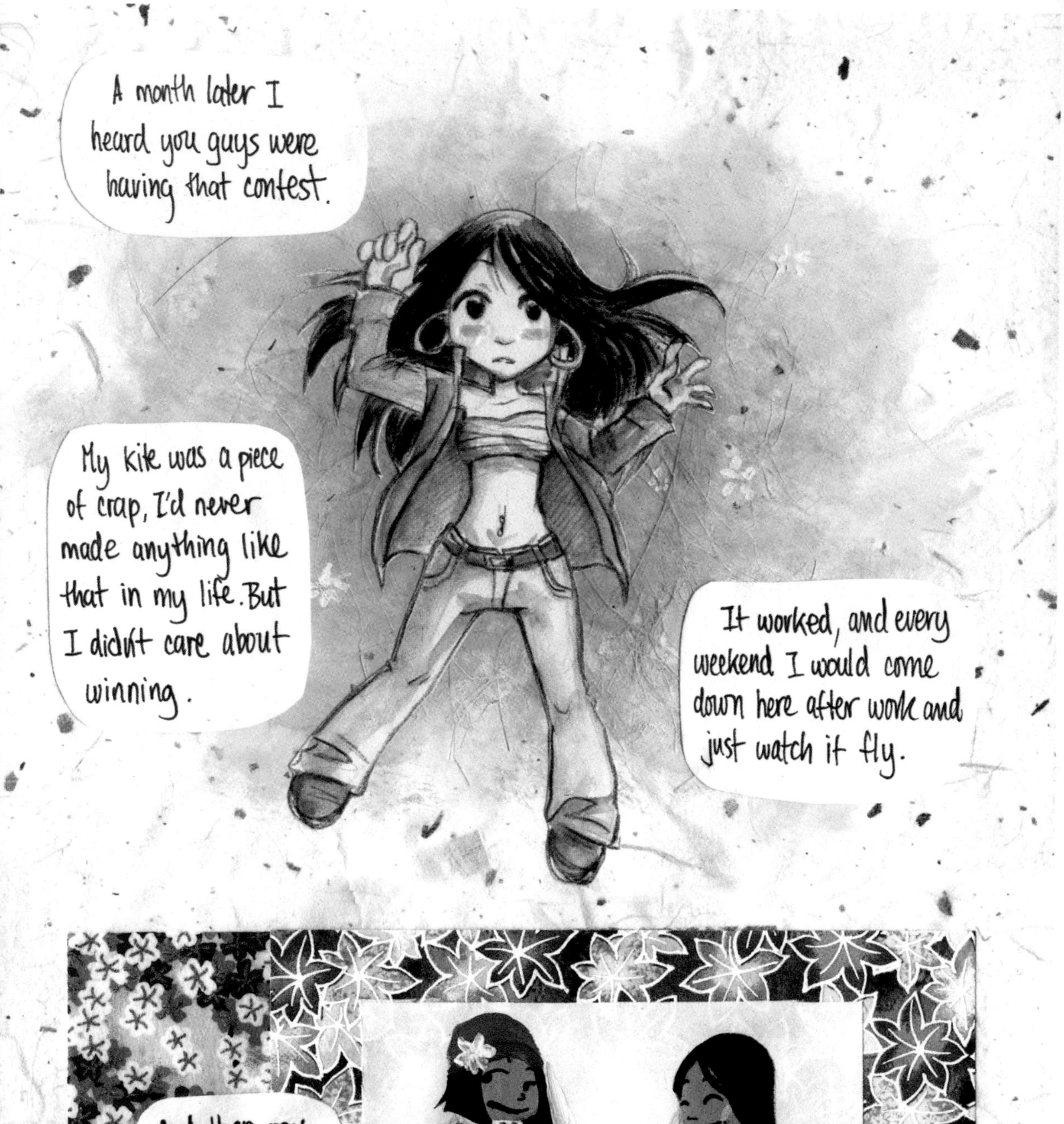
A month later I heard you guys were having that contest.
My kite was a piece of crap, I'd never made anything like that in my life. But I didn't care about winning.
It worked, and every weekend I would come down here after work and just watch it fly.

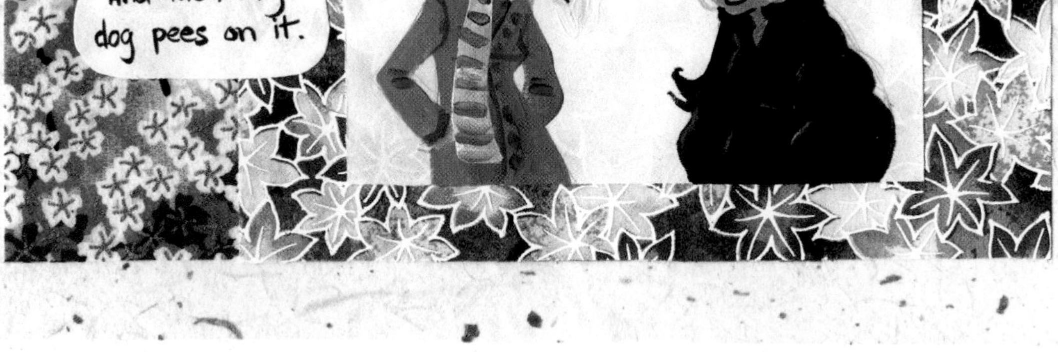
And then my dog pees on it.

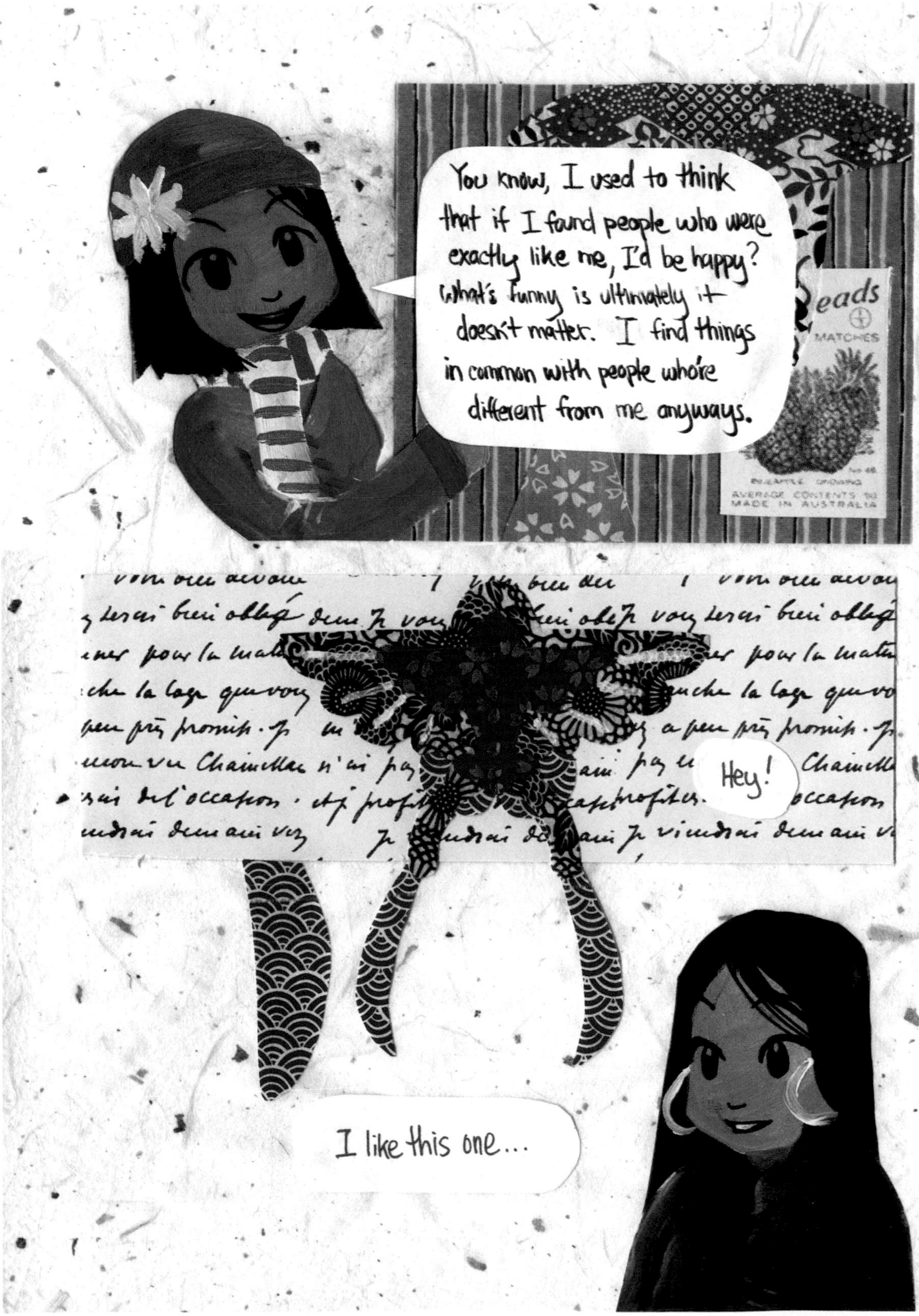
You know, I used to think that if I found people who were exactly like me, I'd be happy? What's funny is ultimately it doesn't matter. I find things in common with people who're different from me anyways.
MATCHES
MADE IN AUSTRALIA
Hey!
I like this one...

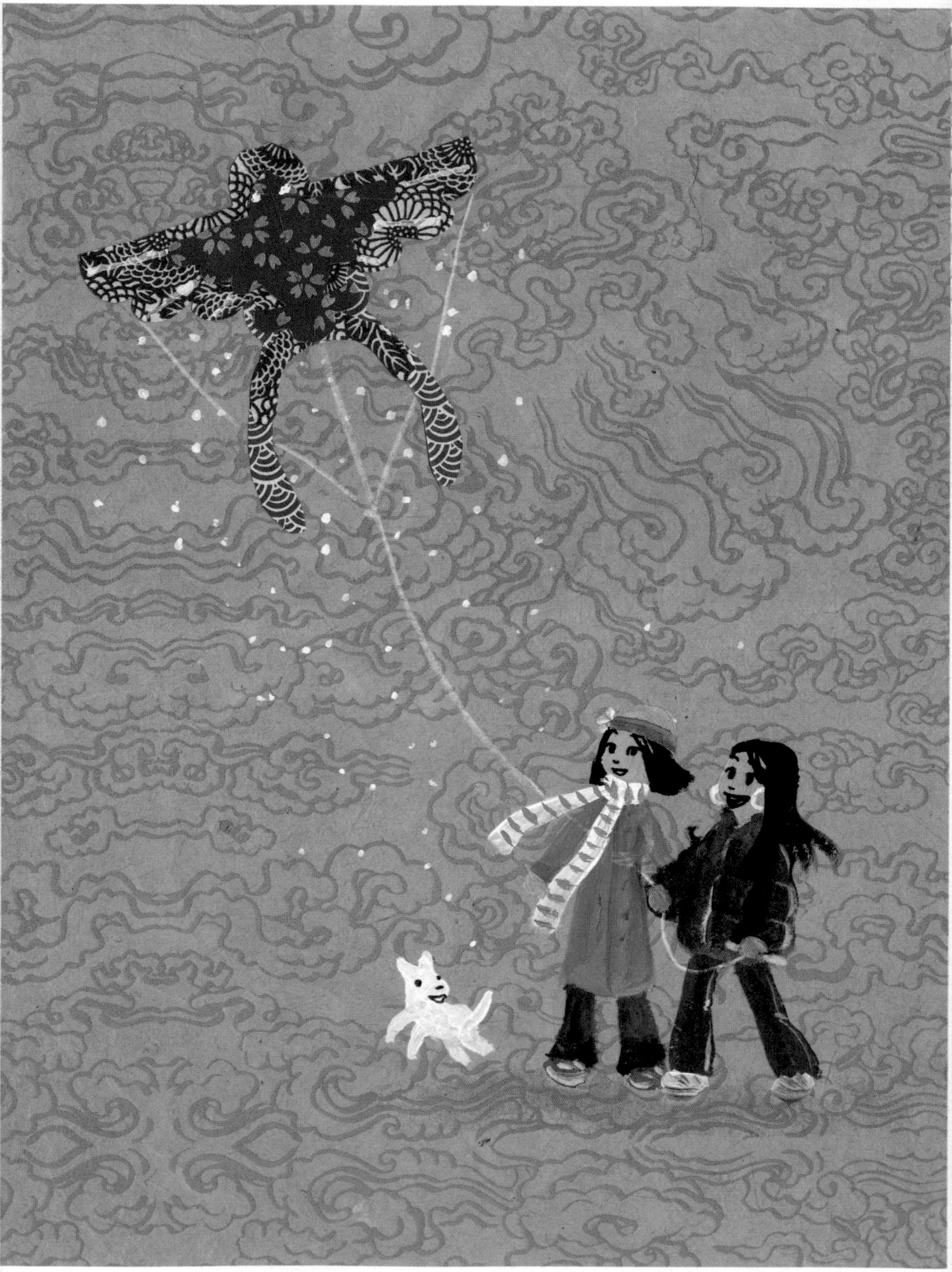

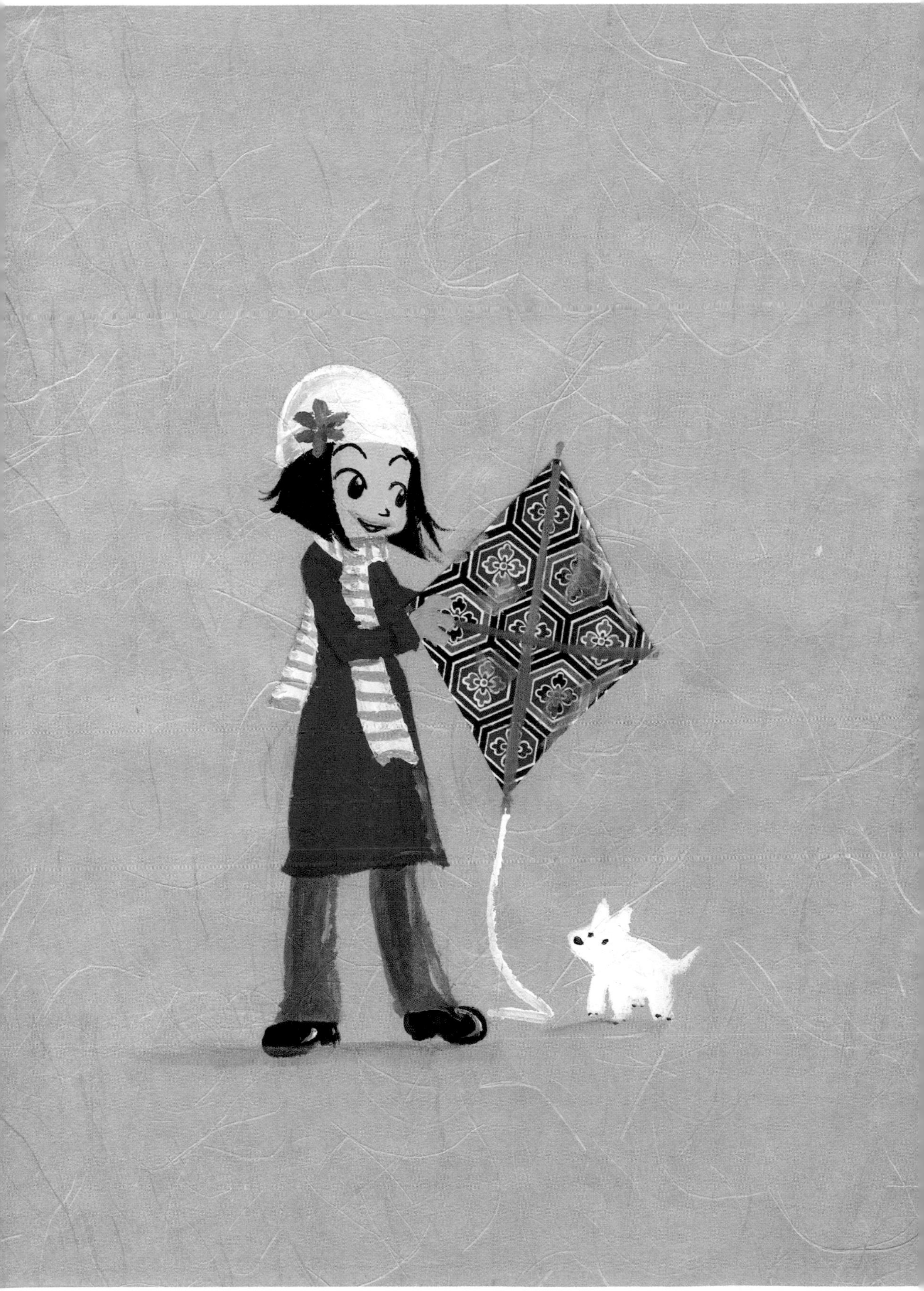

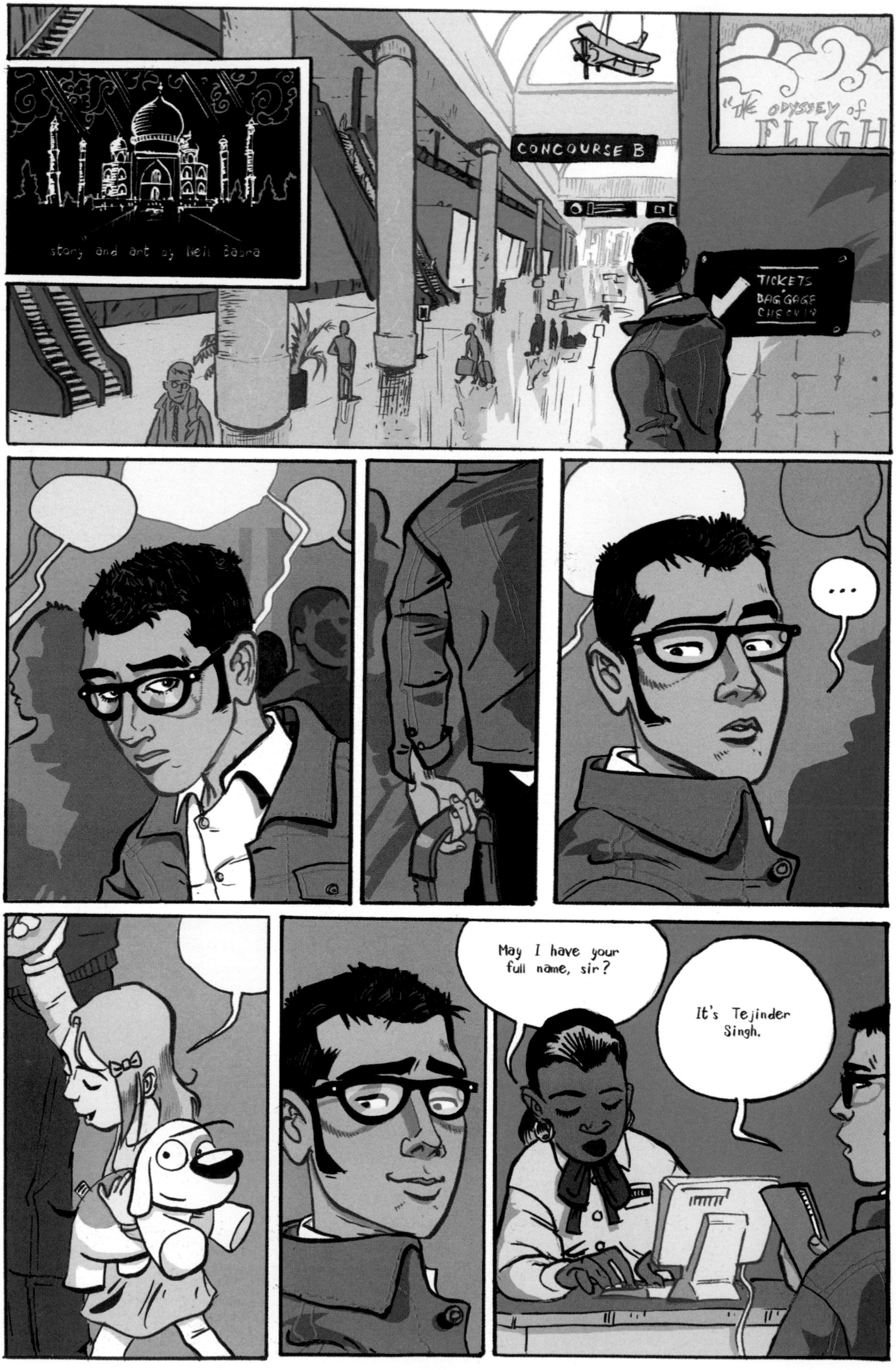

story and art by Neil Babra
"THE ODYSSEY of FLIGH
CONCOURSE B
TICKETS
BAGGAGE CHECK IN
...
May I have your full name, sir?
It's Tejinder Singh.

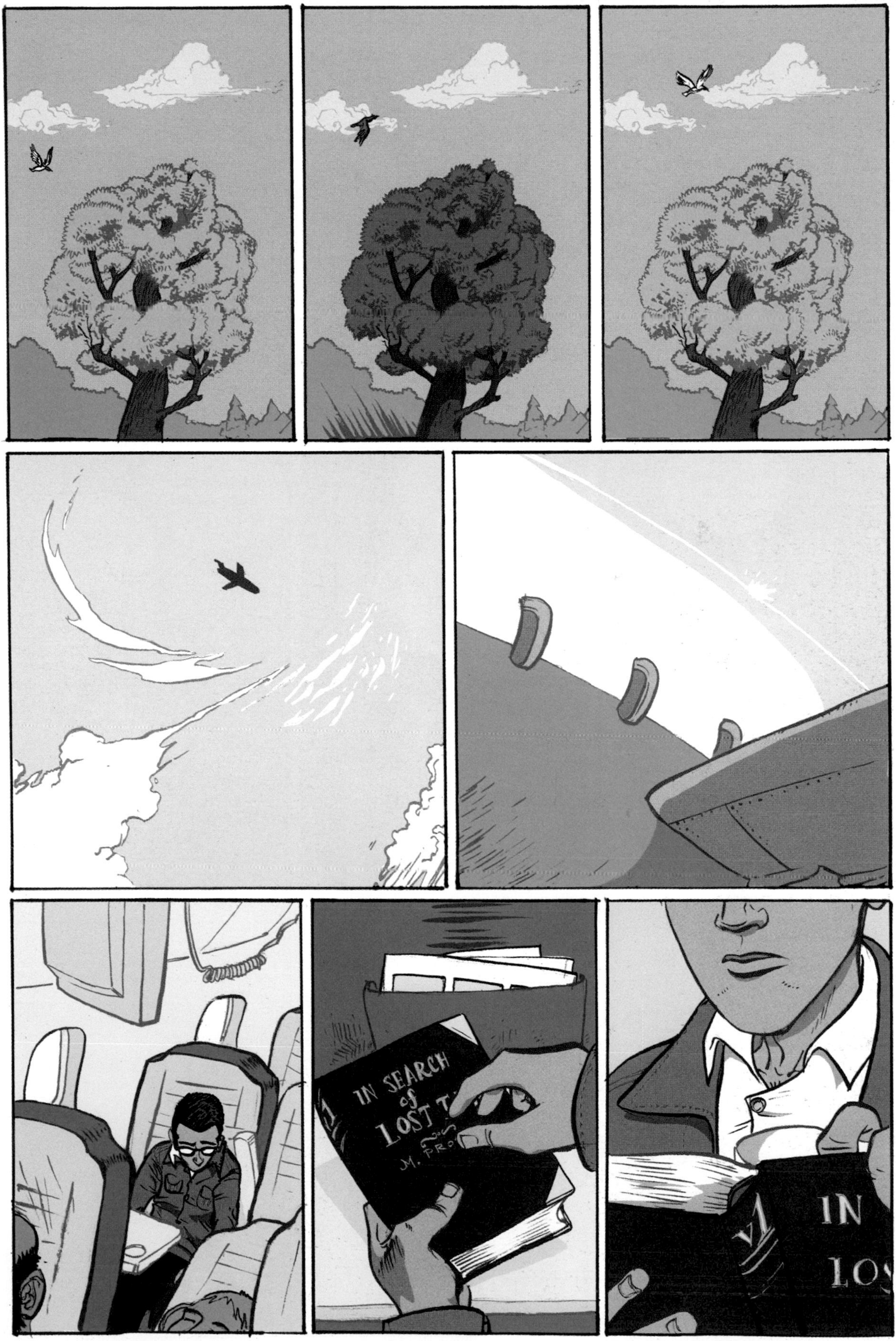
IN SEARCH of LOST T
M. PRO
IN
LOS

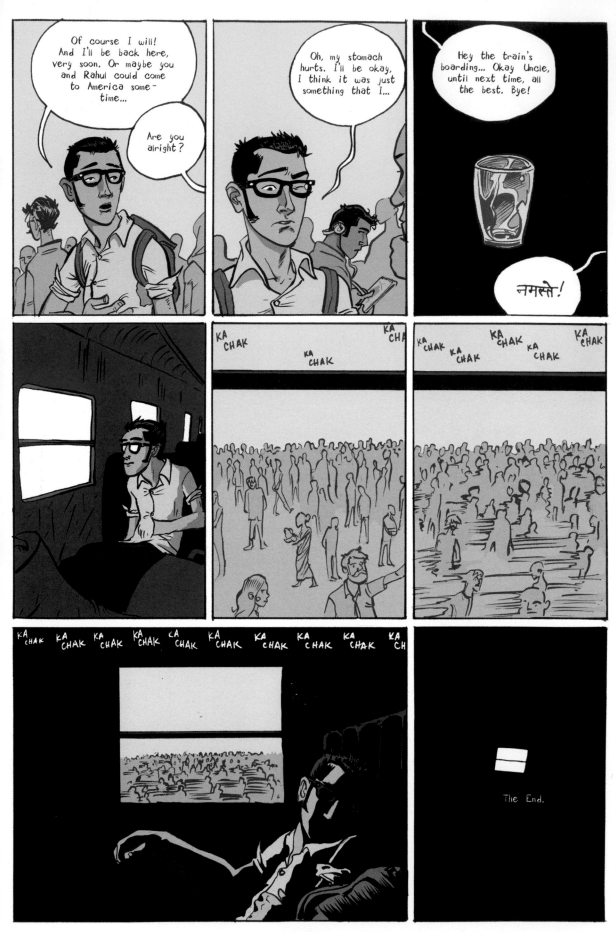

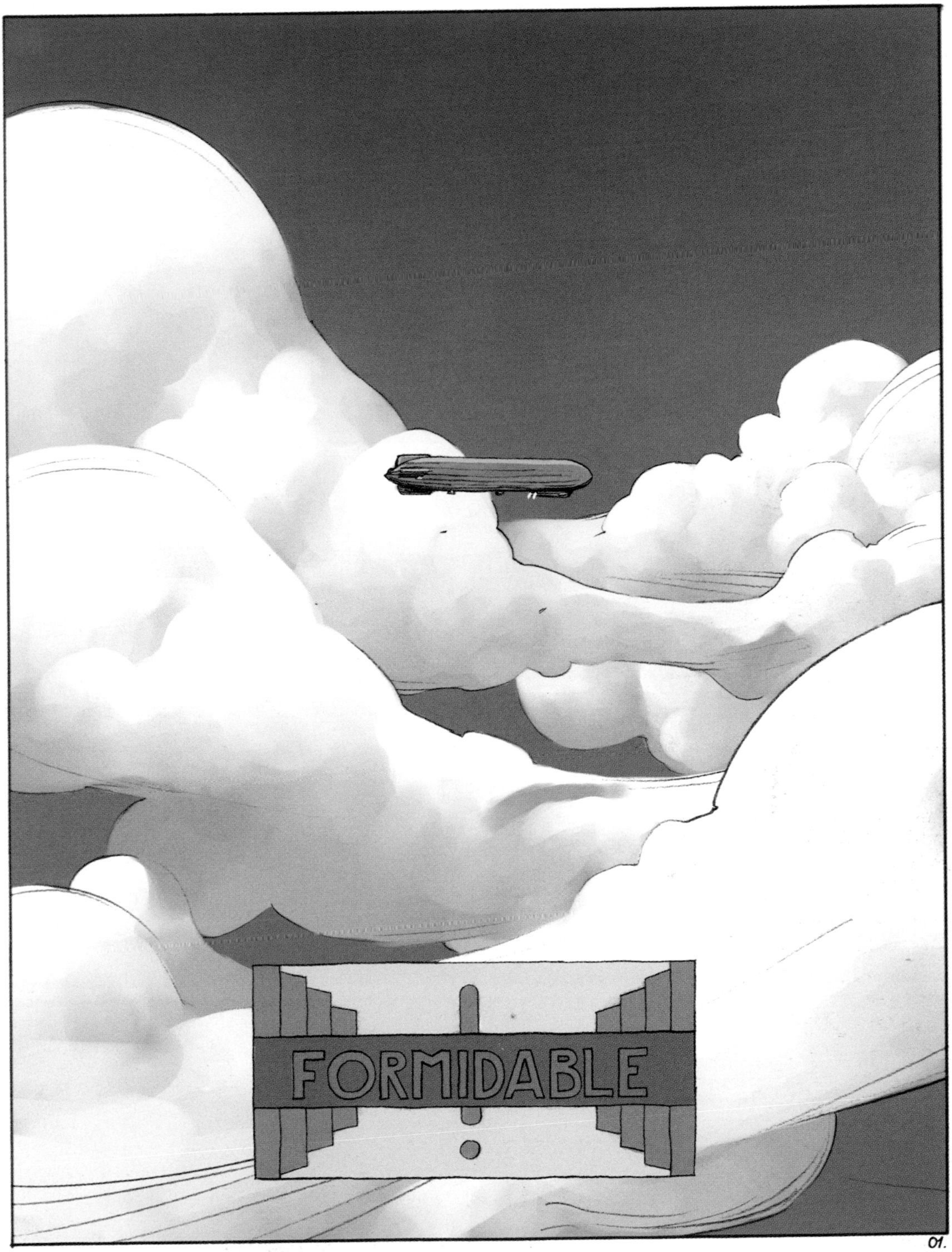
FORMIDABLE
01.

by Bengal

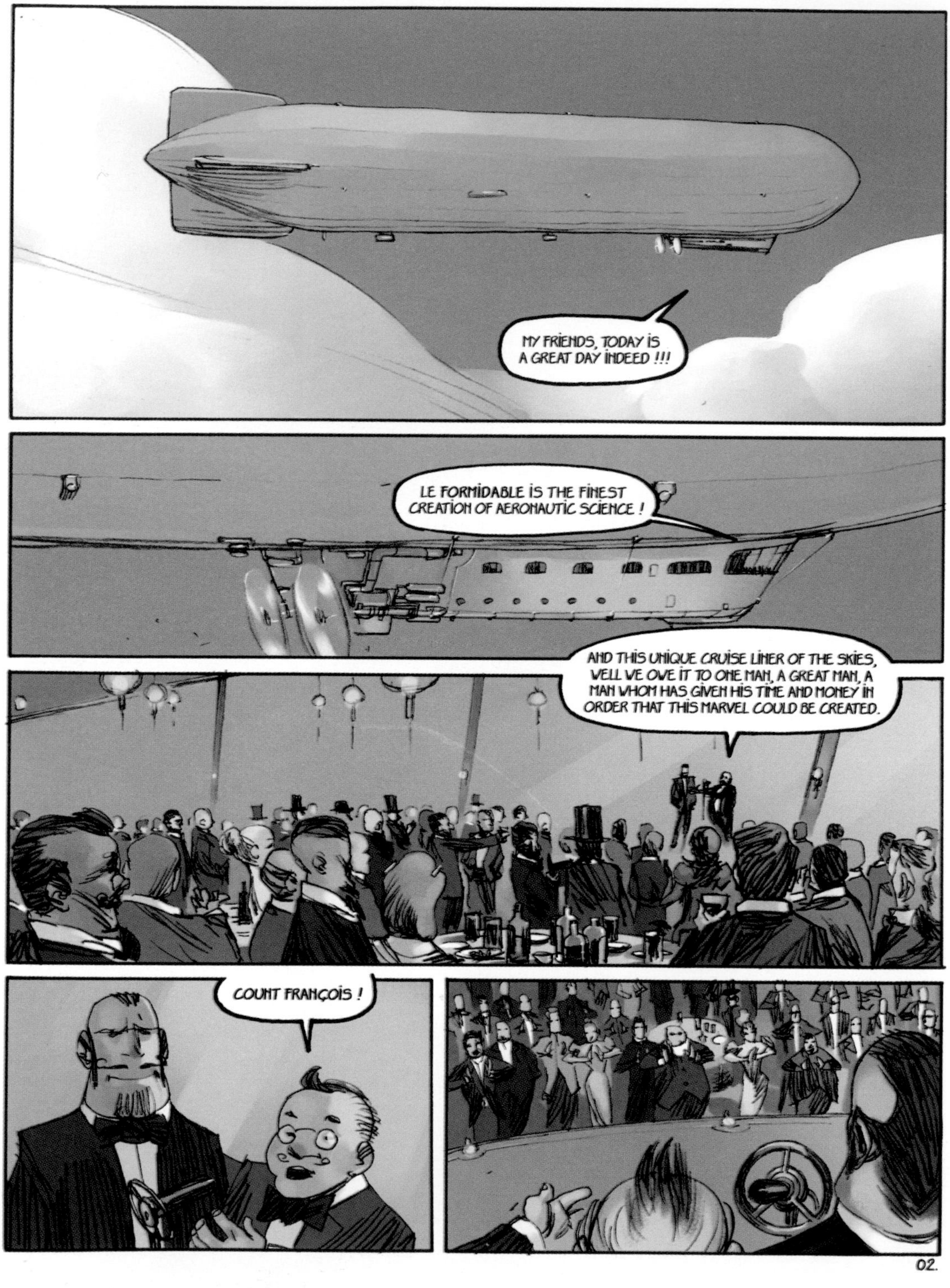
MY FRIENDS, TODAY IS A GREAT DAY INDEED !!!
LE FORMIDABLE IS THE FINEST CREATION OF AERONAUTIC SCIENCE !
AND THIS UNIQUE CRUISE LINER OF THE SKIES, WELL WE OWE IT TO ONE MAN, A GREAT MAN, A MAN WHOM HAS GIVEN HIS TIME AND MONEY IN ORDER THAT THIS MARVEL COULD BE CREATED.
COUNT FRANÇOIS !
02.

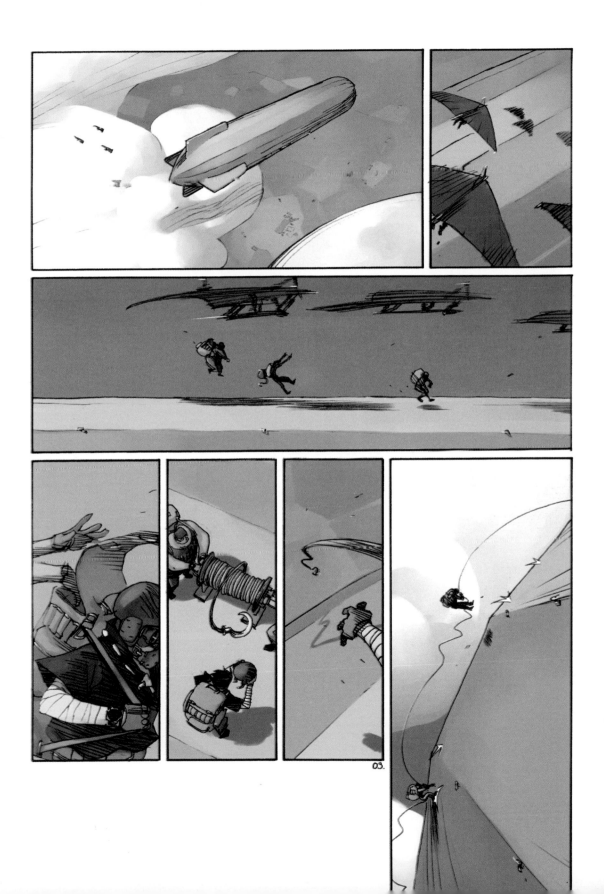

03.

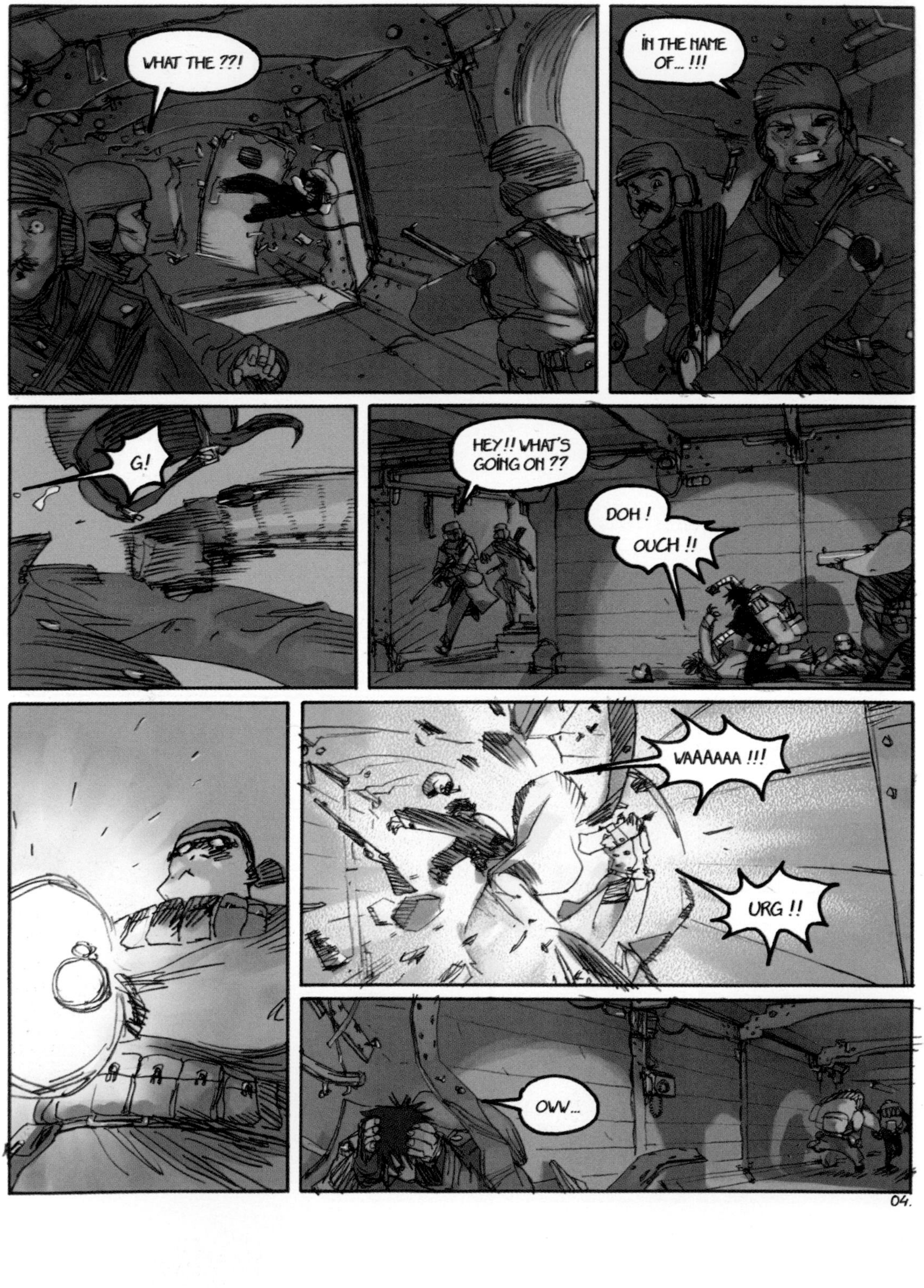
WHAT THE ??!
IN THE NAME OF... !!!
G!
HEY!! WHAT'S GOING ON ??
DOH !
OUCH !!
WAAAAAA !!!
URG !!
OWW...
04.

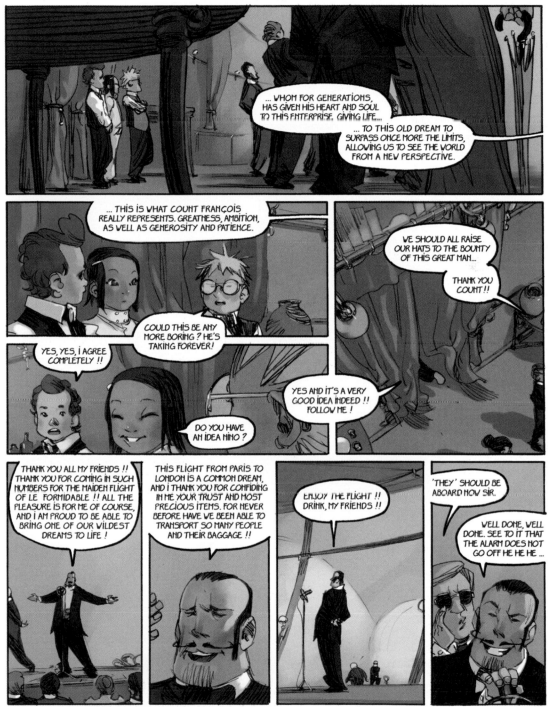

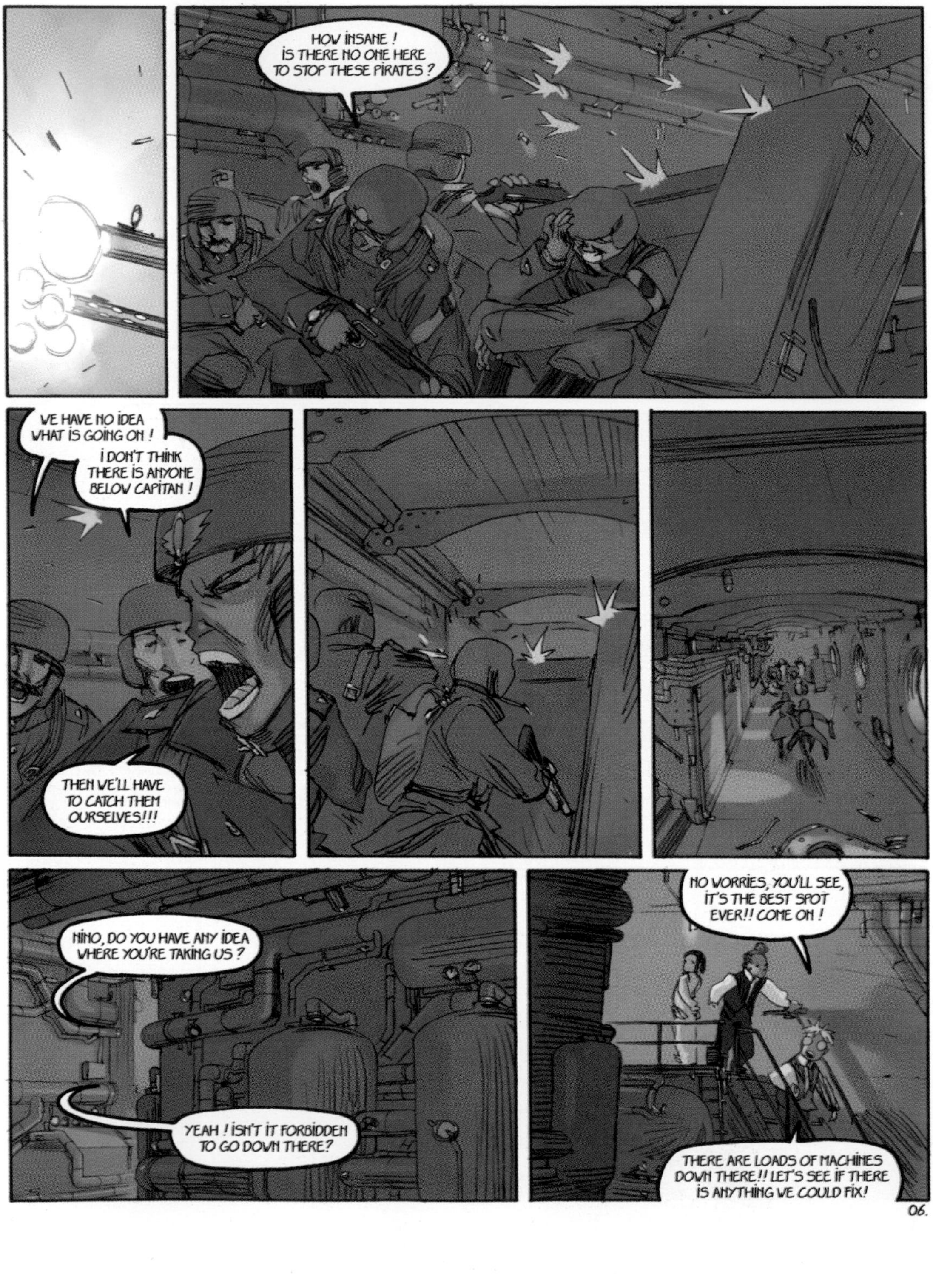
HOW INSANE ! IS THERE NO ONE HERE TO STOP THESE PIRATES ?
WE HAVE NO IDEA WHAT IS GOING ON !
I DON'T THINK THERE IS ANYONE BELOW CAPITAN !
THEN WE'LL HAVE TO CATCH THEM OURSELVES!!!
NINO, DO YOU HAVE ANY IDEA WHERE YOU'RE TAKING US ?
YEAH ! ISN'T IT FORBIDDEN TO GO DOWN THERE?
NO WORRIES, YOU'LL SEE, IT'S THE BEST SPOT EVER!! COME ON !
THERE ARE LOADS OF MACHINES DOWN THERE!! LET'S SEE IF THERE IS ANYTHING WE COULD FIX!
06.

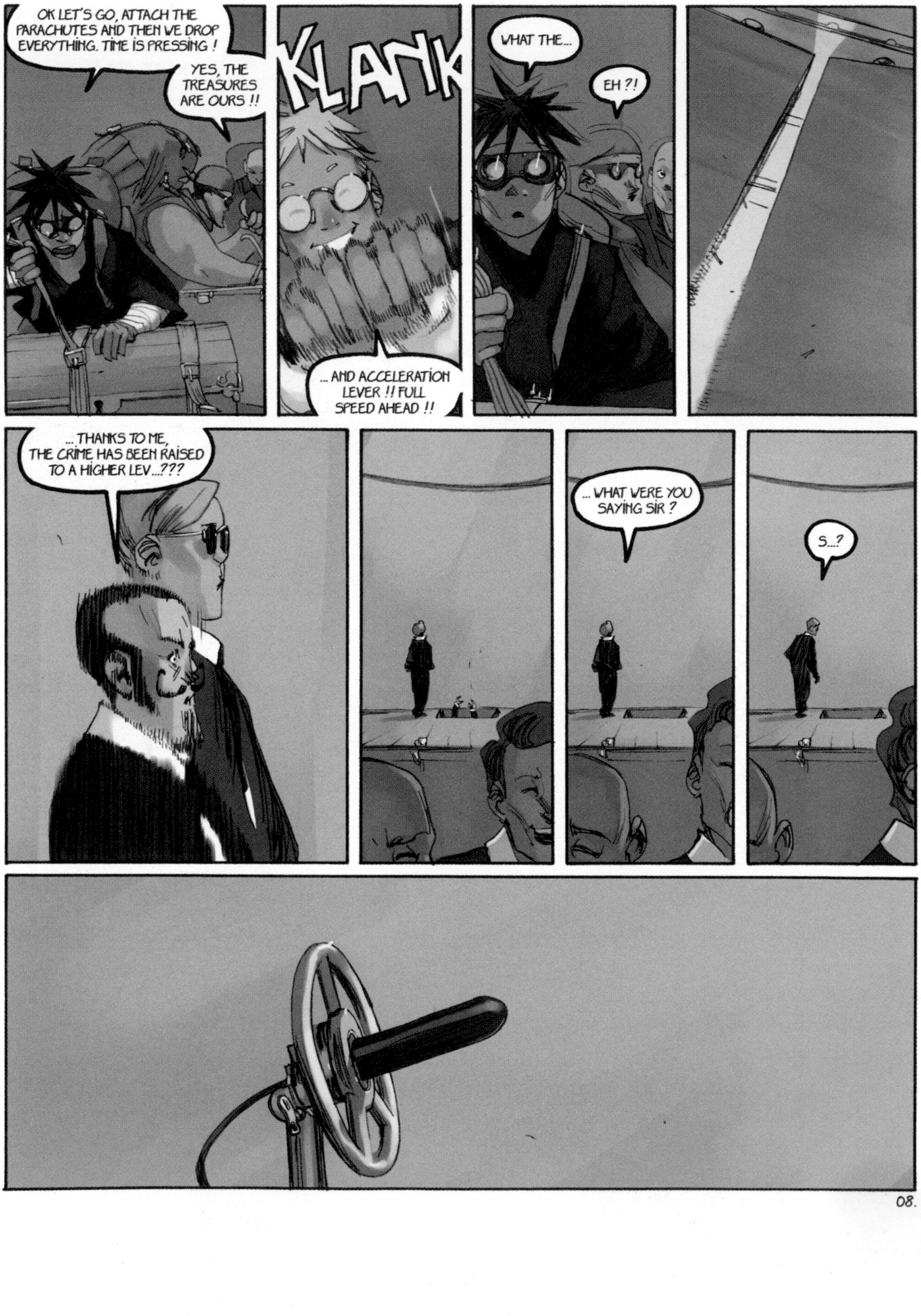
OK LET'S GO, ATTACH THE PARACHUTES AND THEN WE DROP EVERYTHING. TIME IS PRESSING !
YES, THE TREASURES ARE OURS !!
KLANK
... AND ACCELERATION LEVER !! FULL SPEED AHEAD !!
WHAT THE...
EH ?!
... THANKS TO ME, THE CRIME HAS BEEN RAISED TO A HIGHER LEV...???
... WHAT WERE YOU SAYING SIR ?
S...?
08.

"Outside My Window" by Khang Le

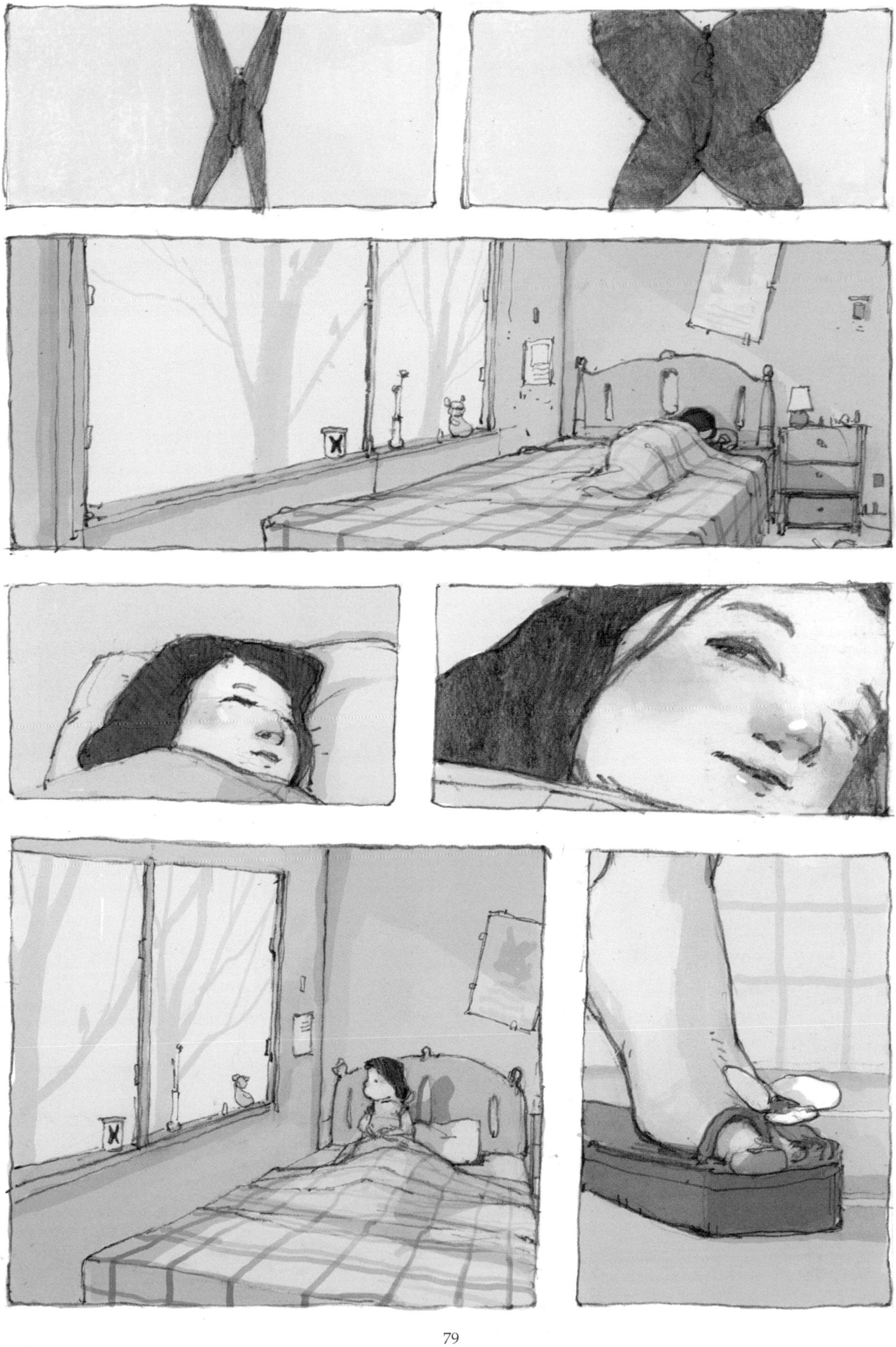

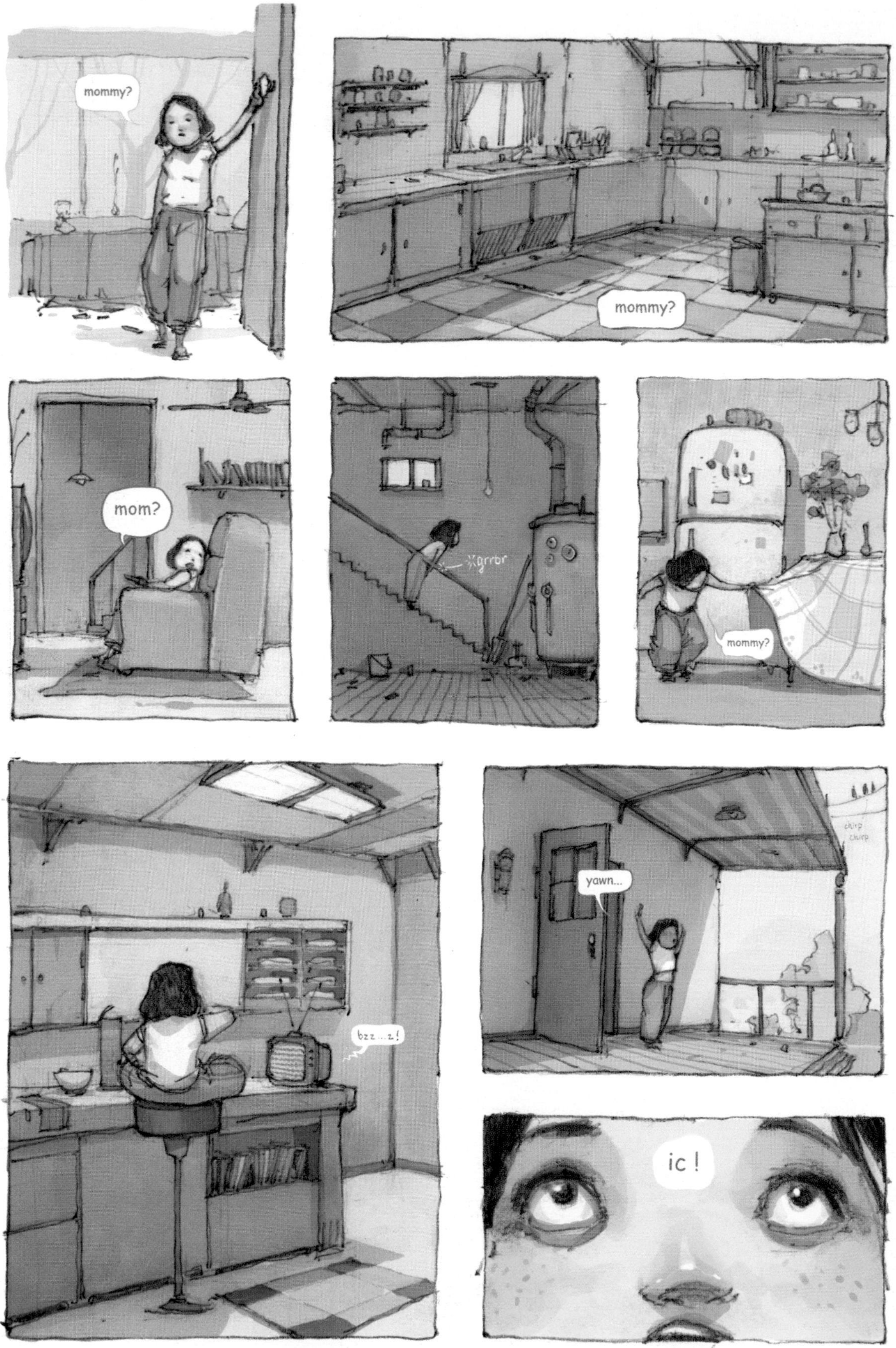
mommy?
mommy?
mom?
grrbr
mommy?
bzz...z!
chirp
chirp
yawn...
ic !

chirp
chirp
Hi!
uh..hello
!

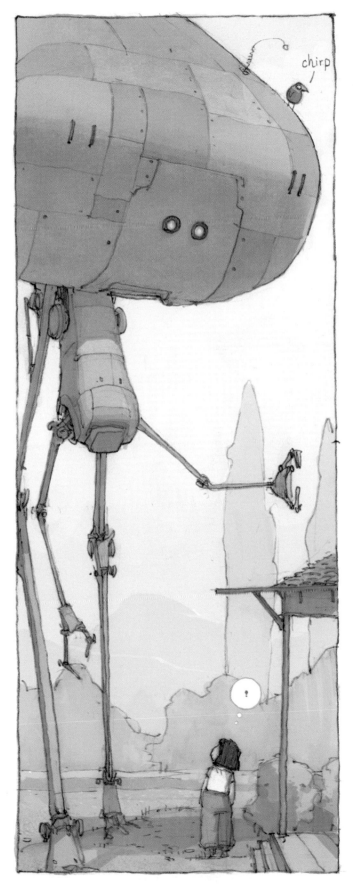

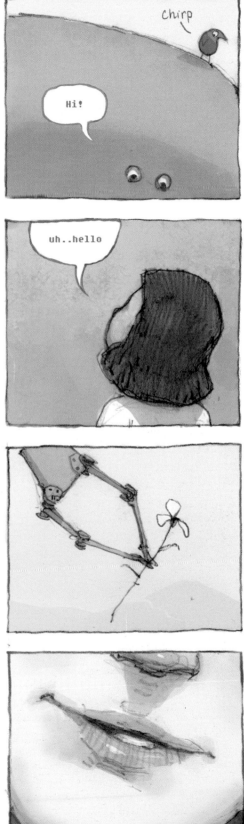

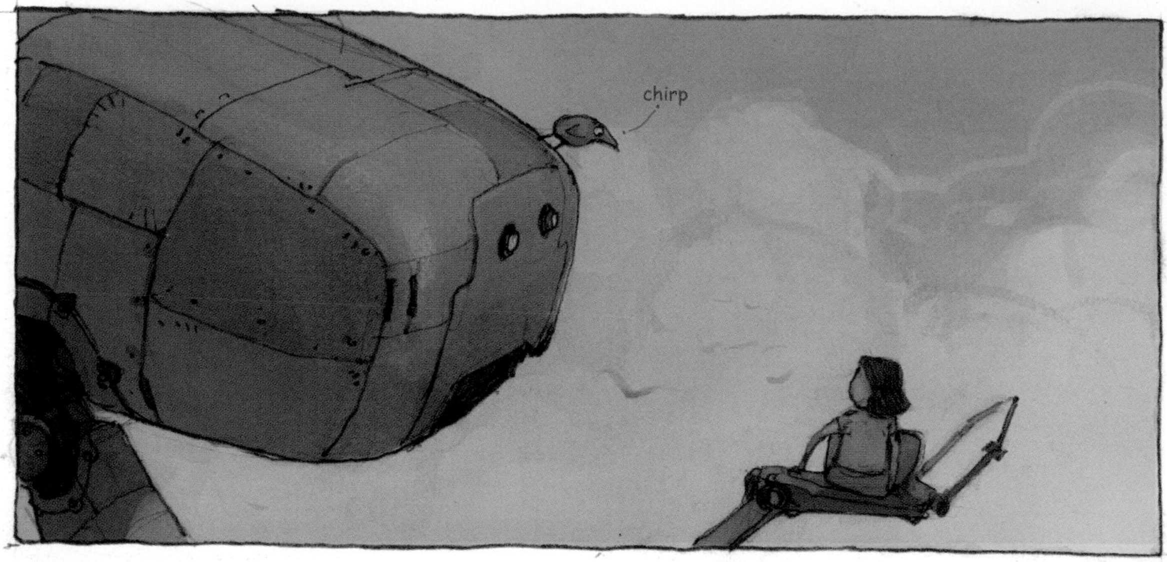
chirp

So what's your name?
Donna. And yours?
Hmm..let's see...you can call me Ulys.
Okay...Ulys. I don't mean to be rude but you're not gonna eat me are you?
Or replace my brain with computer chips and stuff. I saw it on TV once.
Ech...no...of course not. I just want to be your friend. It gets lonely here.
What is this place? I can see my house below but I don't recognize anything else.
Where are my parents? my neighbors? my street?

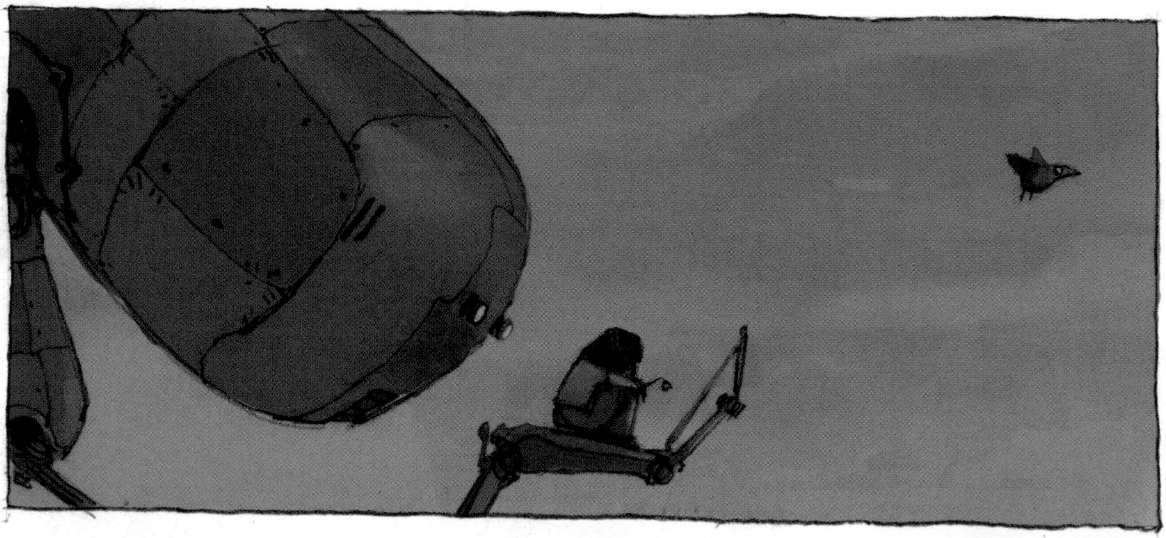

...it's a bit too complicated to explain. I've been watching you,
through the glass. And I brought you here.
This is another place.
But my house is right below. That's my home...isn't it?
Donna, this is my world. I built your home from my memory.
I wanted your transition to be a comfortable one.
In this place, I can give you everything...anything you want.
Just as long as you stay.
I want to go home.

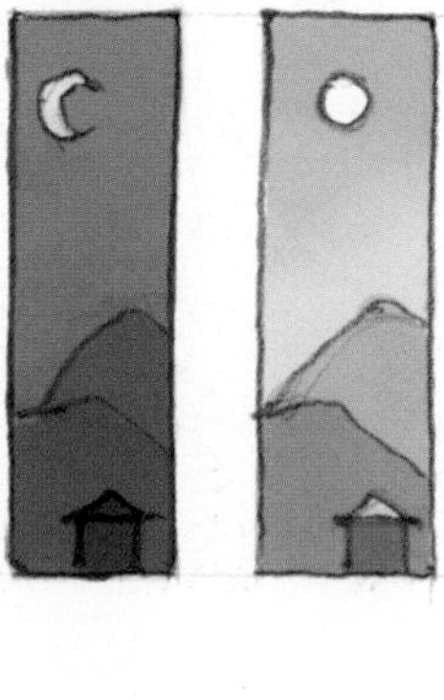

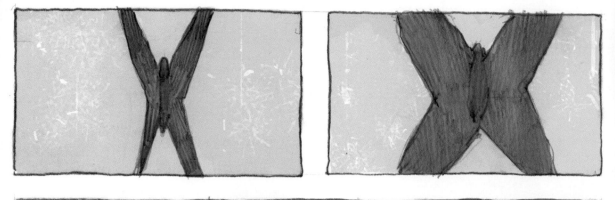

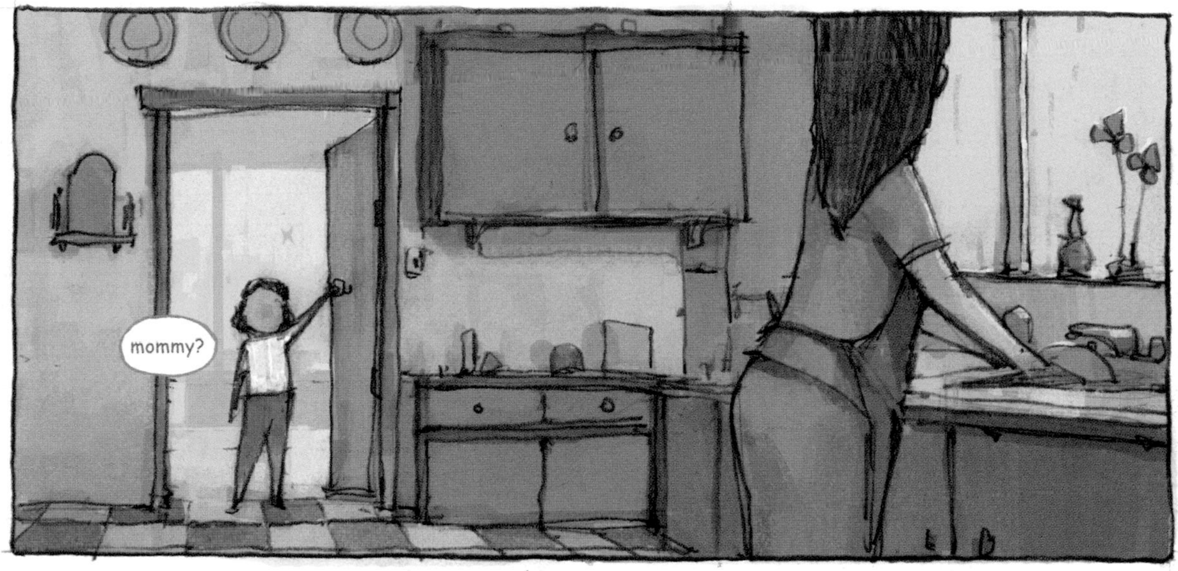
mommy?

THE END.

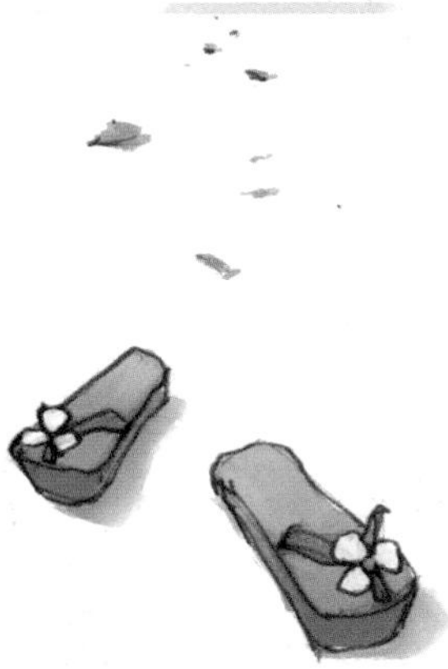

Story and pictures by Chris Appelhans

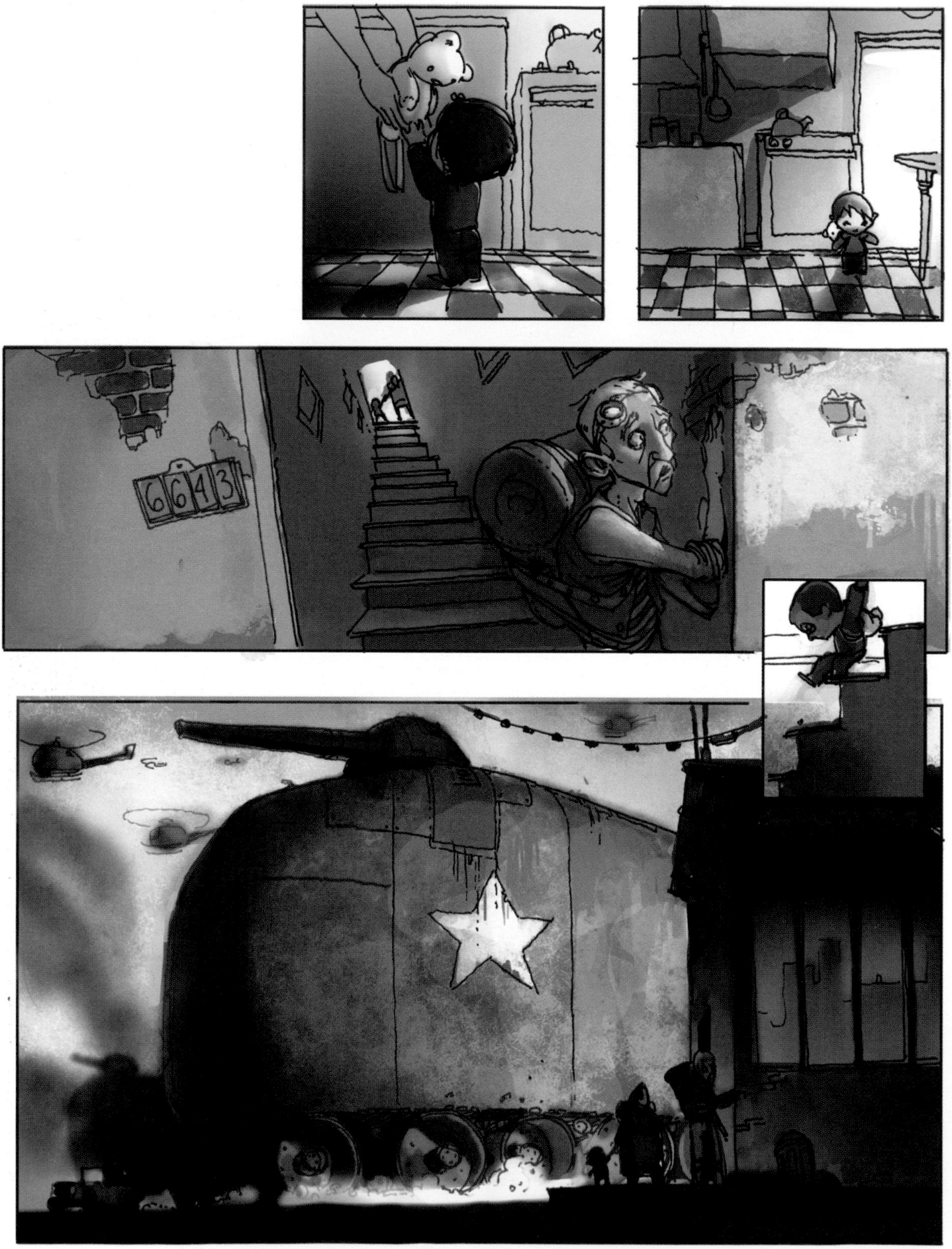
6643

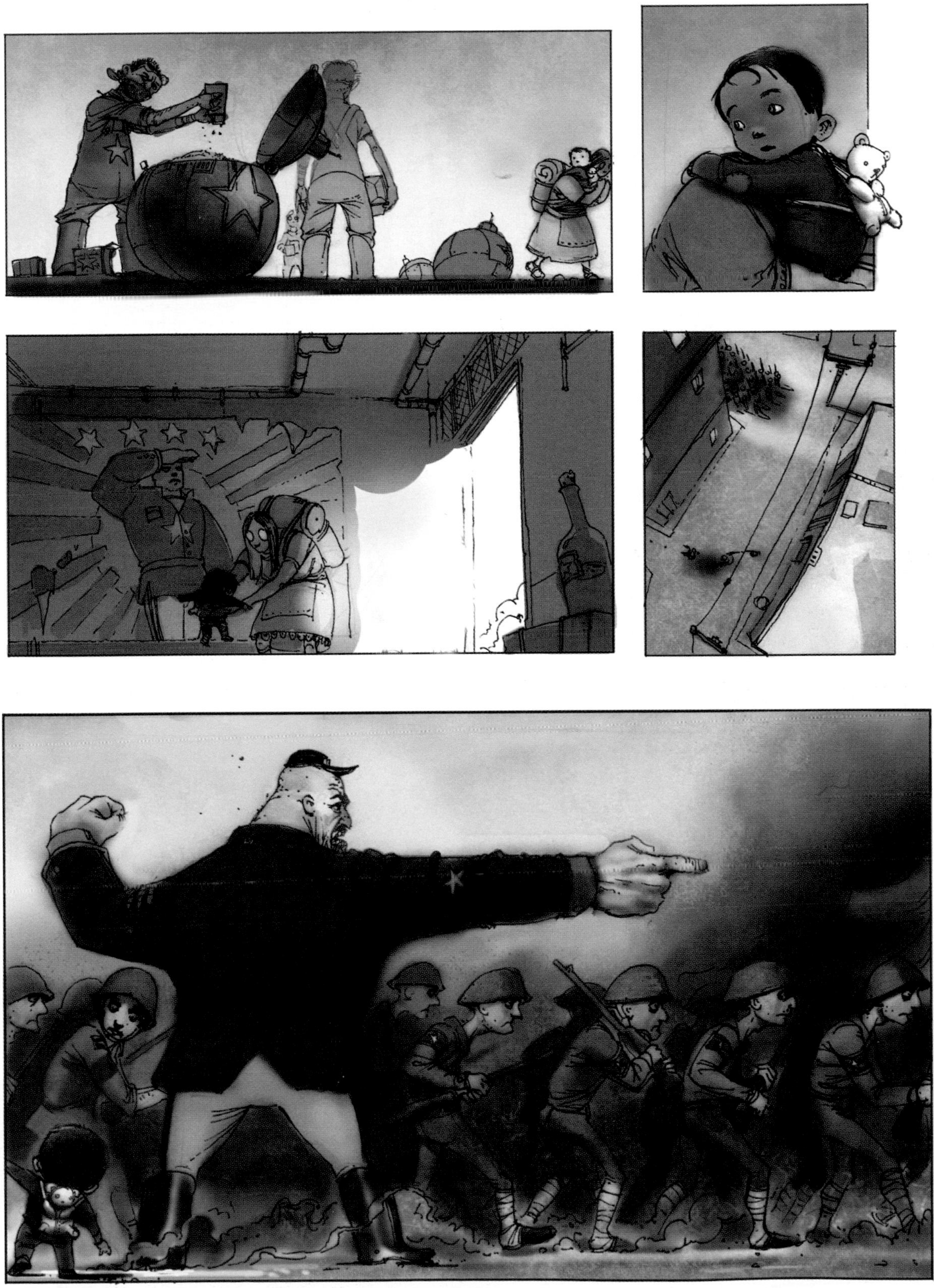

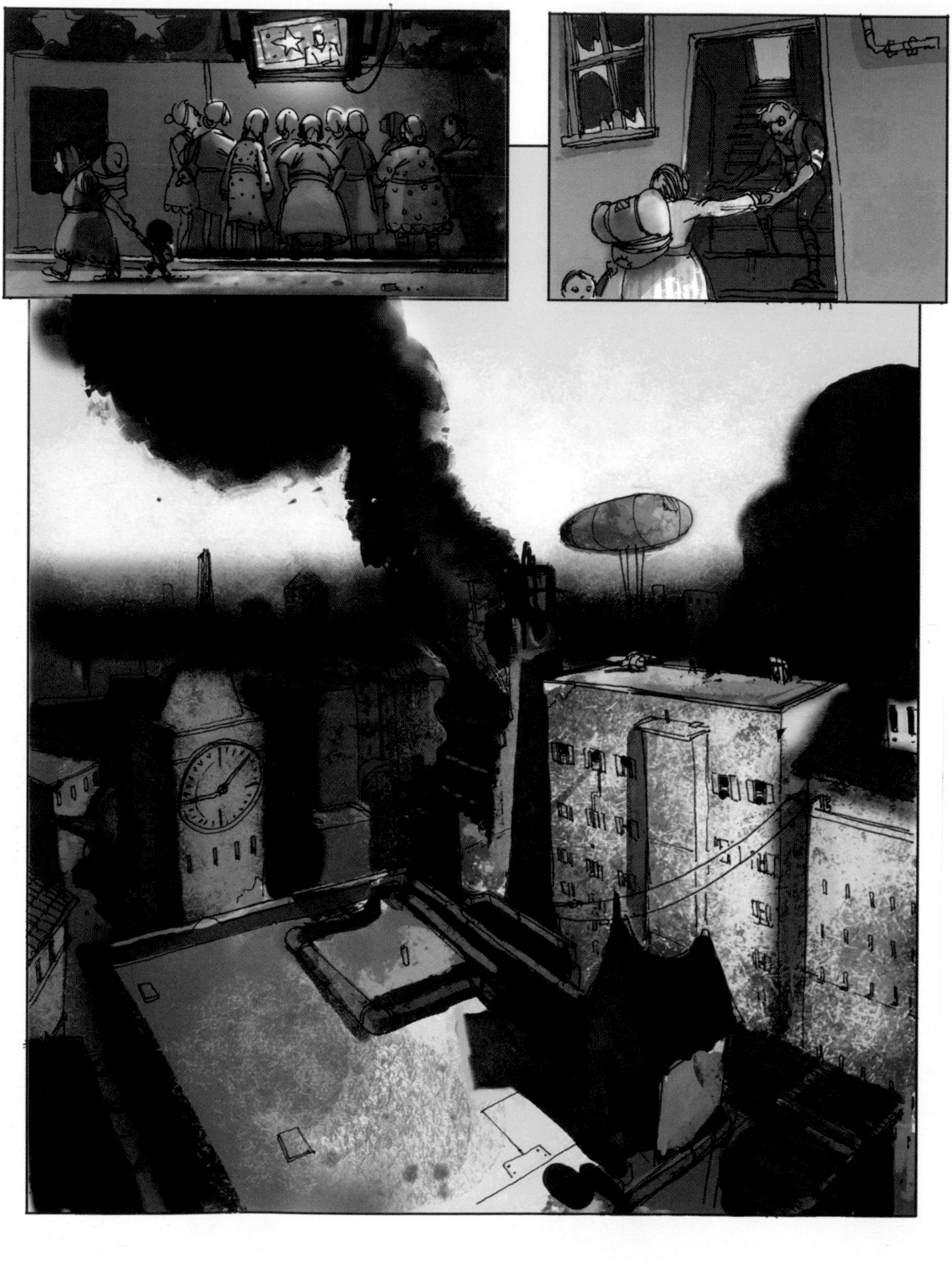

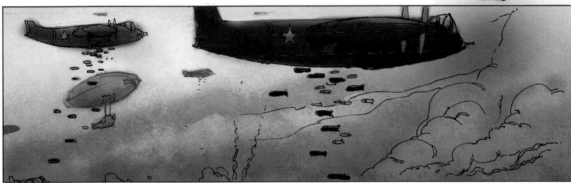

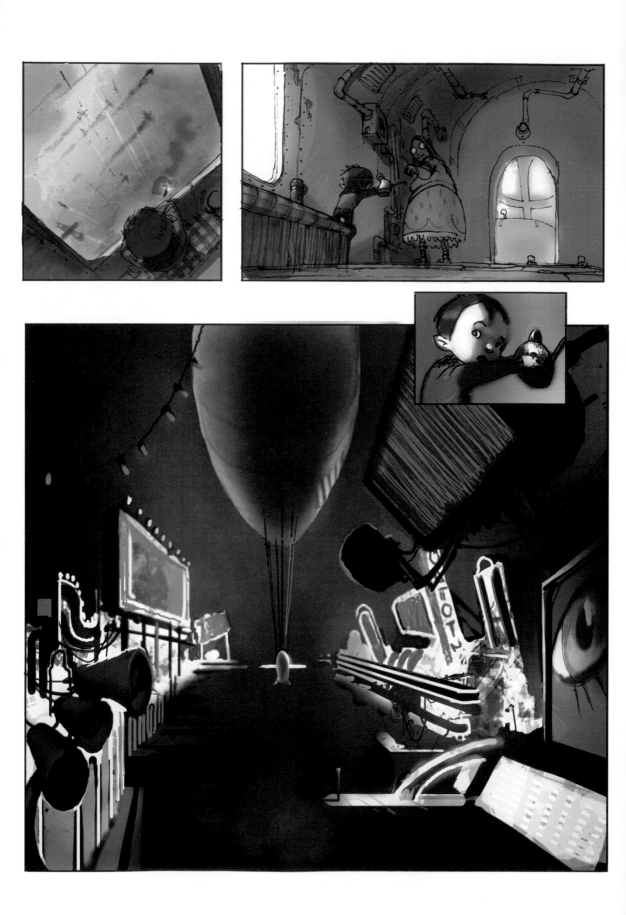

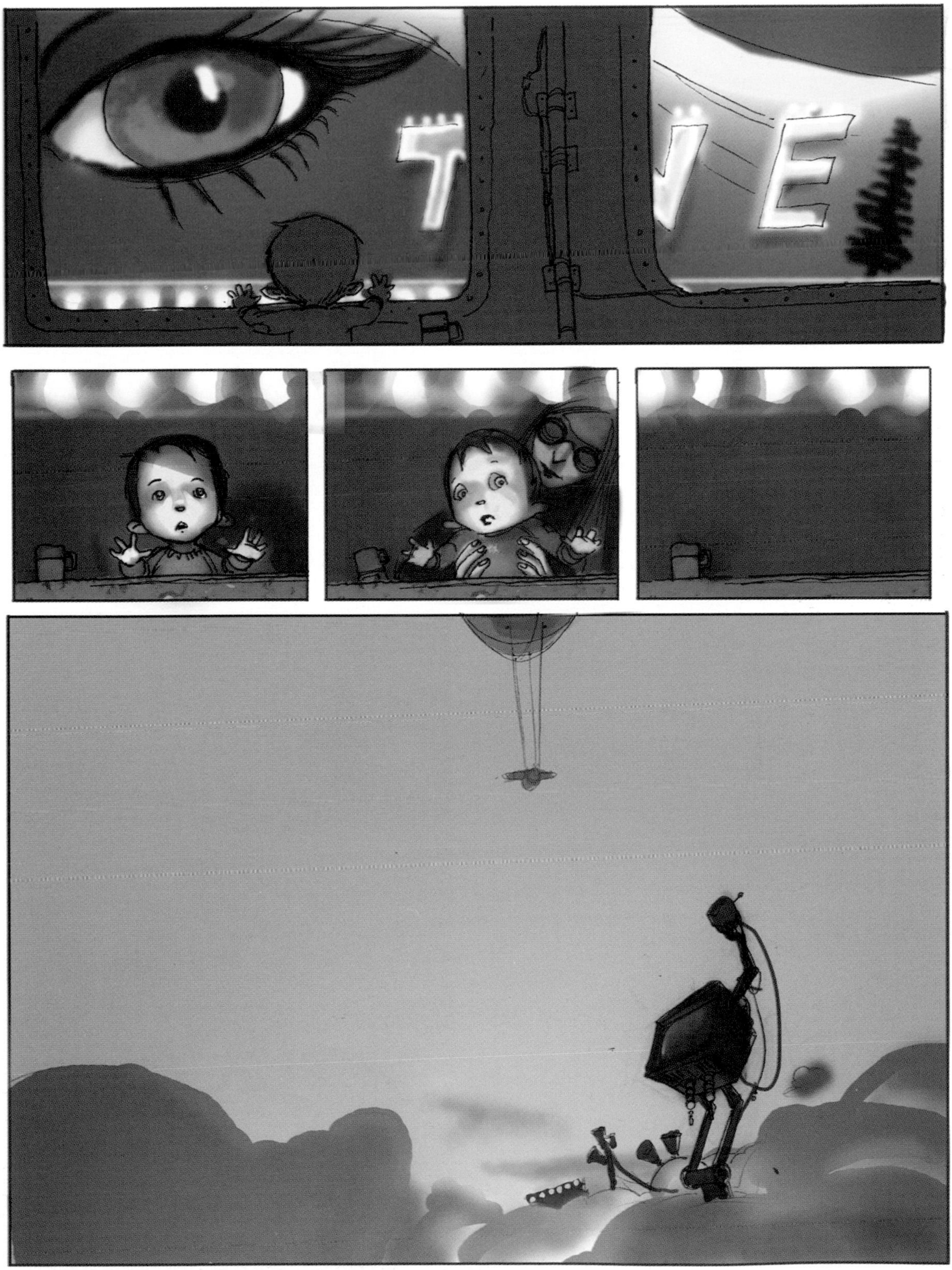

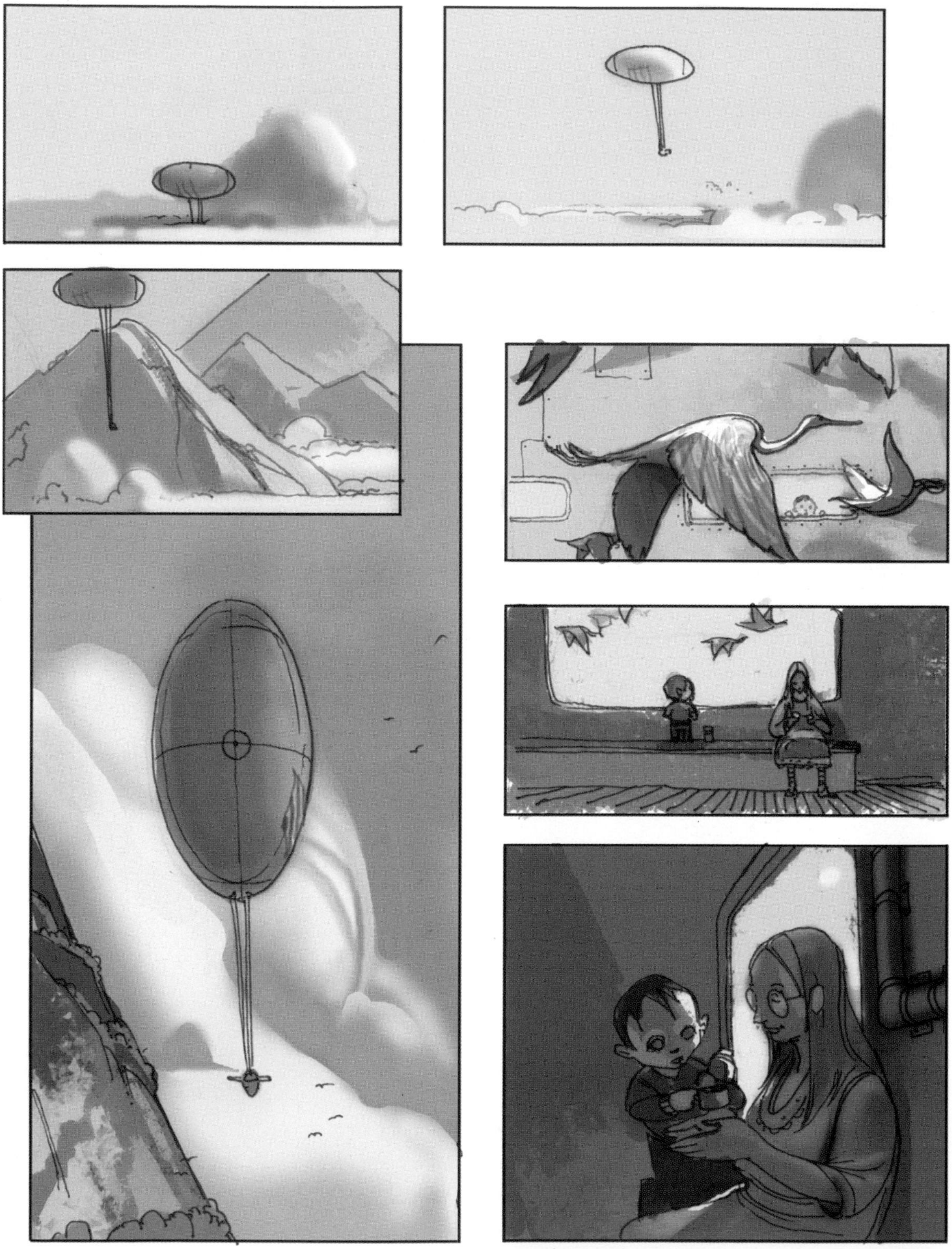

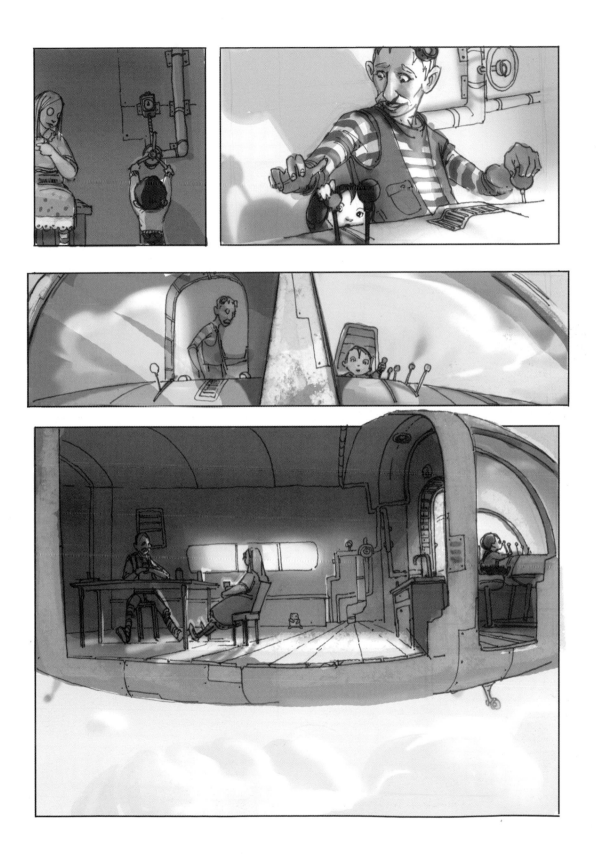

for MoM and DAD

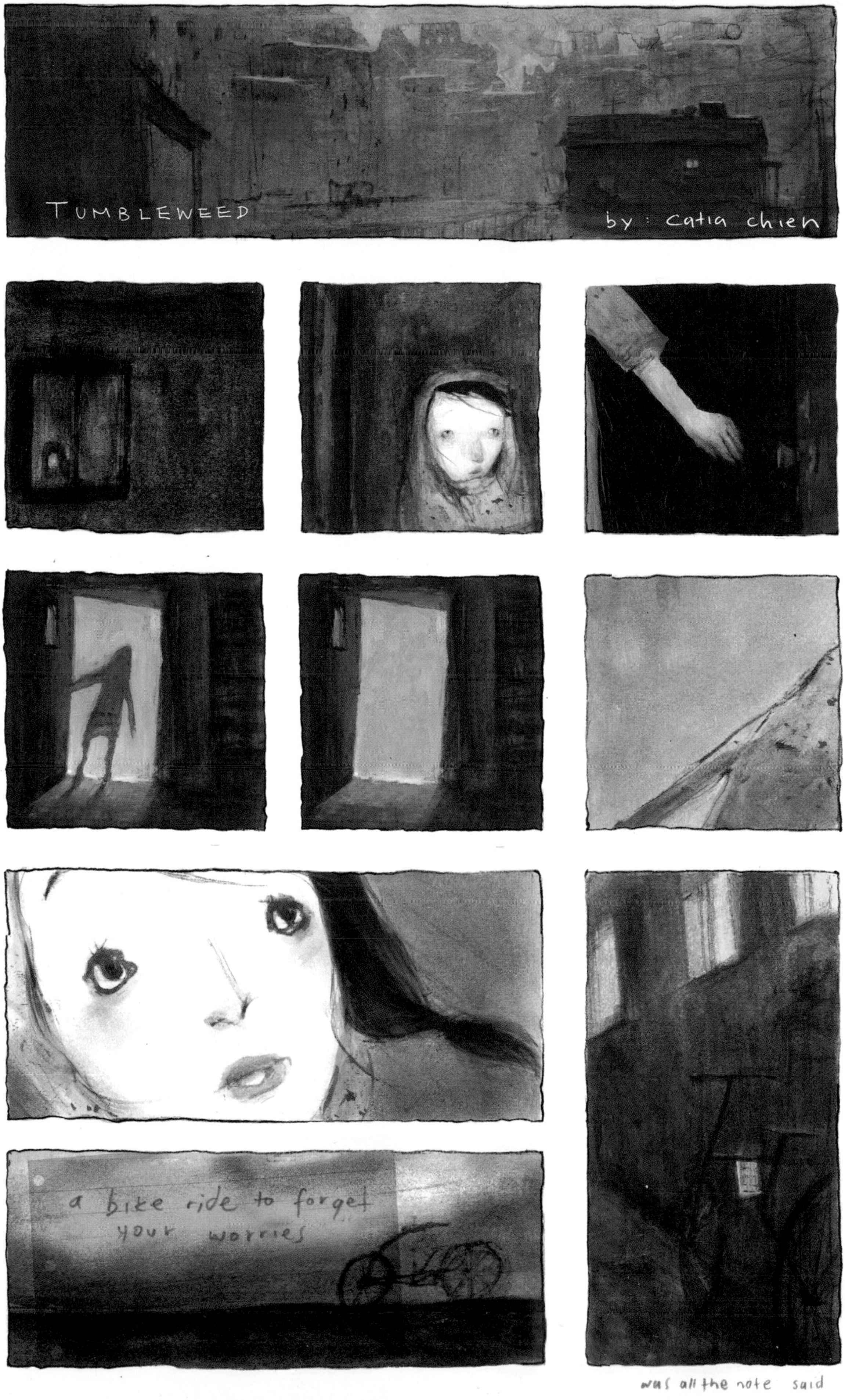
TUMBLEWEED
by: catia chien
a bike ride to forget
your worries
was all the note said

and off I went following a stranger's advice I took a shortcut through the city

to avoid traffic

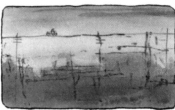

pedaled down and out of town

into

the quiet space

between tall trees

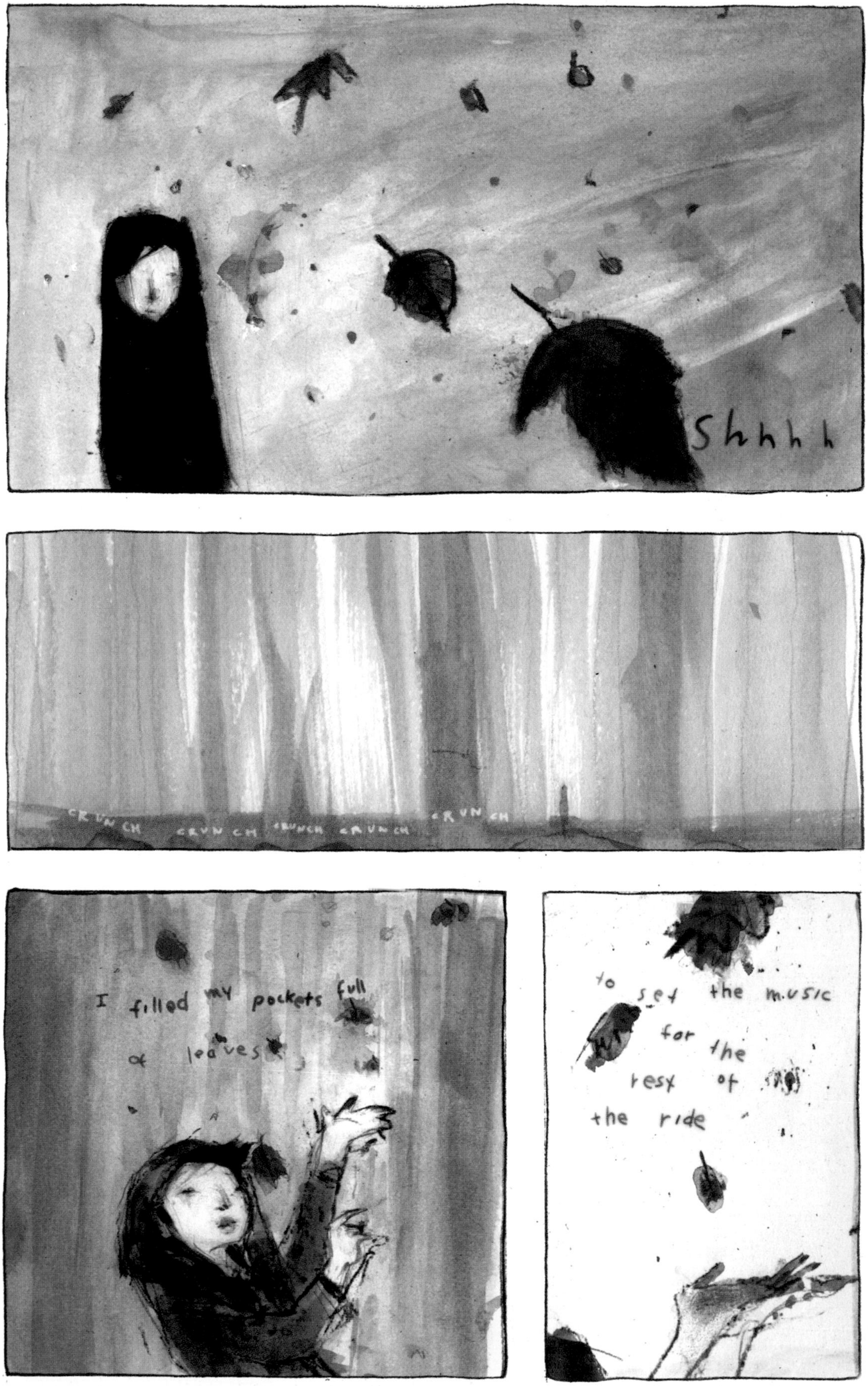
Shhhh
CRUNCH CRUNCH CRUNCH CRUNCH CRUNCH
I filled my pockets full of leaves
to set the music for the rest of the ride

CRUNCH
CRUNCH
CRUNCH
CRUNCH
CRUNCH
SPLASH

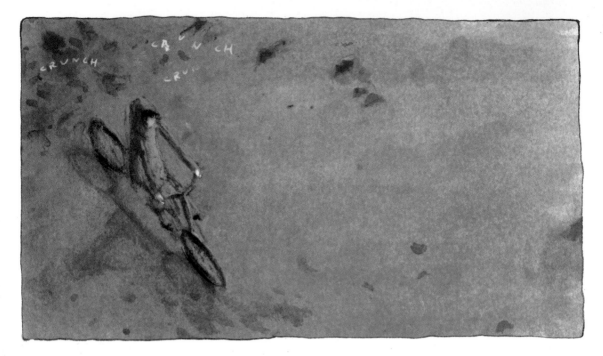

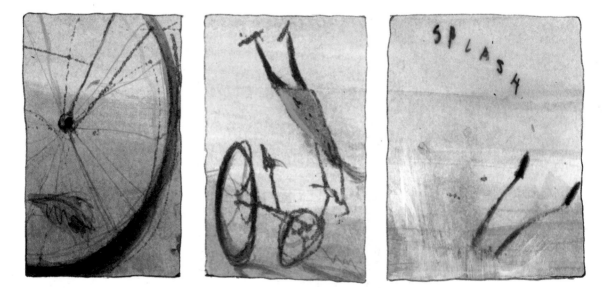

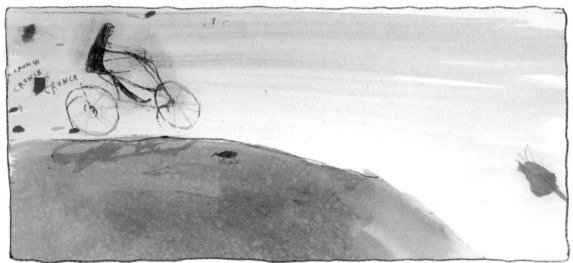

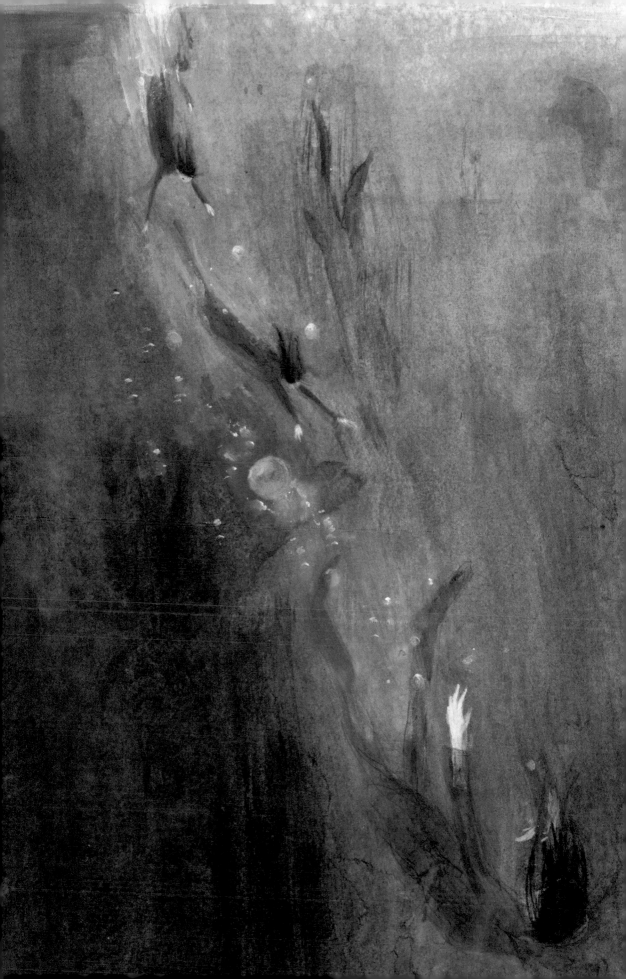

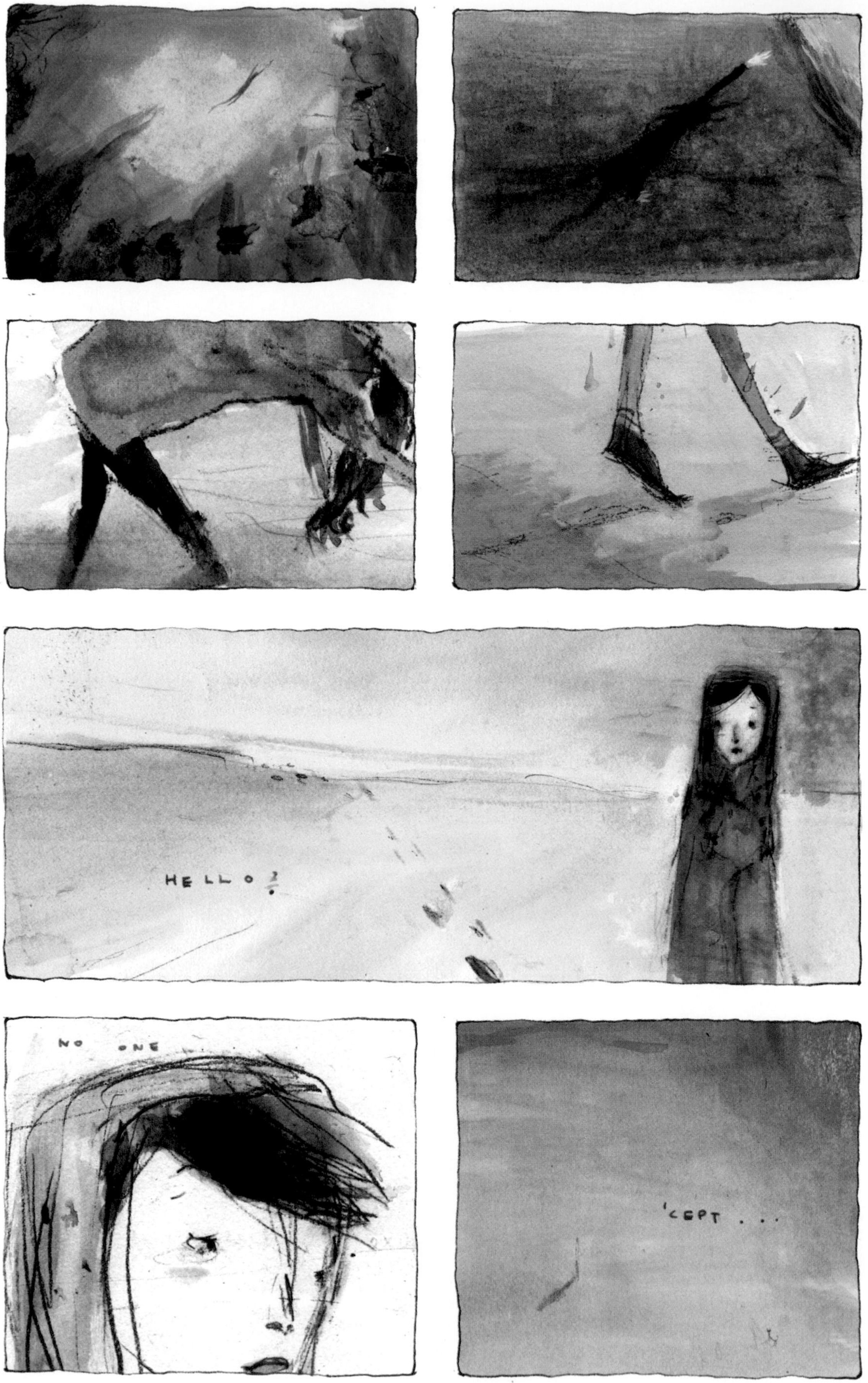
HELLO?
NO ONE...
'CEPT ...

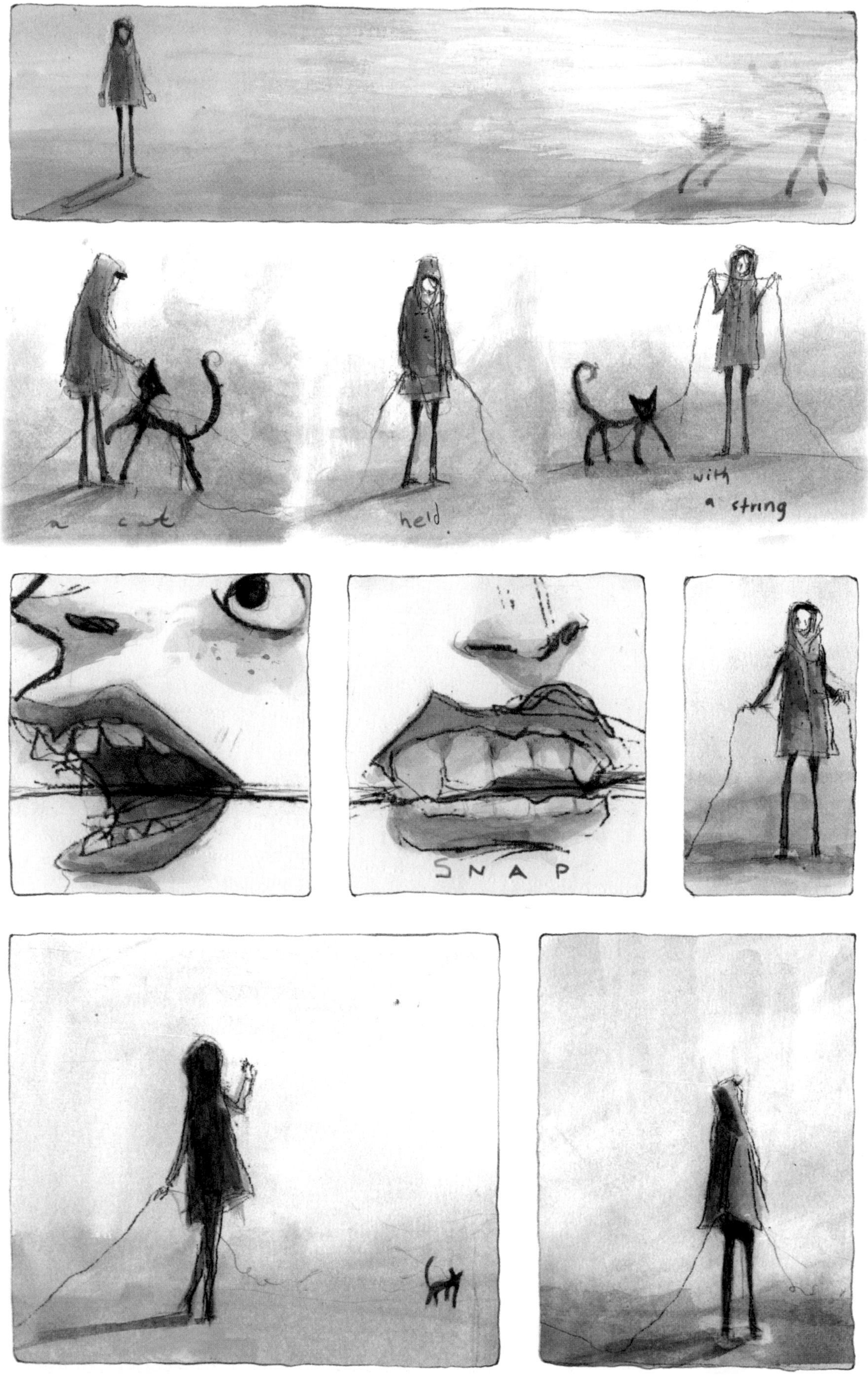
a cat
held
with a string
SNAP

I followed the string

till'our hands met in a light handshake

A sudden Raincloud passed

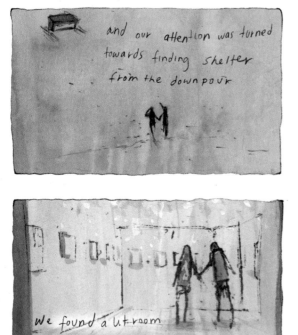

and our attention was turned towards finding shelter from the downpour

We found a litroom

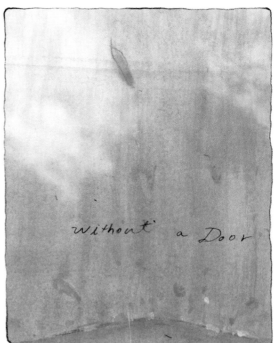

without a Door

104

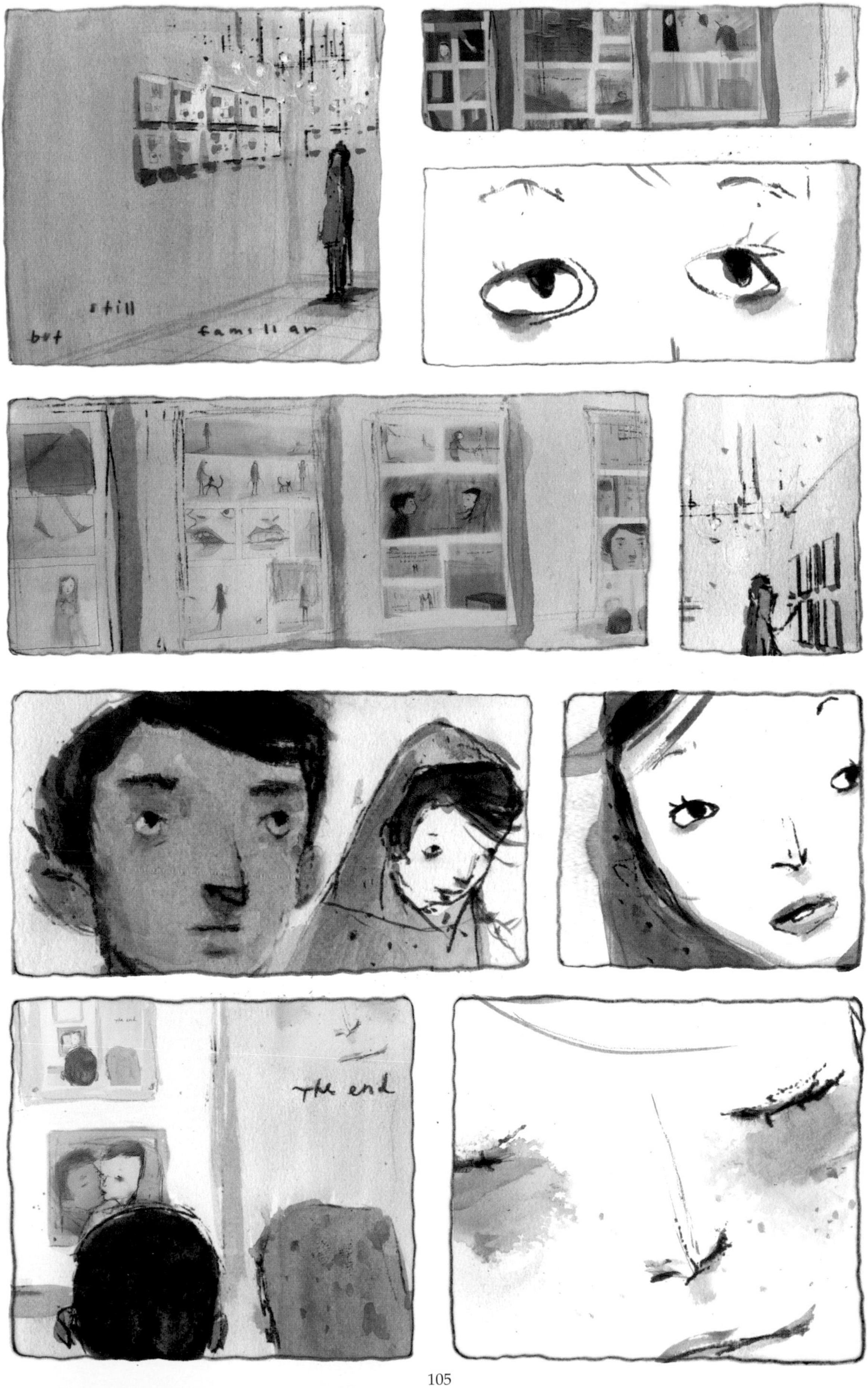
but
still
familiar
the end

Fall

by Catia chien

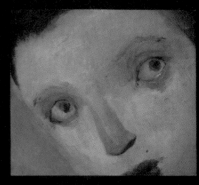
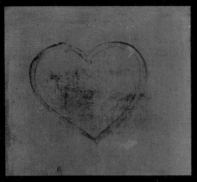
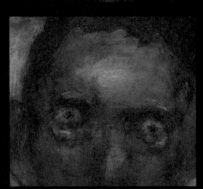

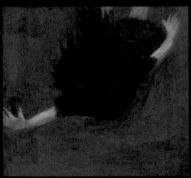

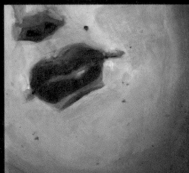

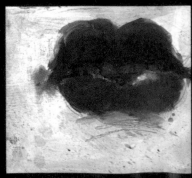
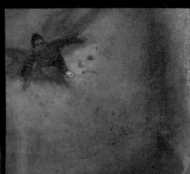

June.

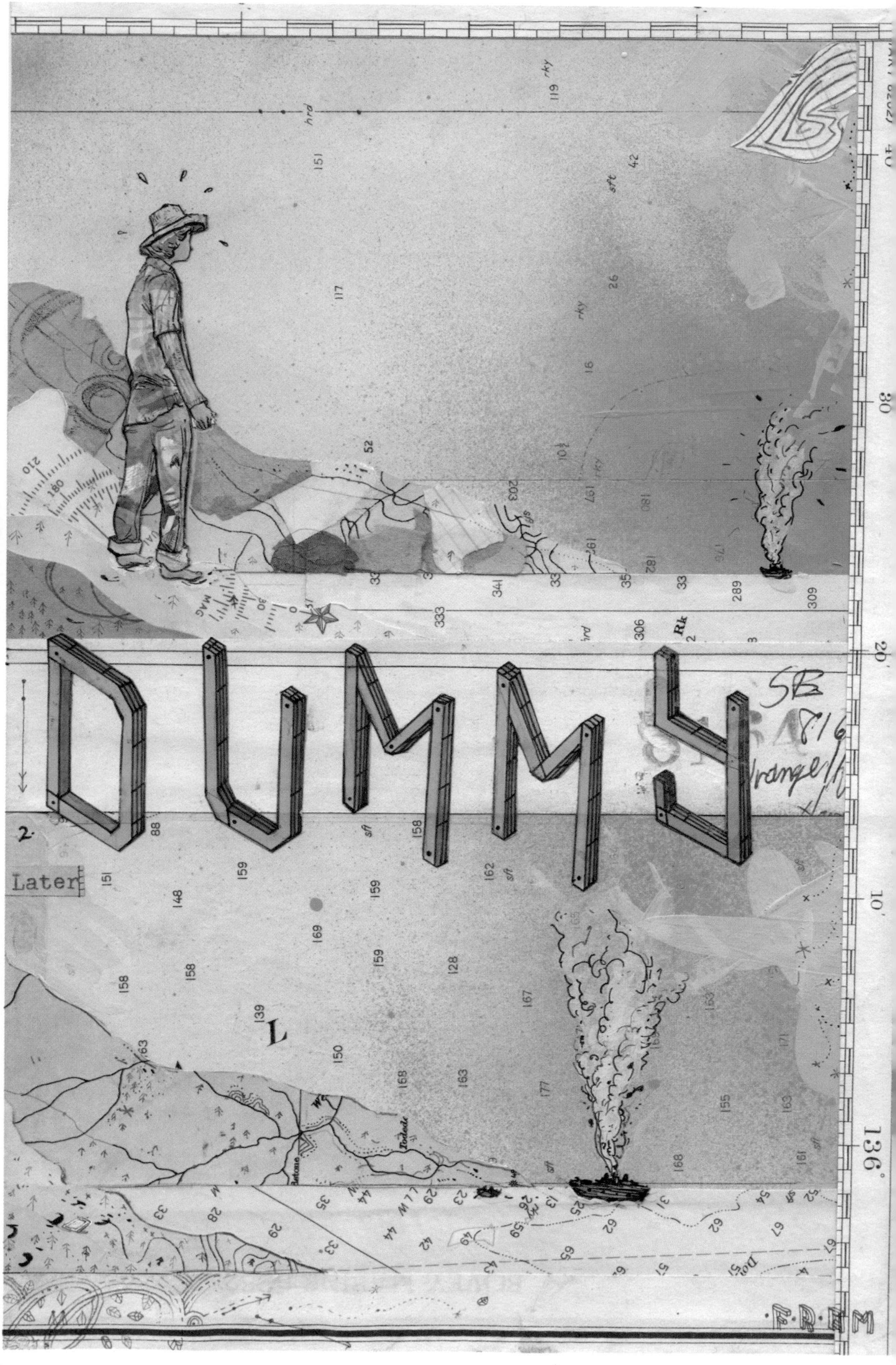
DUMMY
Later

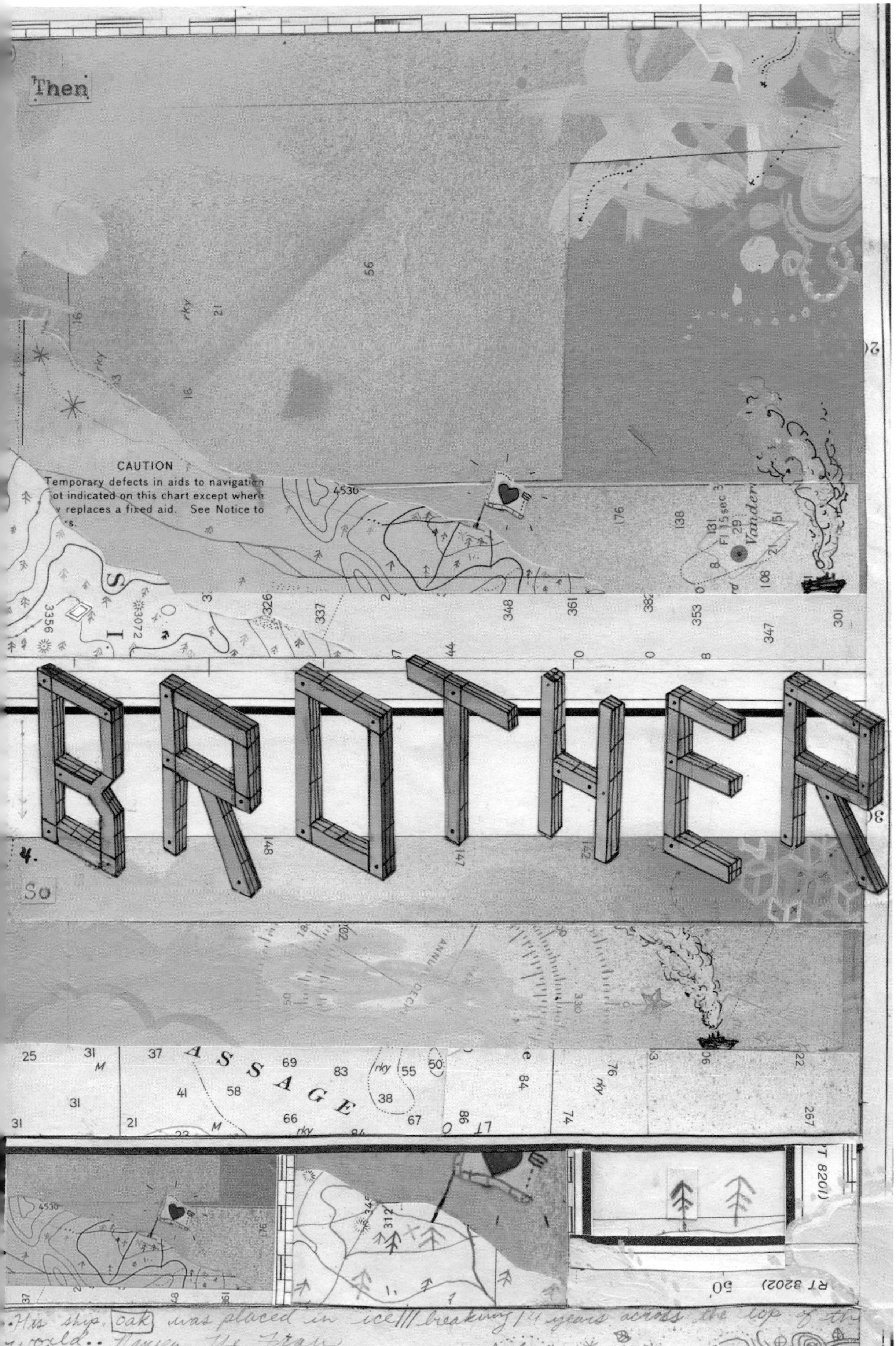

Then
CAUTION
Temporary defects in aids to navigation
ot indicated on this chart except where
y replaces a fixed aid. See Notice to
BROTHER
So
ASSAGE
His ship oak was placed in ice /// breaking / 4 years across the top of the
world.. Nansen The Fram
Walking in the dark, holding your tongue while the prattle

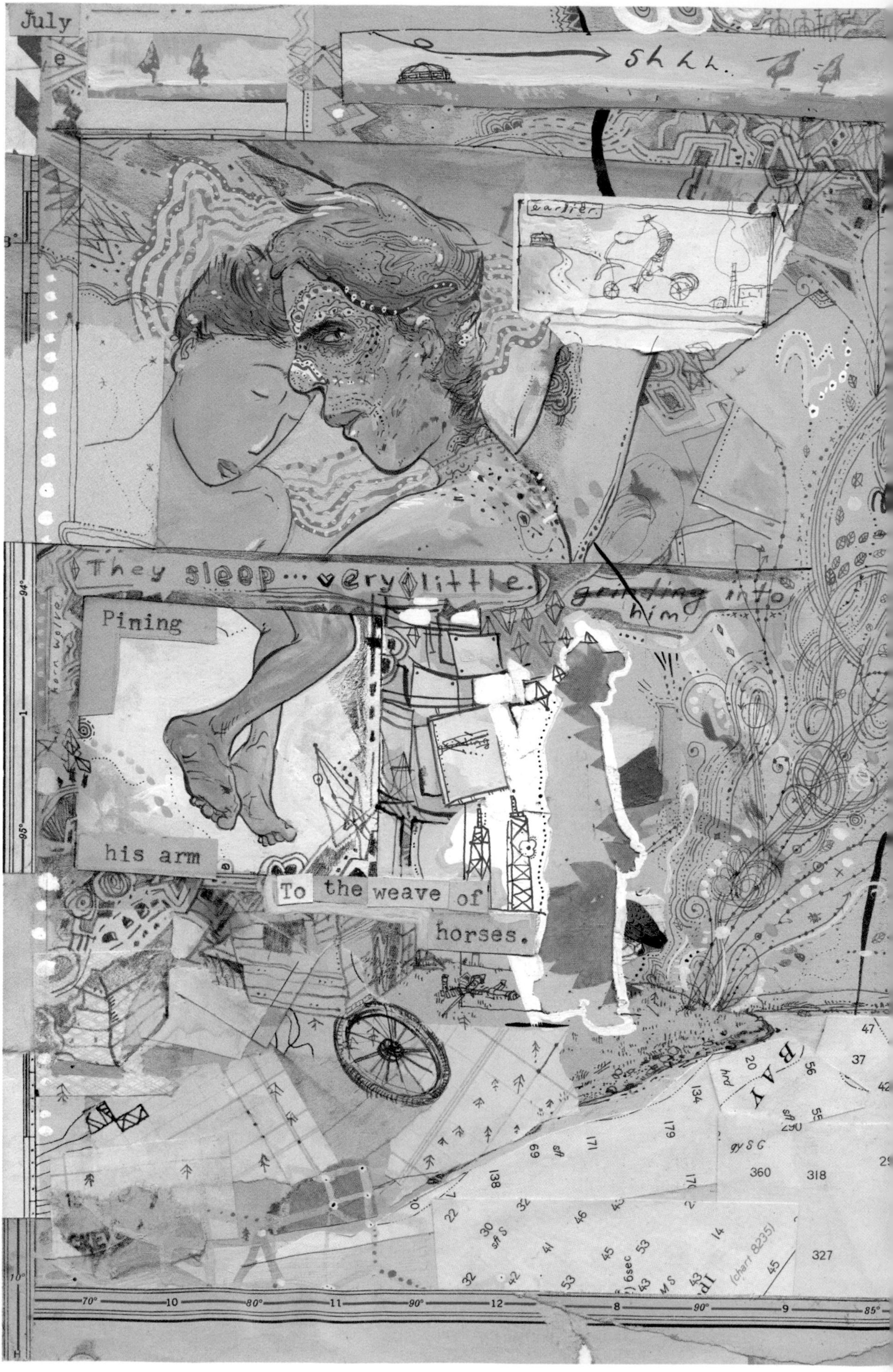

July
Shhh.
earlier.
They sleep... very little.
grinding into him
Pining
his arm
To the weave of horses.

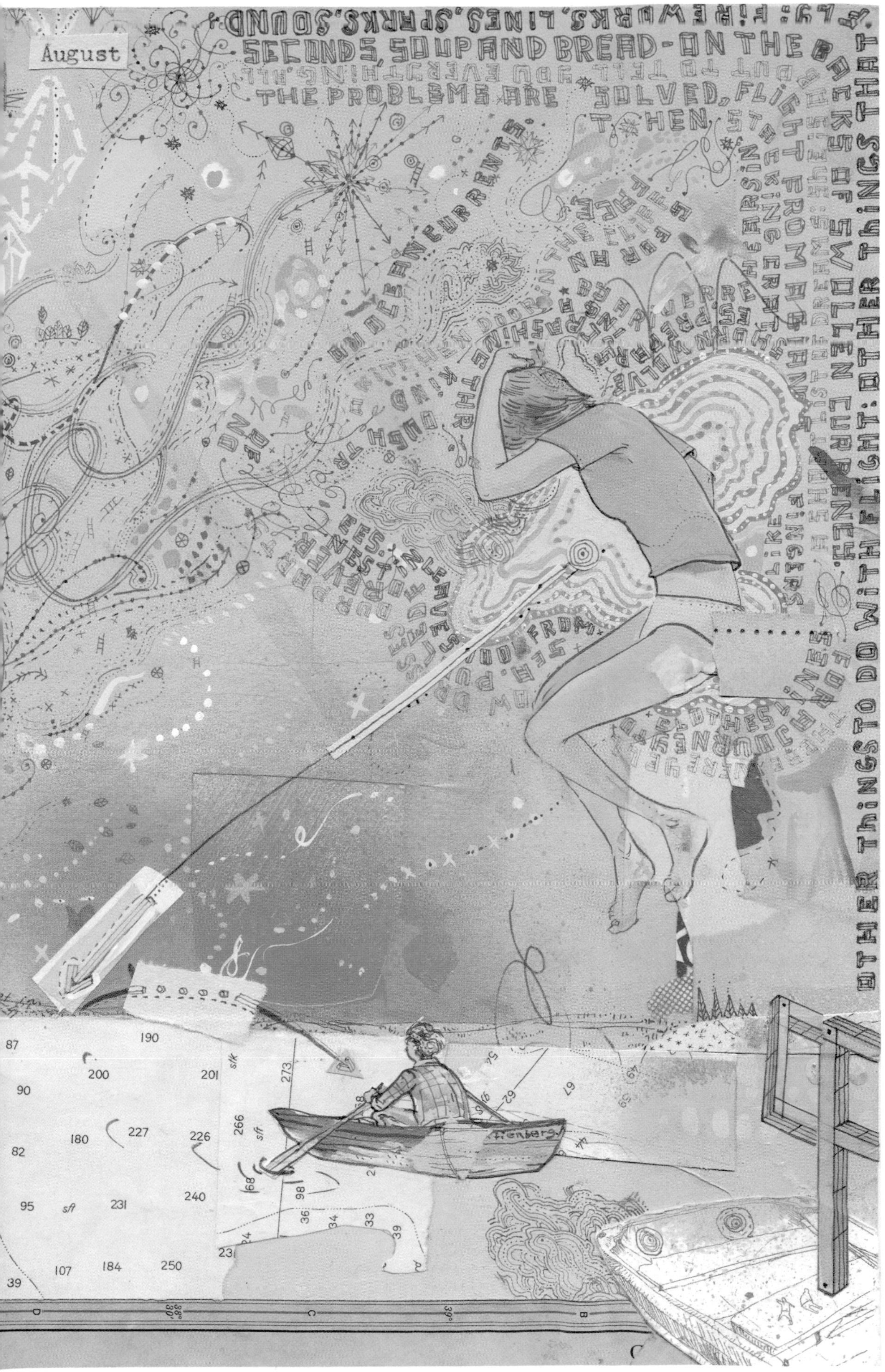

August
SECONDS, SOUP AND BREAD - ON THE
THE PROBLEMS ARE
SOLVED, FLIGHT
THEN,
OTHER THINGS TO DO WITH FLIGHT: THINGS

His boat a red stained account. Full of sea beaten papers. lay down ~~the street~~ on the strand line.

In the kitchen men held bouyant // the whisper of drinking. All else neglected for a door Later in bed as he strained to hear (a plot!) ~~as~~ his door

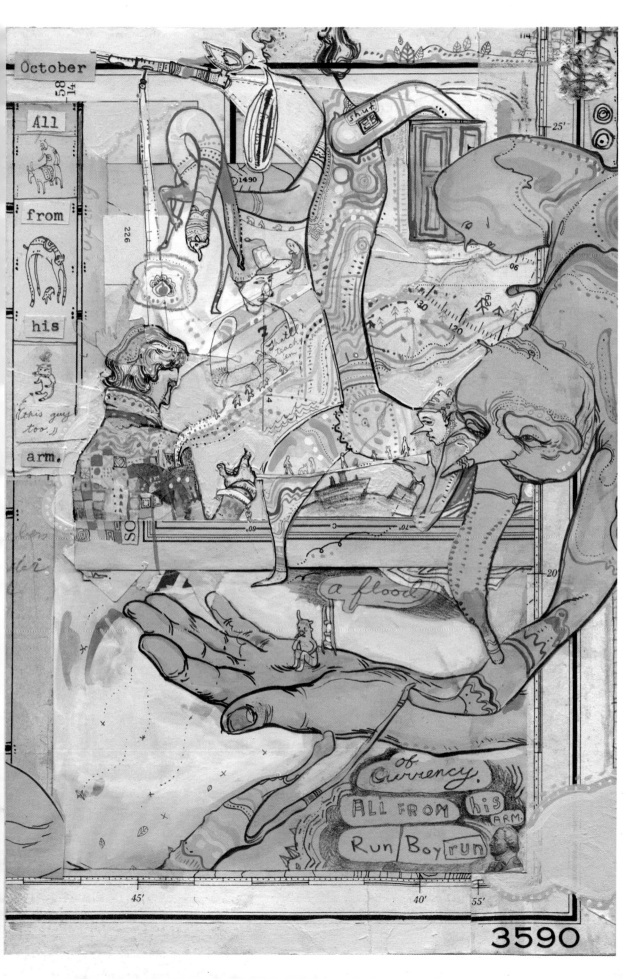

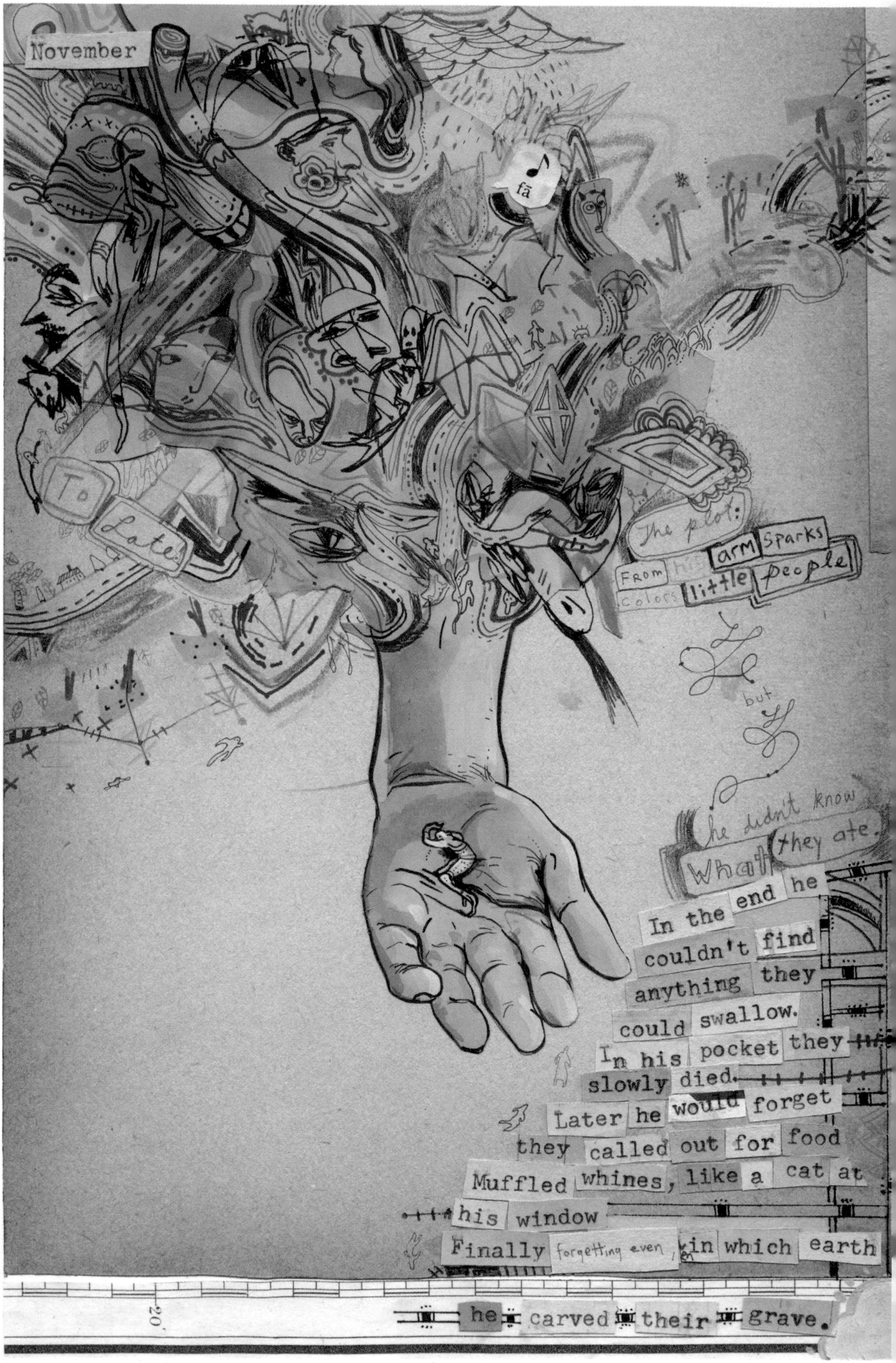
November
fā
To Late
The plot: arm Sparks
From his little people
colors
but
he didn't know
What they ate.
In the end he
couldn't find
anything they
could swallow.
In his pocket they
slowly died.
Later he would forget
they called out for food
Muffled whines, like a cat at
his window
Finally forgetting even in which earth
20
he carved their grave.

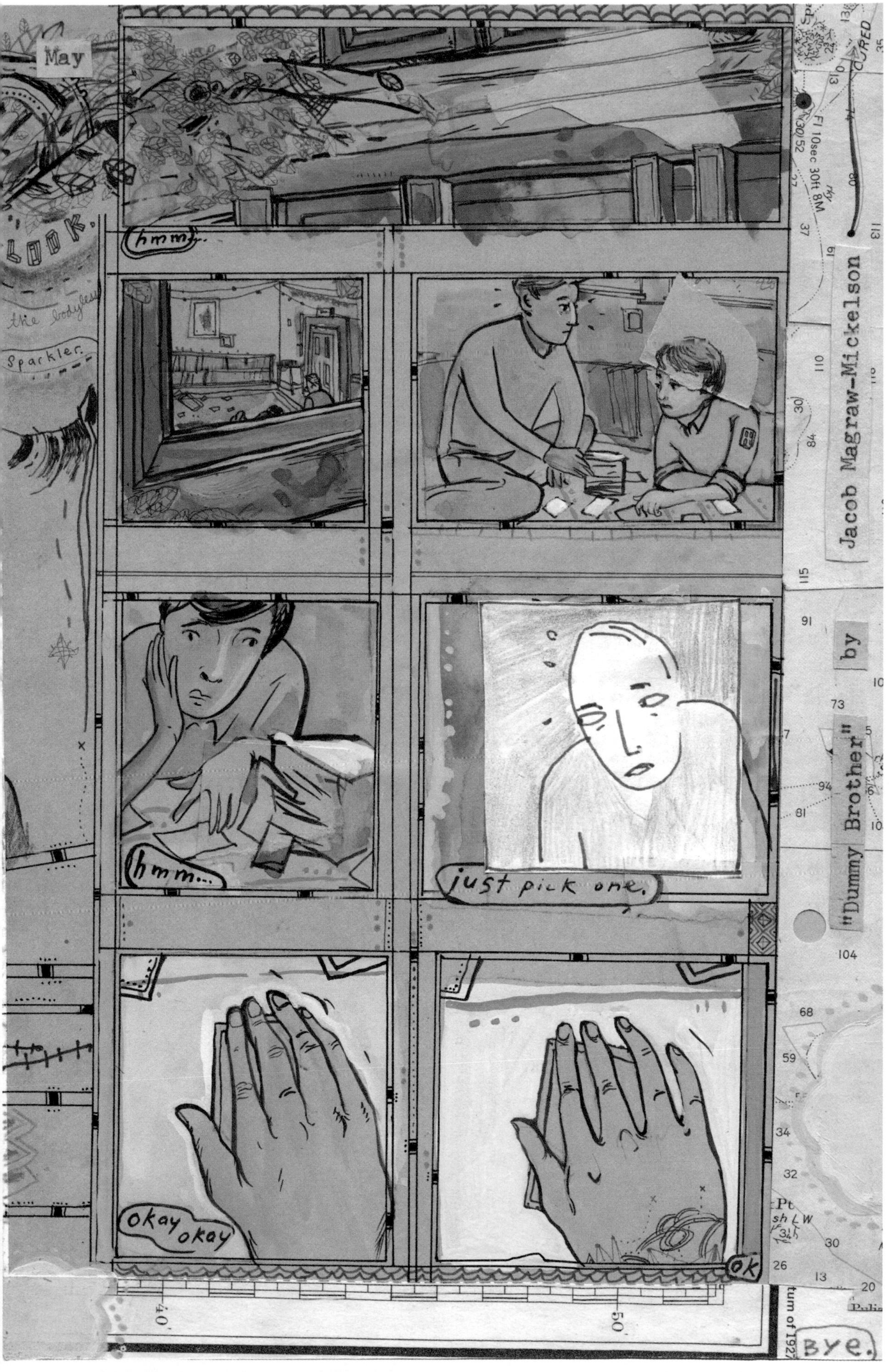

May
LOOK.
the bodyless
sparkler
"Dummy Brother" by Jacob Magraw-Mickelson
hmm...
hmm...
just pick one.
okay okay
ok
Bye.

"All-Time Low" - Story by Dylan Meconis Pictures by Bill Mudron

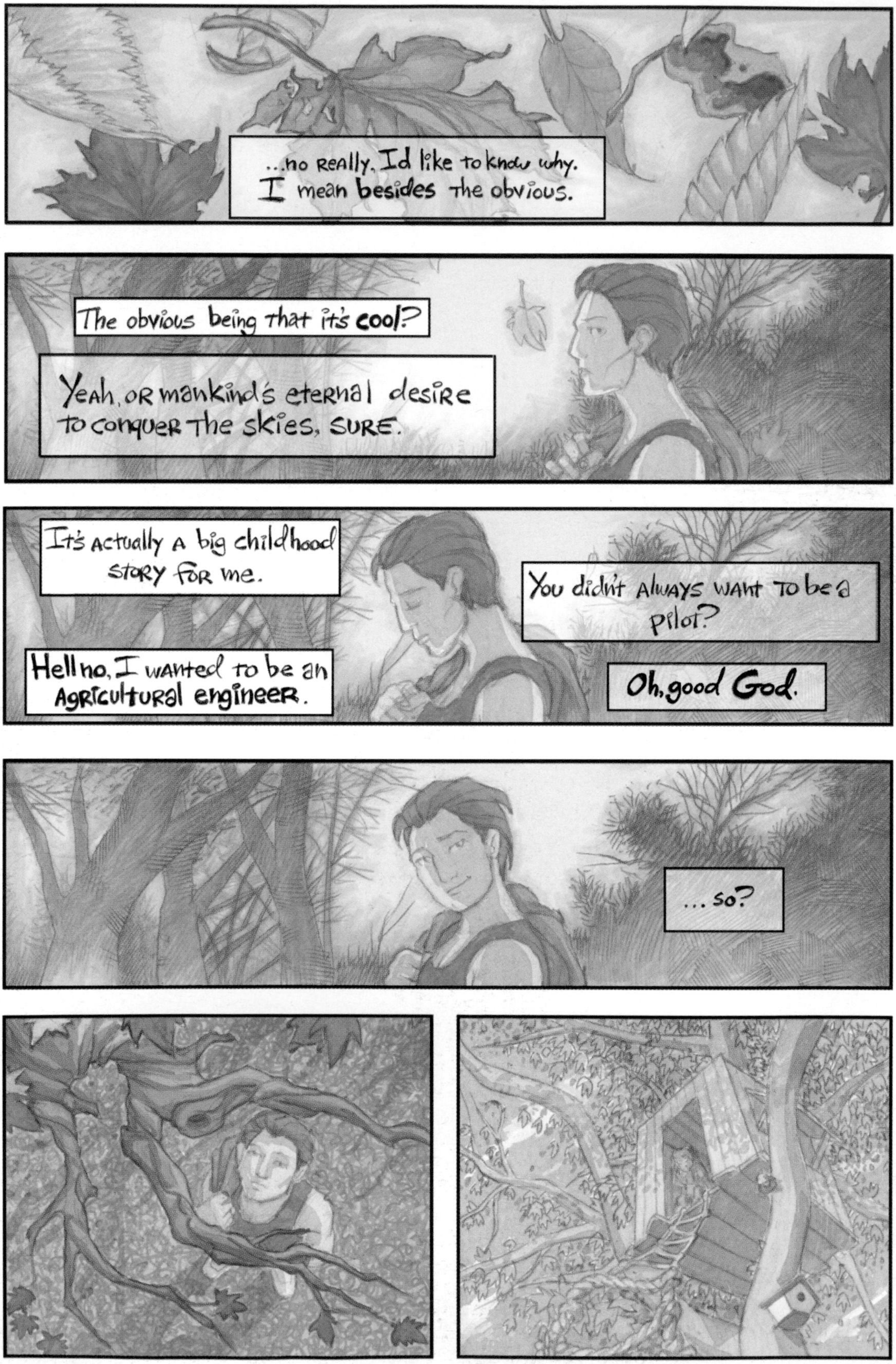
...no Really. Id like to know why.
I mean besides the obvious.
The obvious being that it's cool?
Yeah, or mankind's eternal desire to conquer the skies, sure.
It's actually a big childhood story for me.
You didn't always want to be a pilot?
Hell no, I wanted to be an agricultural engineer.
Oh, good God.
...so?

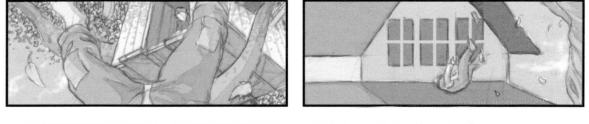

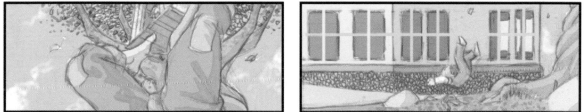

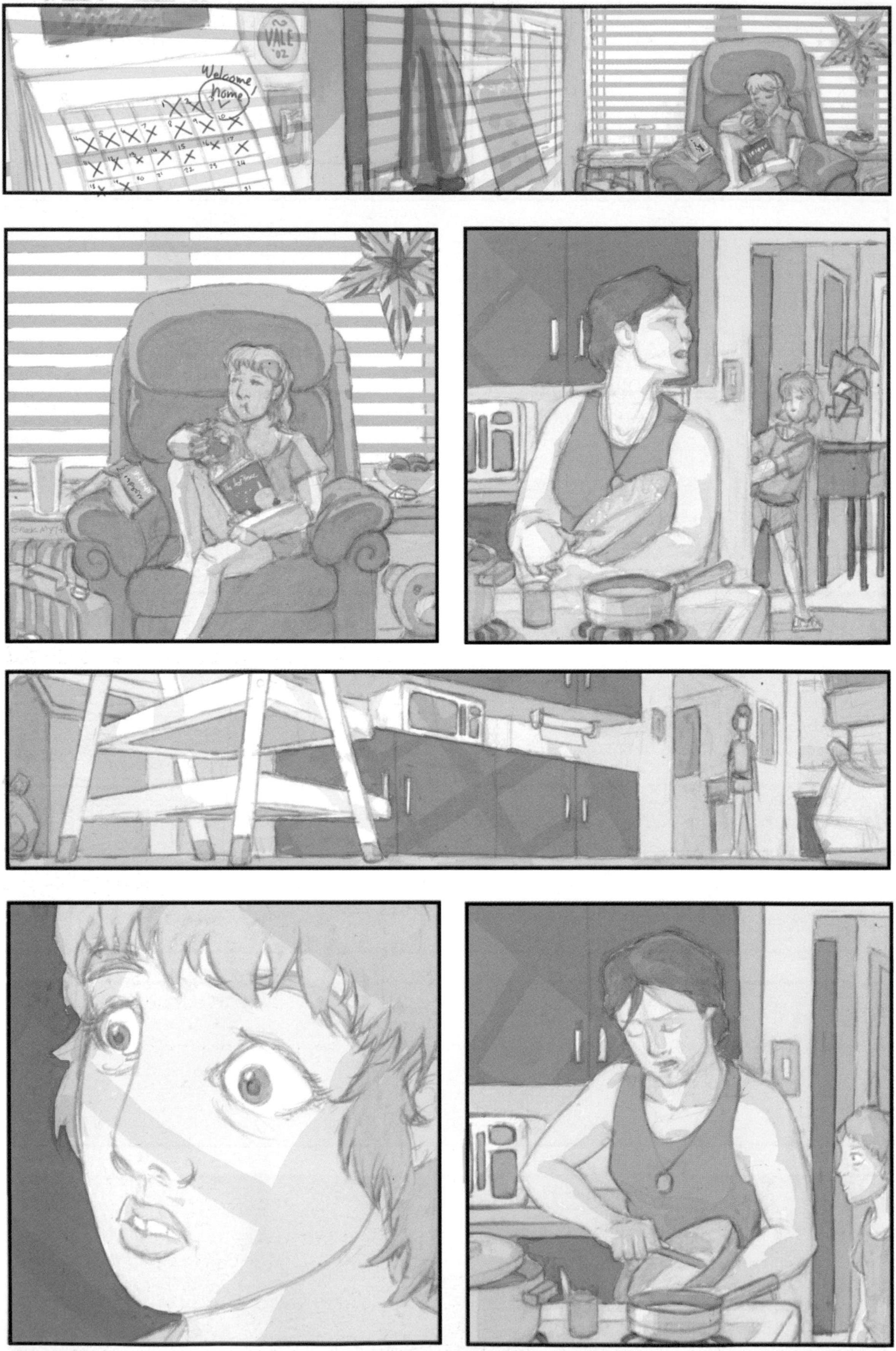
VALE '02
Welcome home!

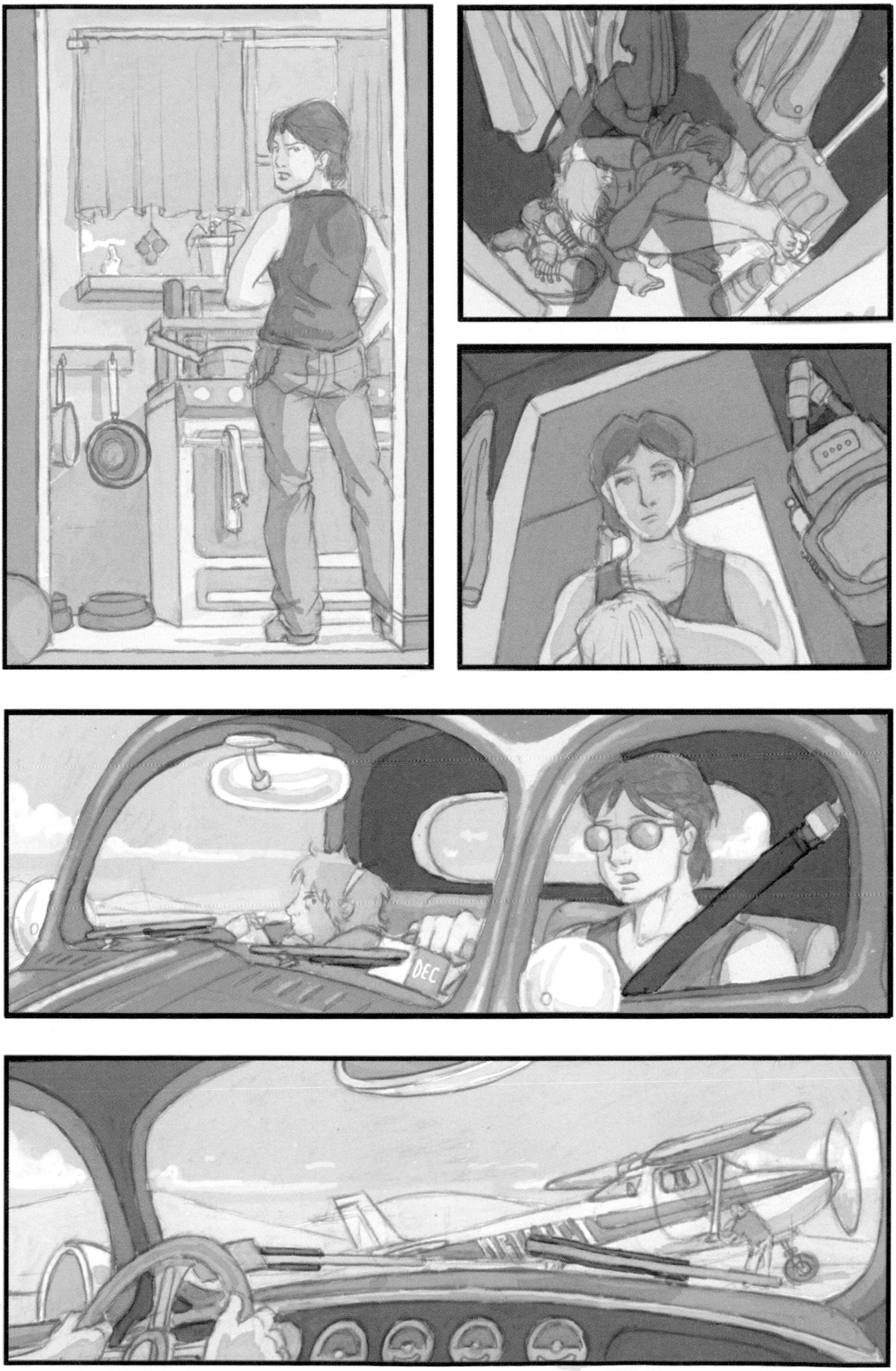
DEC

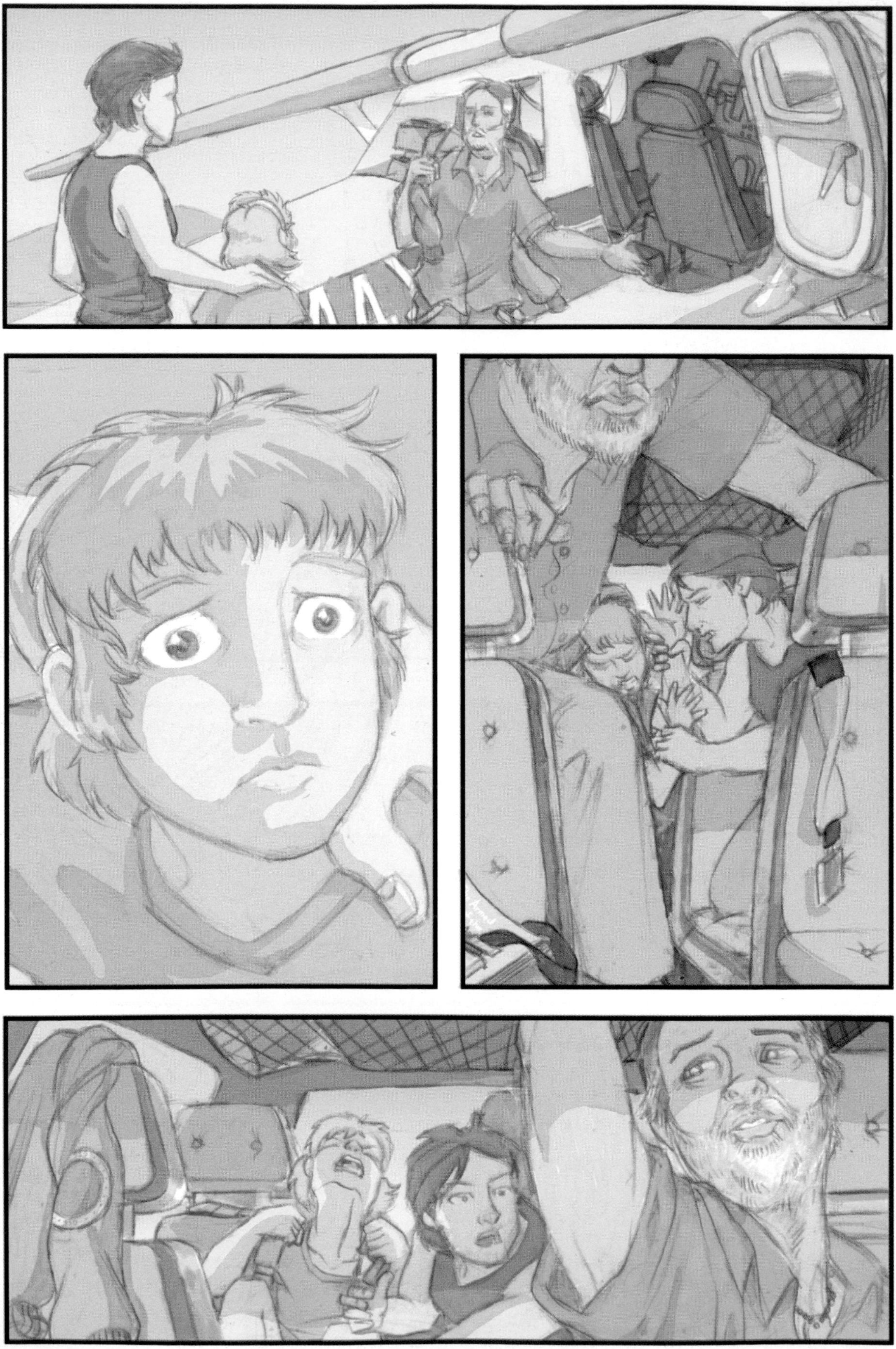

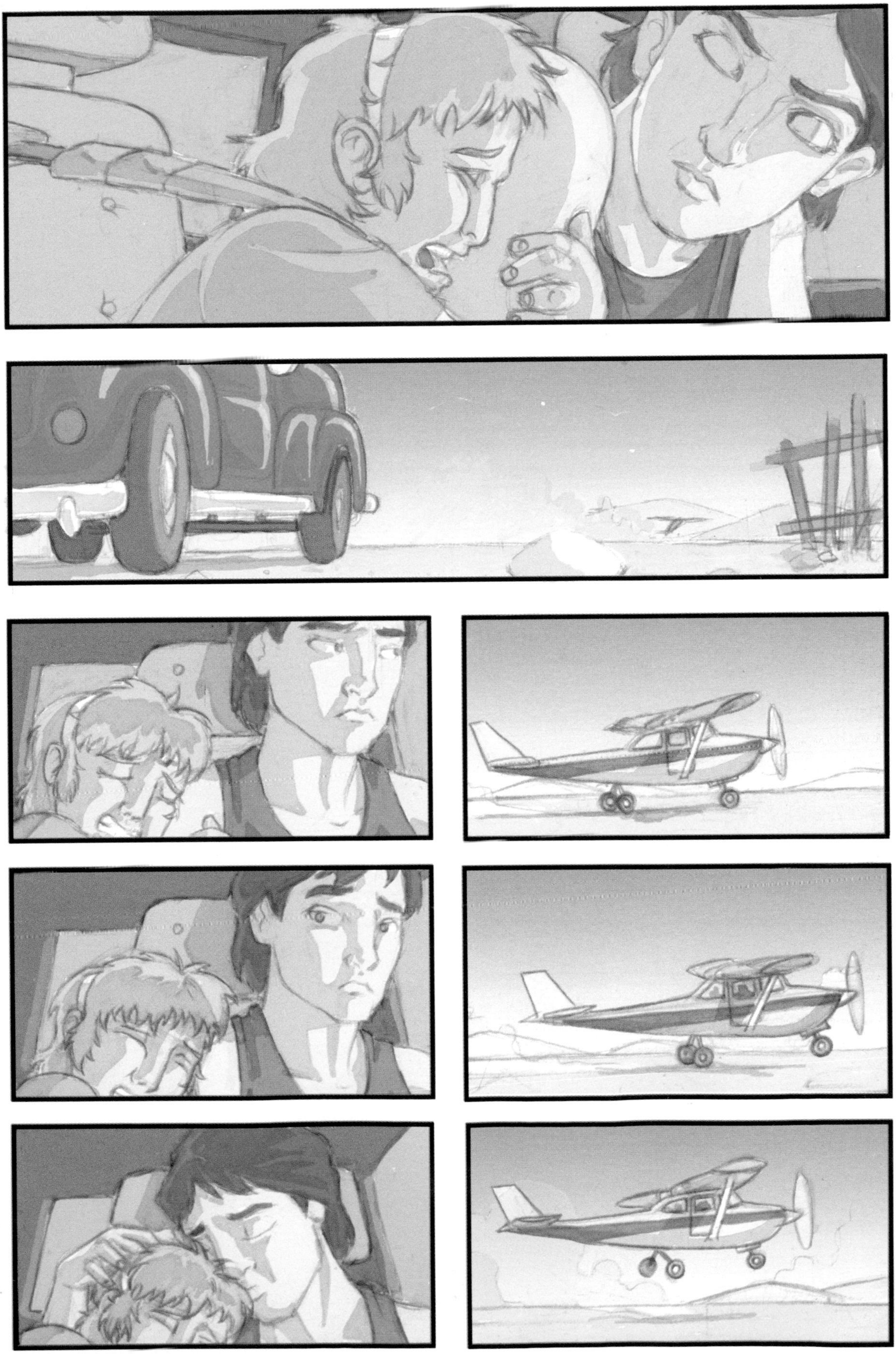

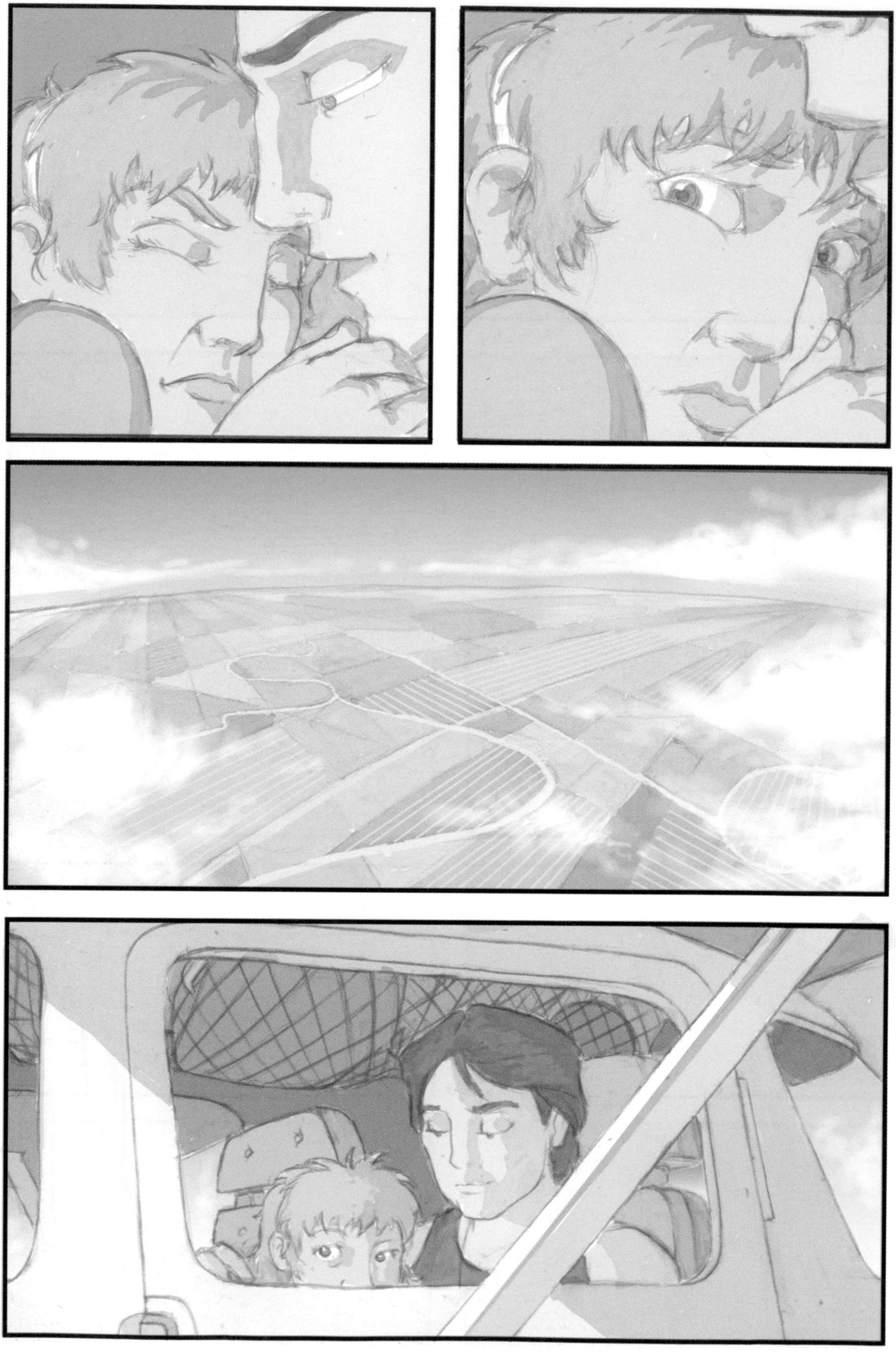

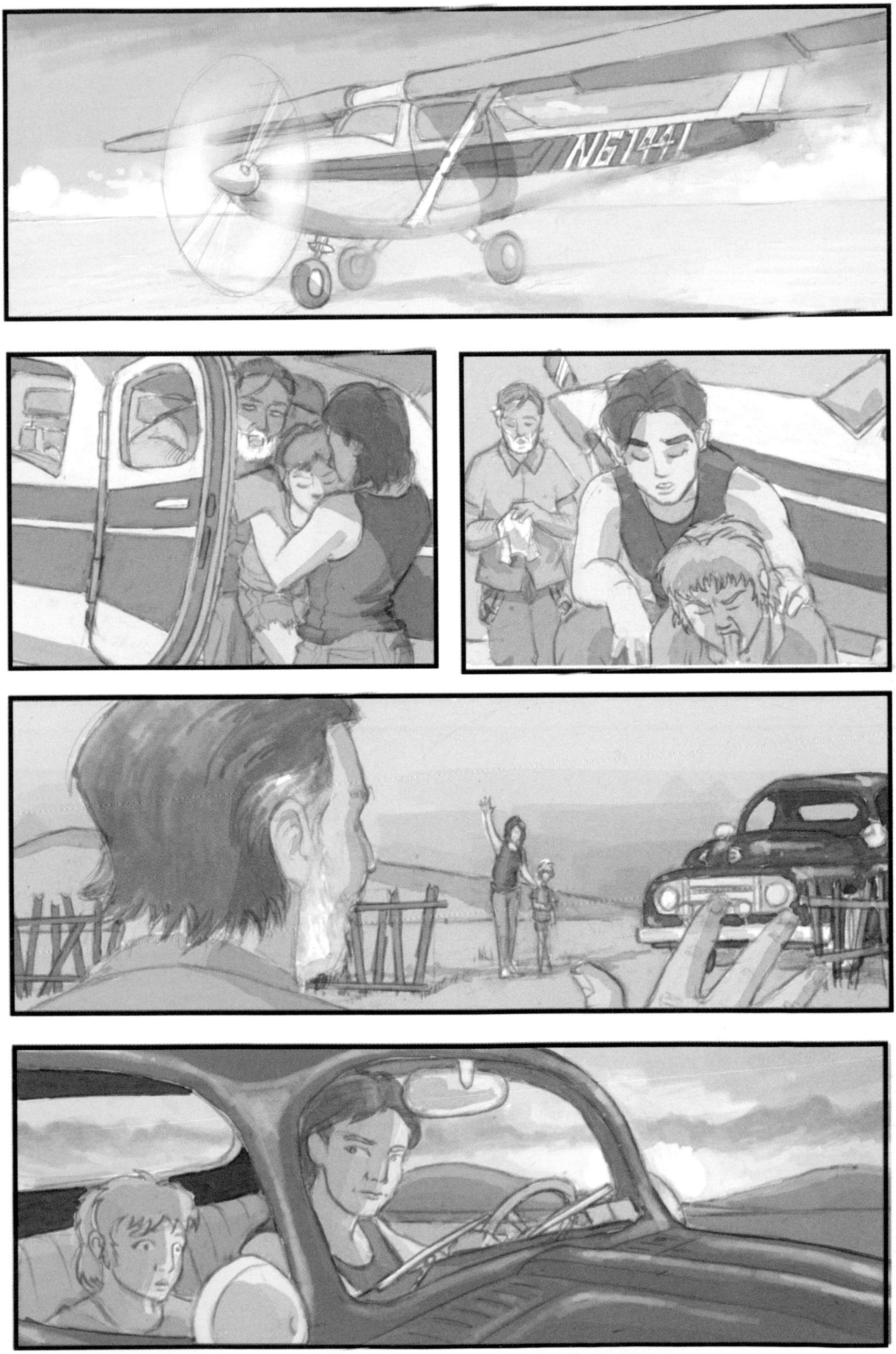
N61441

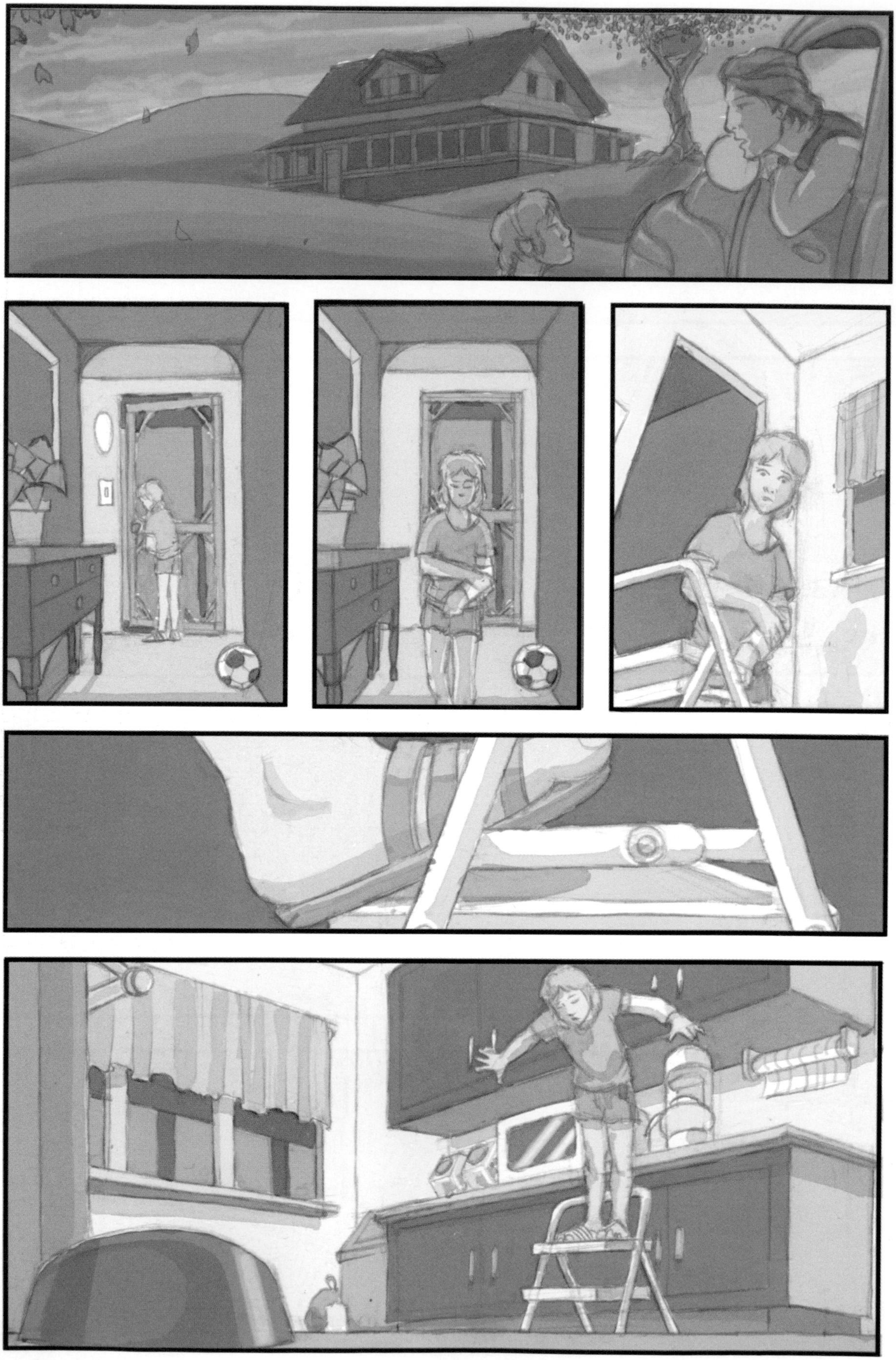

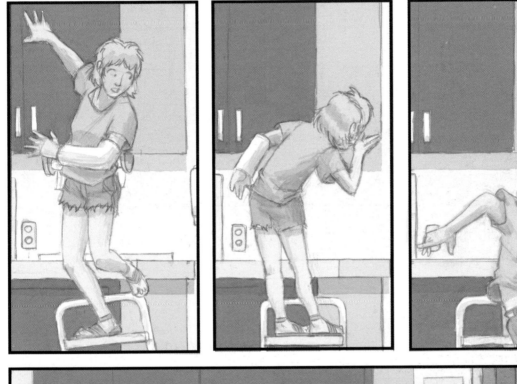

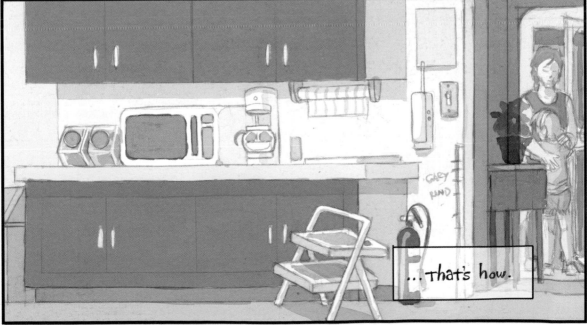

...that's how.

Story: Dylan Meconis - Pictures: Bill Mudron

The Maiden
and
the River Spirit

by Derek Kirk Kim

Once upon a time, a maiden was drinking coffee on the bank of a river after a hard day's work.

So, following the Woodman's example, she told the truth instead. The River Spirit dove in a second time and this time brought up a thermos made of pure silver.

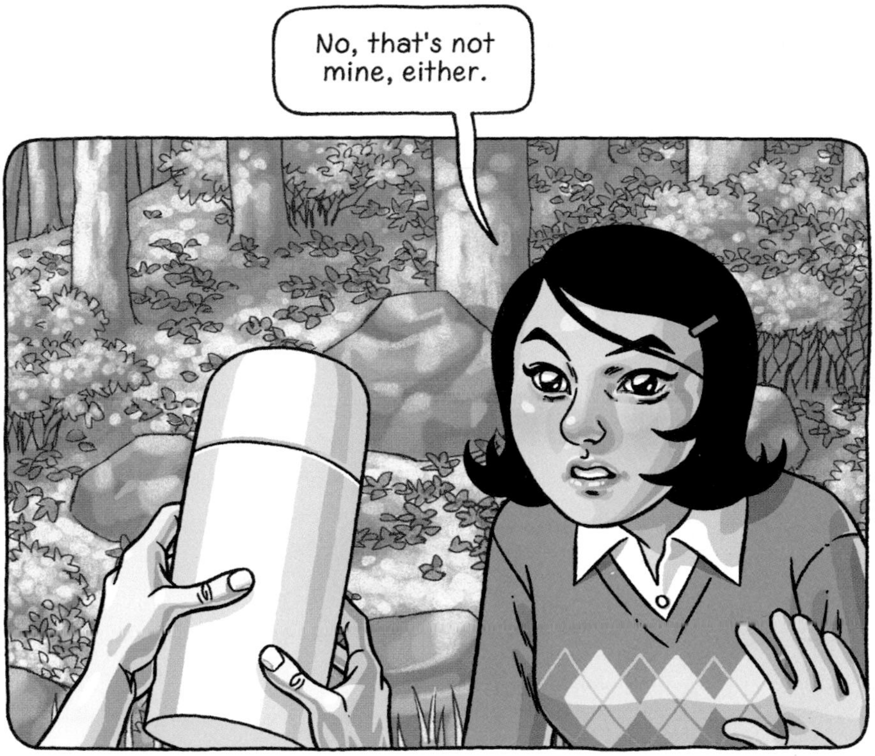
No, that's not mine, either.

One more time the River Spirit dove into the river and this time he brought up the Maiden's thermos.

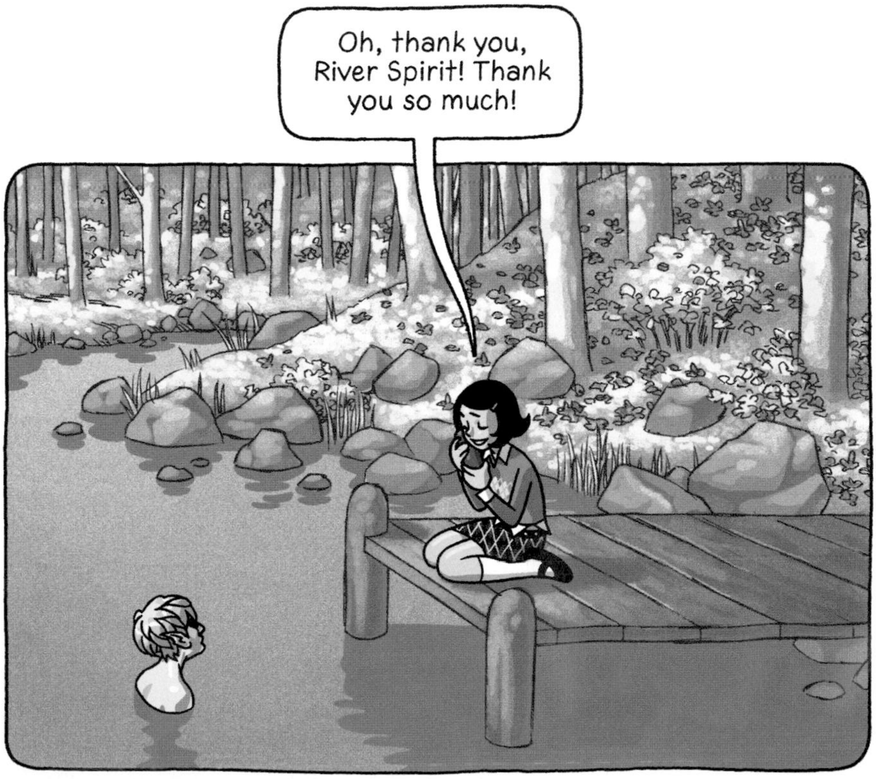
Oh, thank you, River Spirit! Thank you so much!

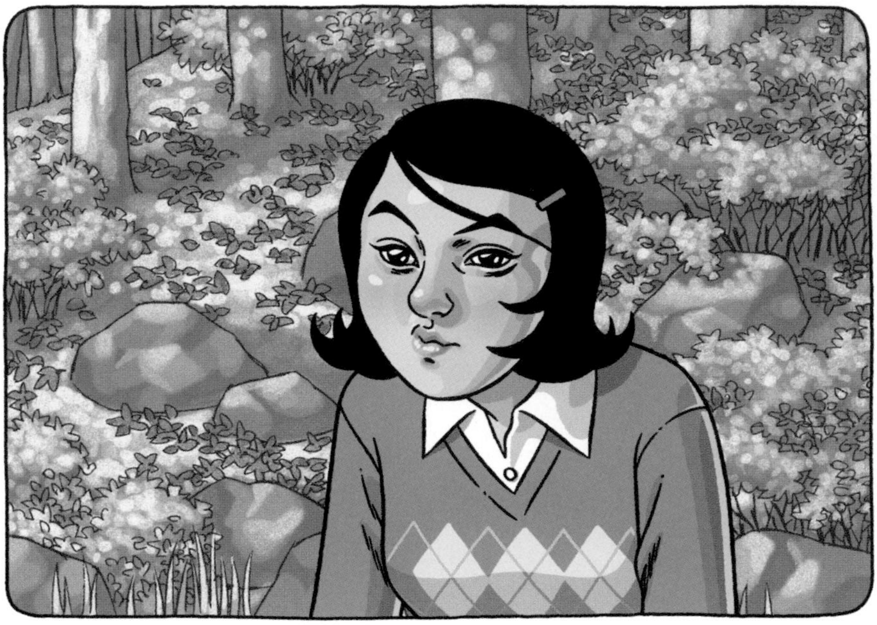

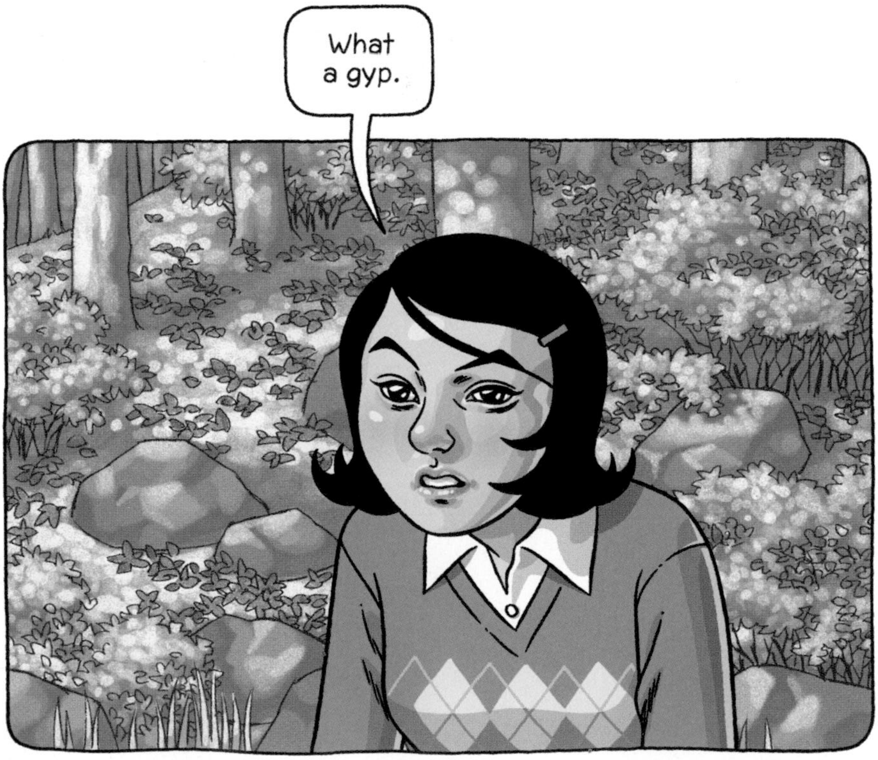
What a gyp.

Moral: Aesop is great on paper.

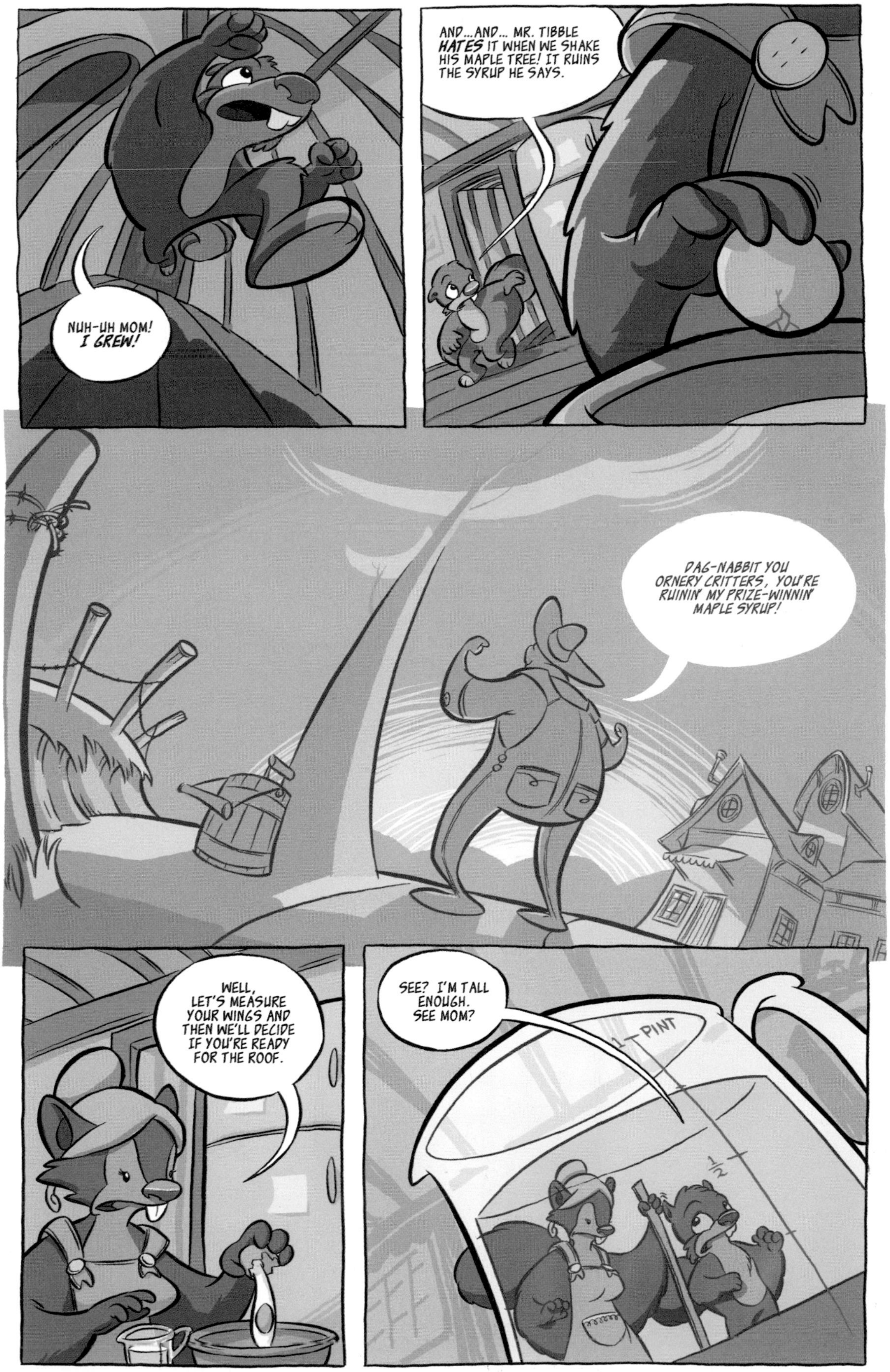
NUH-UH MOM! I GREW!
AND...AND... MR. TIBBLE HATES IT WHEN WE SHAKE HIS MAPLE TREE! IT RUINS THE SYRUP HE SAYS.
DAG-NABBIT YOU ORNERY CRITTERS, YOU'RE RUININ' MY PRIZE-WINNIN' MAPLE SYRUP!
WELL, LET'S MEASURE YOUR WINGS AND THEN WE'LL DECIDE IF YOU'RE READY FOR THE ROOF.
SEE? I'M TALL ENOUGH. SEE MOM?
1 PINT
1/2

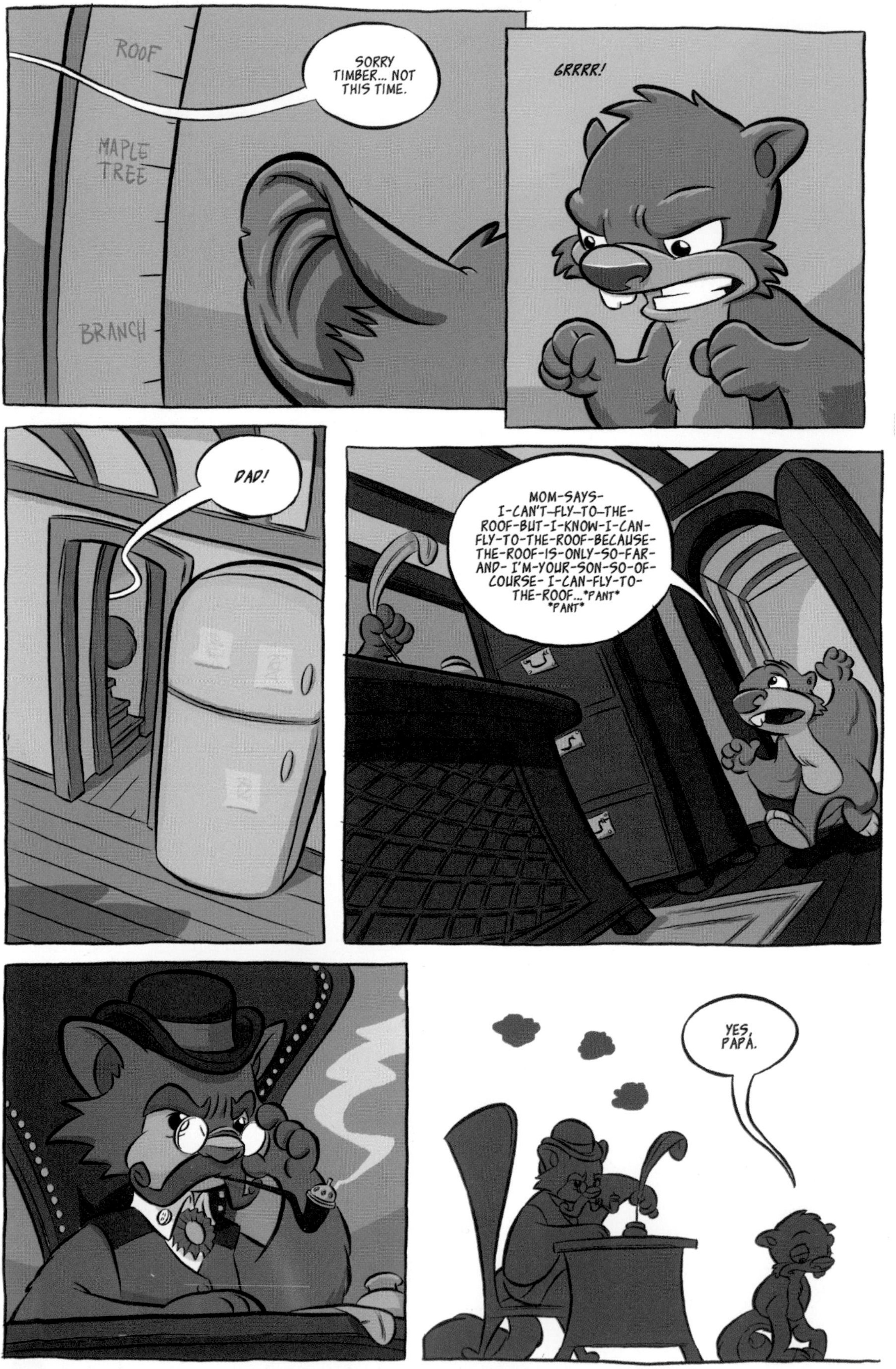
ROOF
MAPLE TREE
BRANCH
SORRY TIMBER... NOT THIS TIME.
GRRRR!
DAD!
MOM-SAYS-I-CAN'T-FLY-TO-THE-ROOF-BUT-I-KNOW-I-CAN-FLY-TO-THE-ROOF-BECAUSE-THE-ROOF-IS-ONLY-SO-FAR-AND- I'M-YOUR-SON-SO-OF-COURSE- I-CAN-FLY-TO-THE-ROOF...*PANT* *PANT*
YES, PAPA.

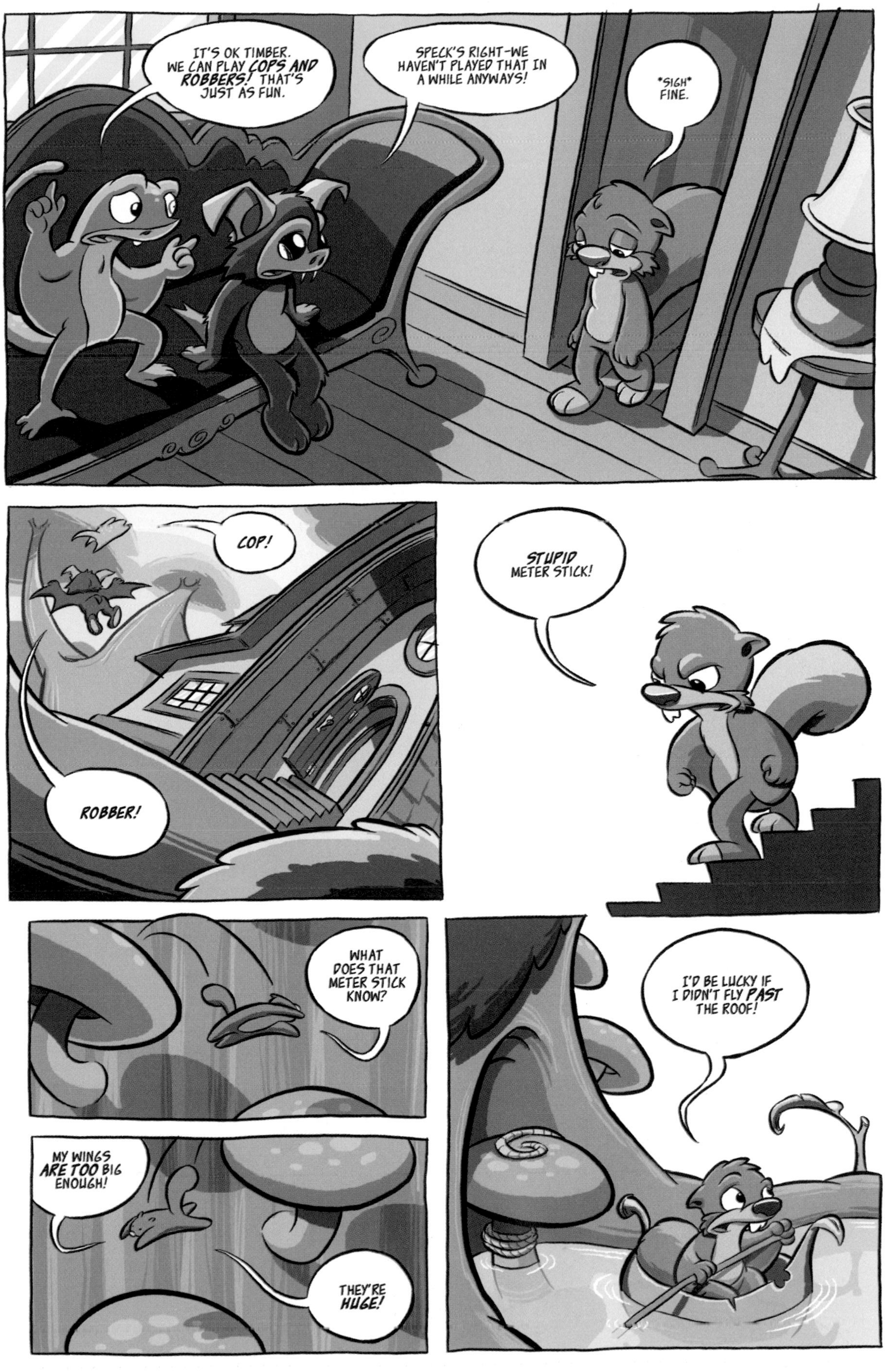
IT'S OK TIMBER. WE CAN PLAY COPS AND ROBBERS! THAT'S JUST AS FUN.
SPECK'S RIGHT-WE HAVEN'T PLAYED THAT IN A WHILE ANYWAYS!
SIGH FINE.
COP!
ROBBER!
STUPID METER STICK!
WHAT DOES THAT METER STICK KNOW?
MY WINGS ARE TOO BIG ENOUGH!
THEY'RE HUGE!
I'D BE LUCKY IF I DIDN'T FLY PAST THE ROOF!

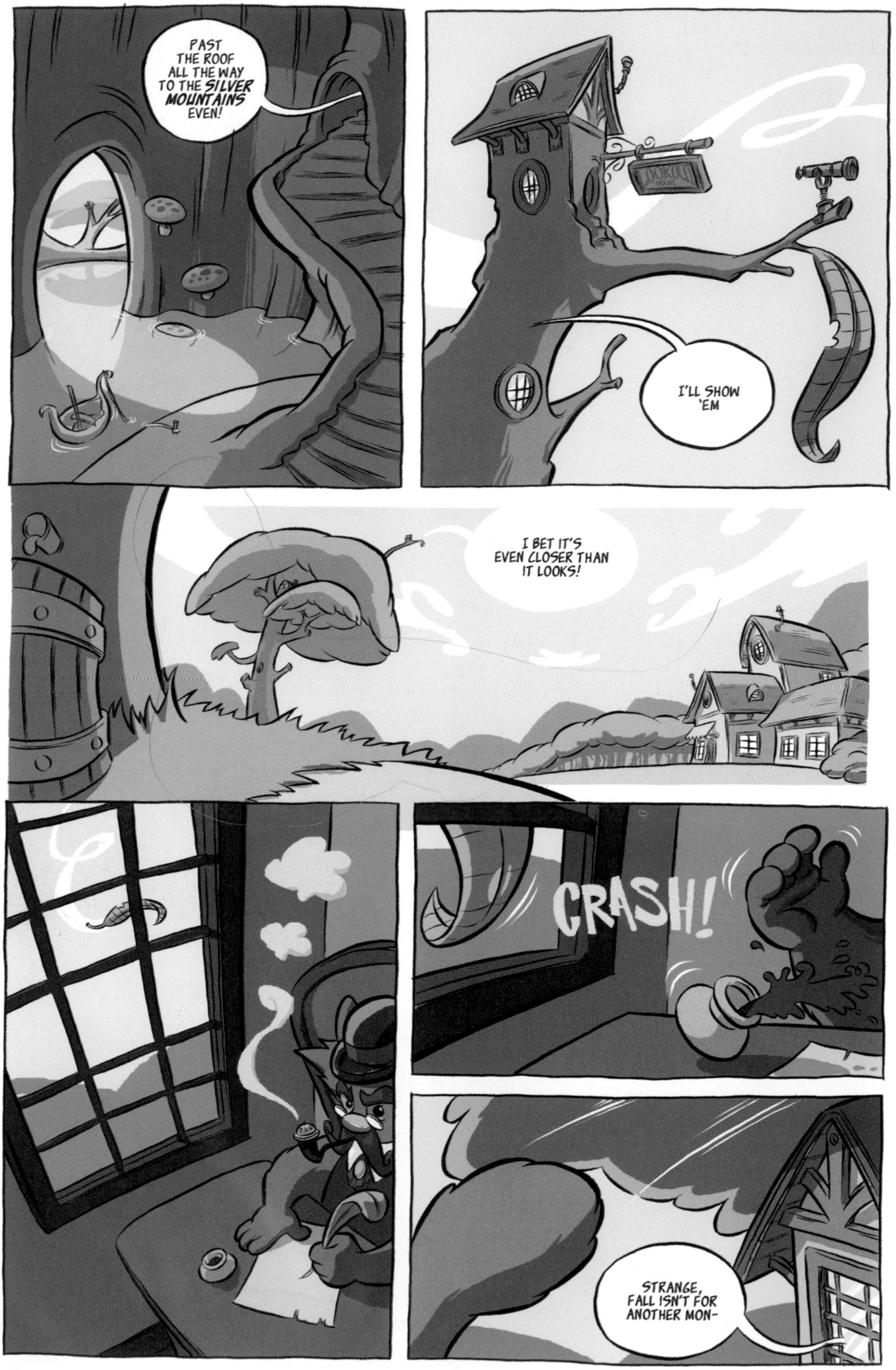
PAST THE ROOF ALL THE WAY TO THE SILVER MOUNTAINS EVEN!
I'LL SHOW 'EM
I BET IT'S EVEN CLOSER THAN IT LOOKS!
CRASH!
STRANGE, FALL ISN'T FOR ANOTHER MON-

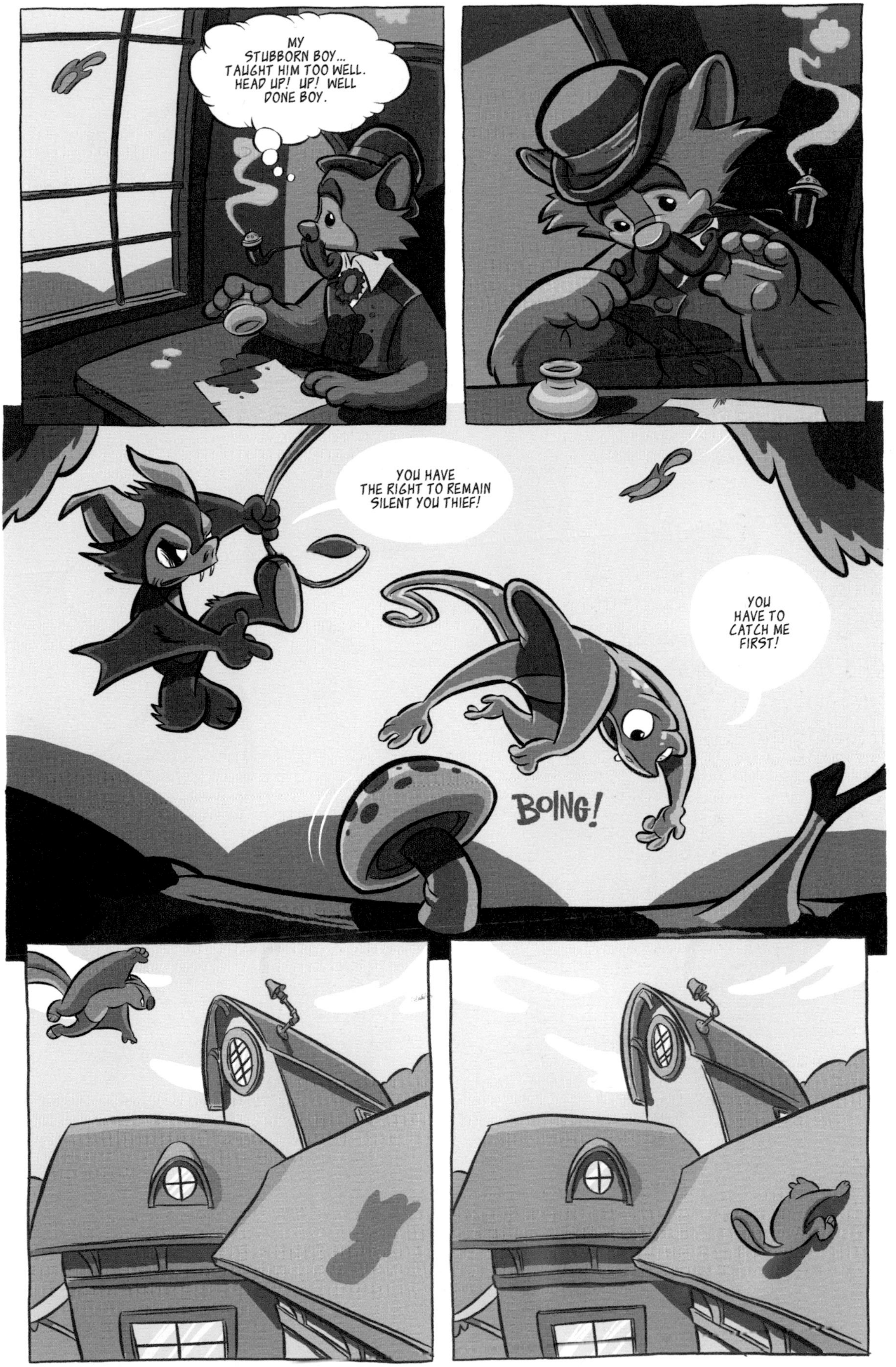
MY STUBBORN BOY... TAUGHT HIM TOO WELL. HEAD UP! UP! WELL DONE BOY.
YOU HAVE THE RIGHT TO REMAIN SILENT YOU THIEF!
YOU HAVE TO CATCH ME FIRST!
BOING!

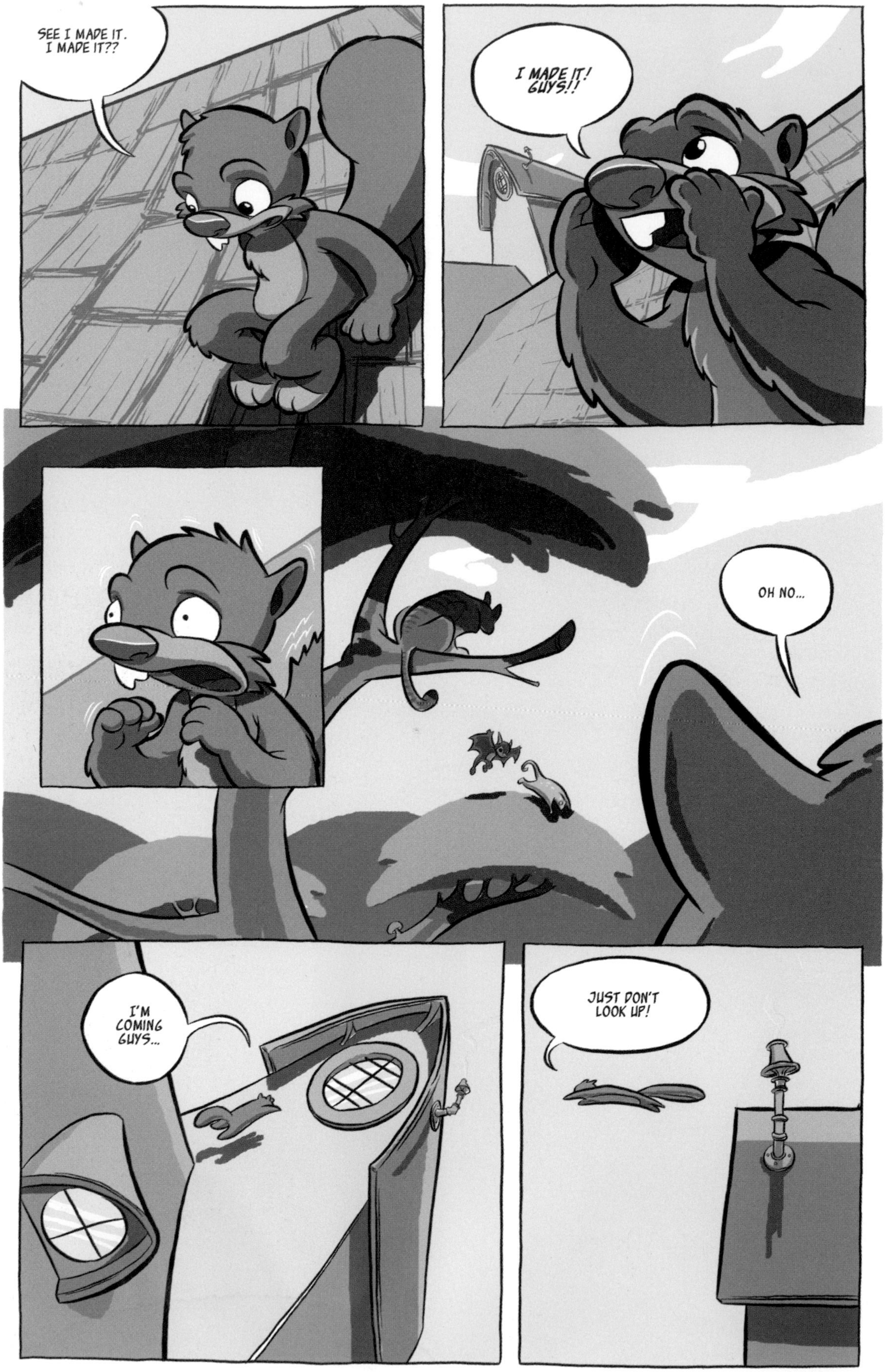
SEE I MADE IT.
I MADE IT??
I MADE IT!
GUYS!!
OH NO...
I'M
COMING
GUYS...
JUST DON'T
LOOK UP!

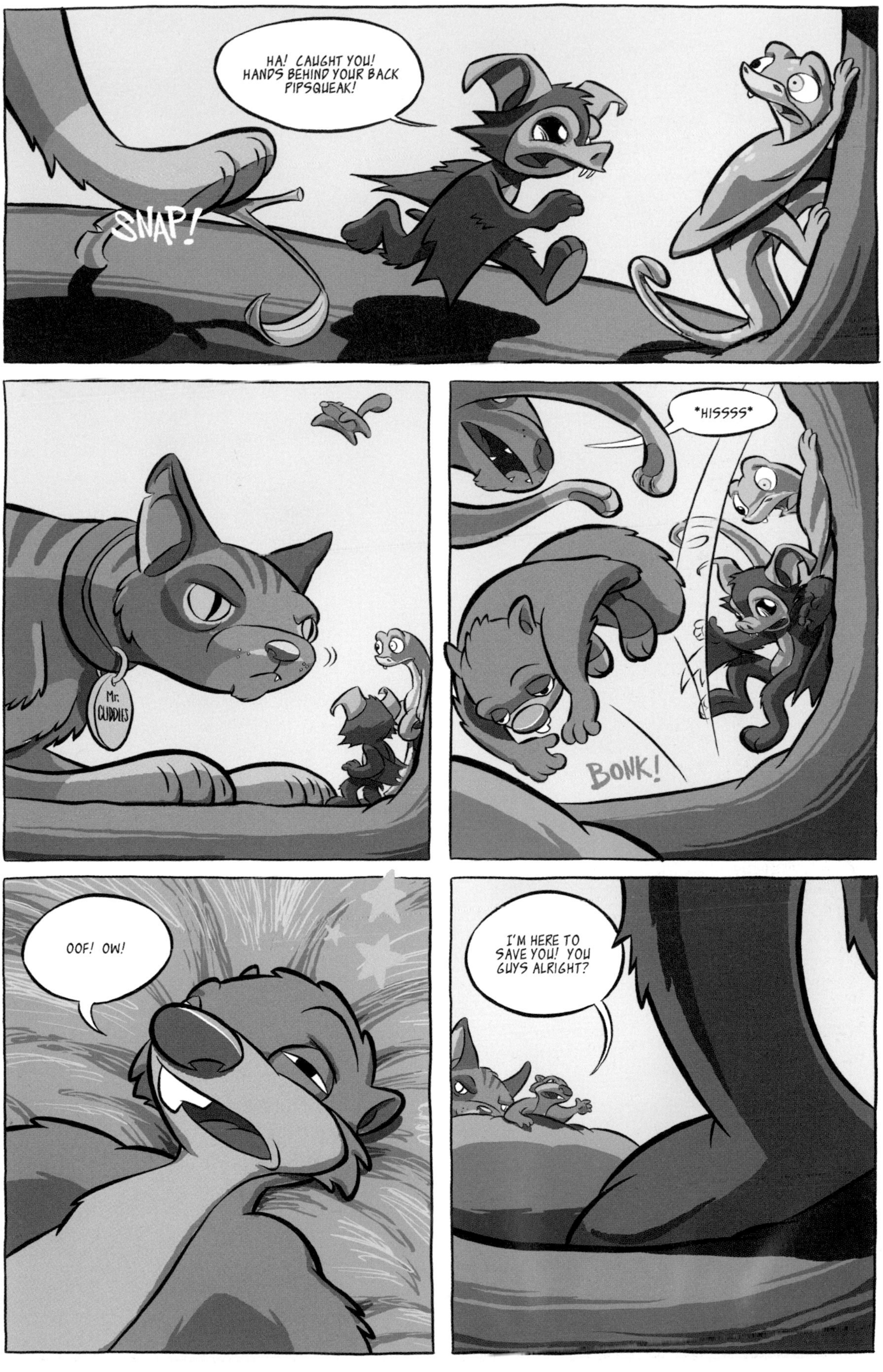
HA! CAUGHT YOU! HANDS BEHIND YOUR BACK PIPSQUEAK!
SNAP!
Mr. CUDDLES
HISSSS
BONK!
OOF! OW!
I'M HERE TO SAVE YOU! YOU GUYS ALRIGHT?

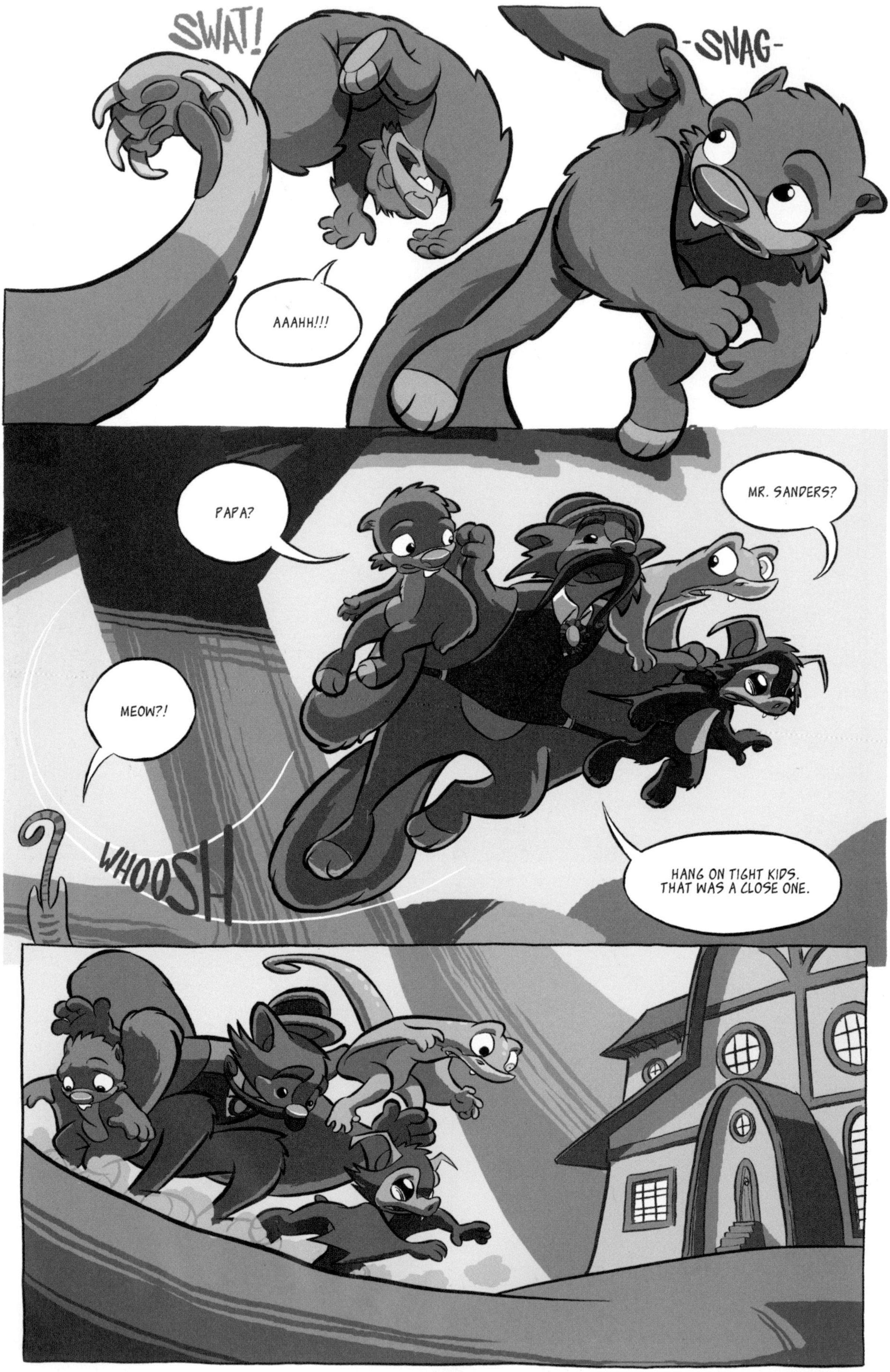
SWAT!
-SNAG-
AAAHH!!!
PAPA?
MR. SANDERS?
MEOW?!
WHOOSH
HANG ON TIGHT KIDS.
THAT WAS A CLOSE ONE.

"Tug McTaggart - Circus Detective" by Phil Craven

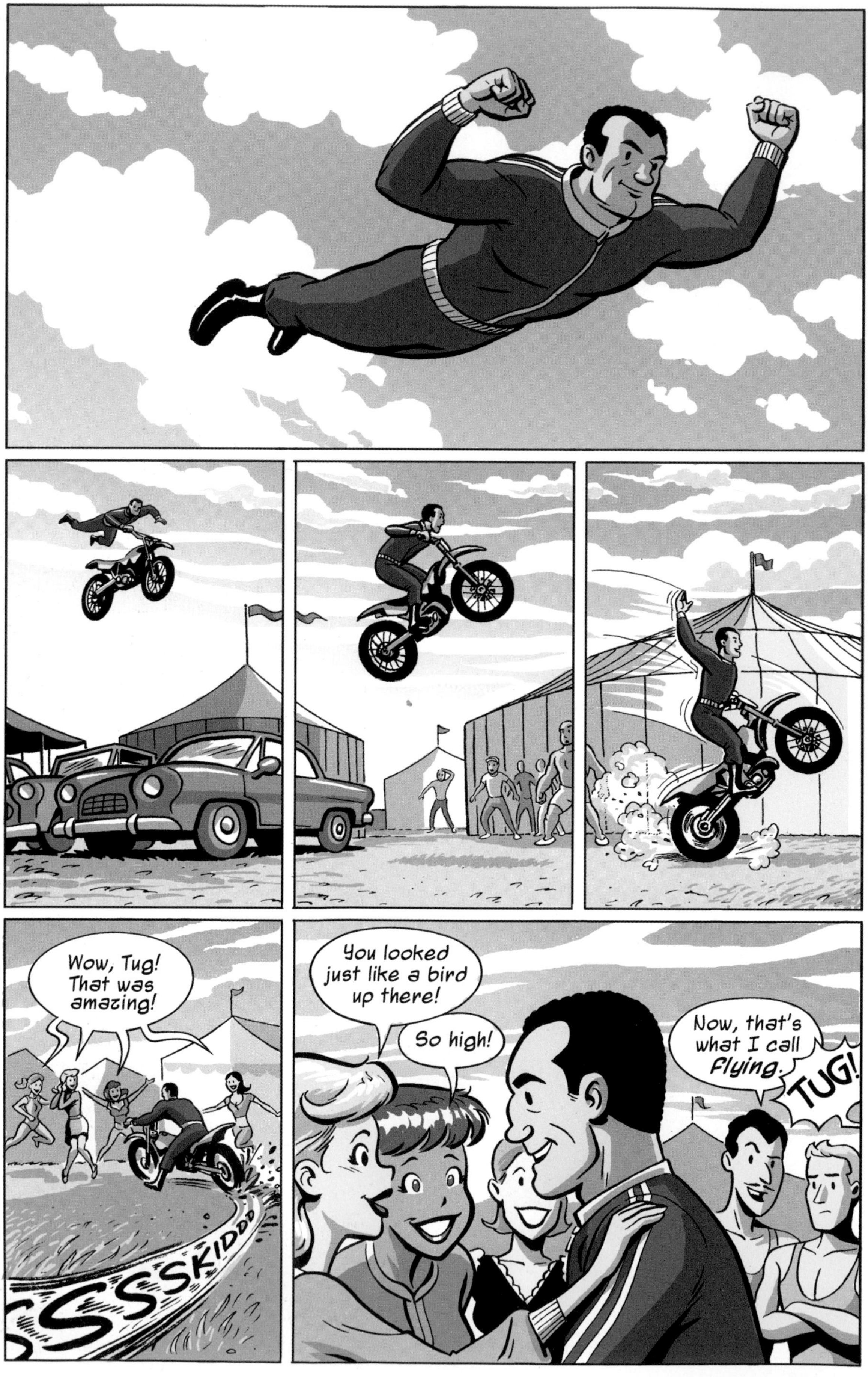
Wow, Tug! That was amazing!
SSSSKIDDD
You looked just like a bird up there!
So high!
Now, that's what I call flying.
TUG!

"Deep Blue" by Phil Craven

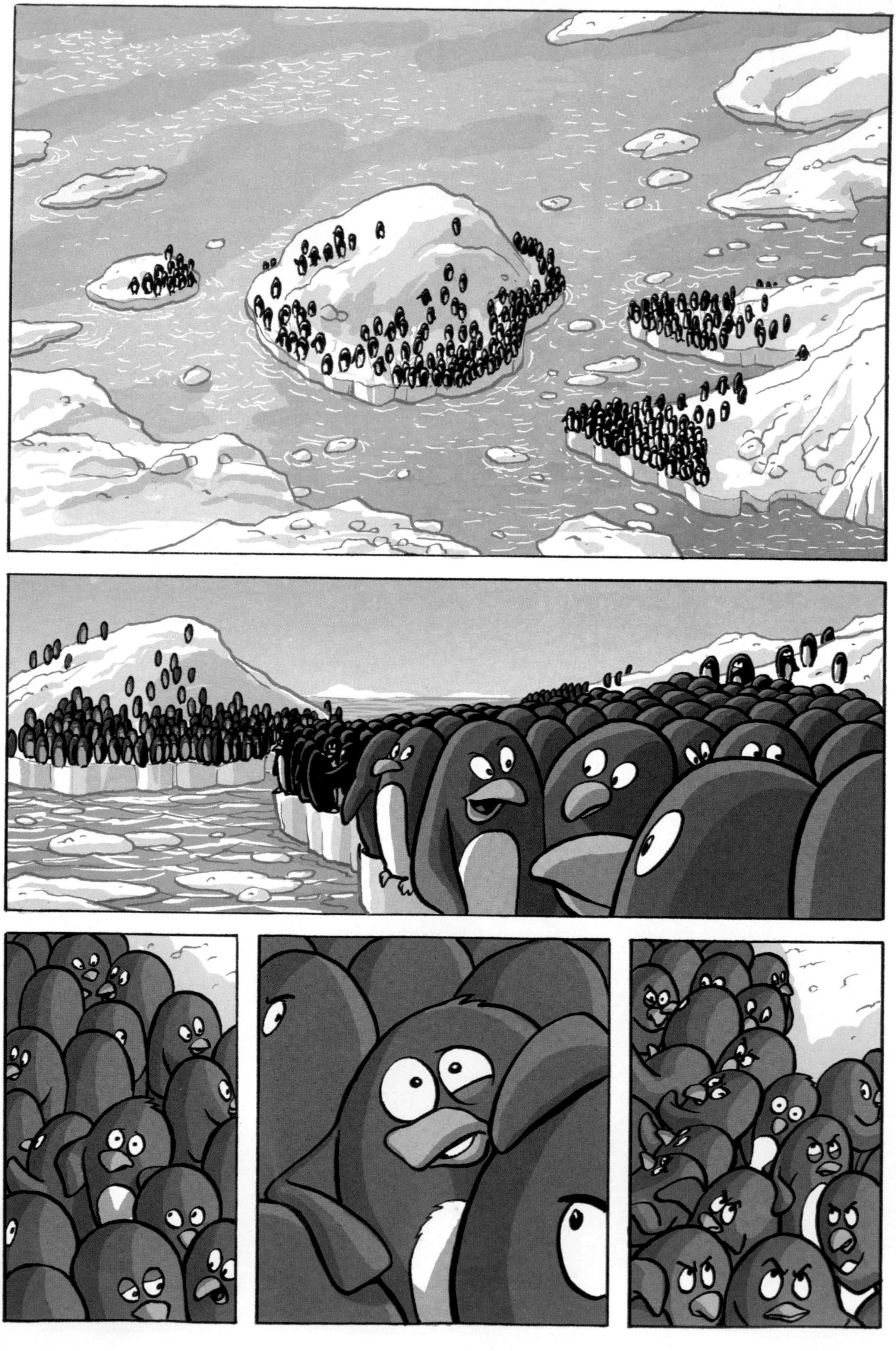

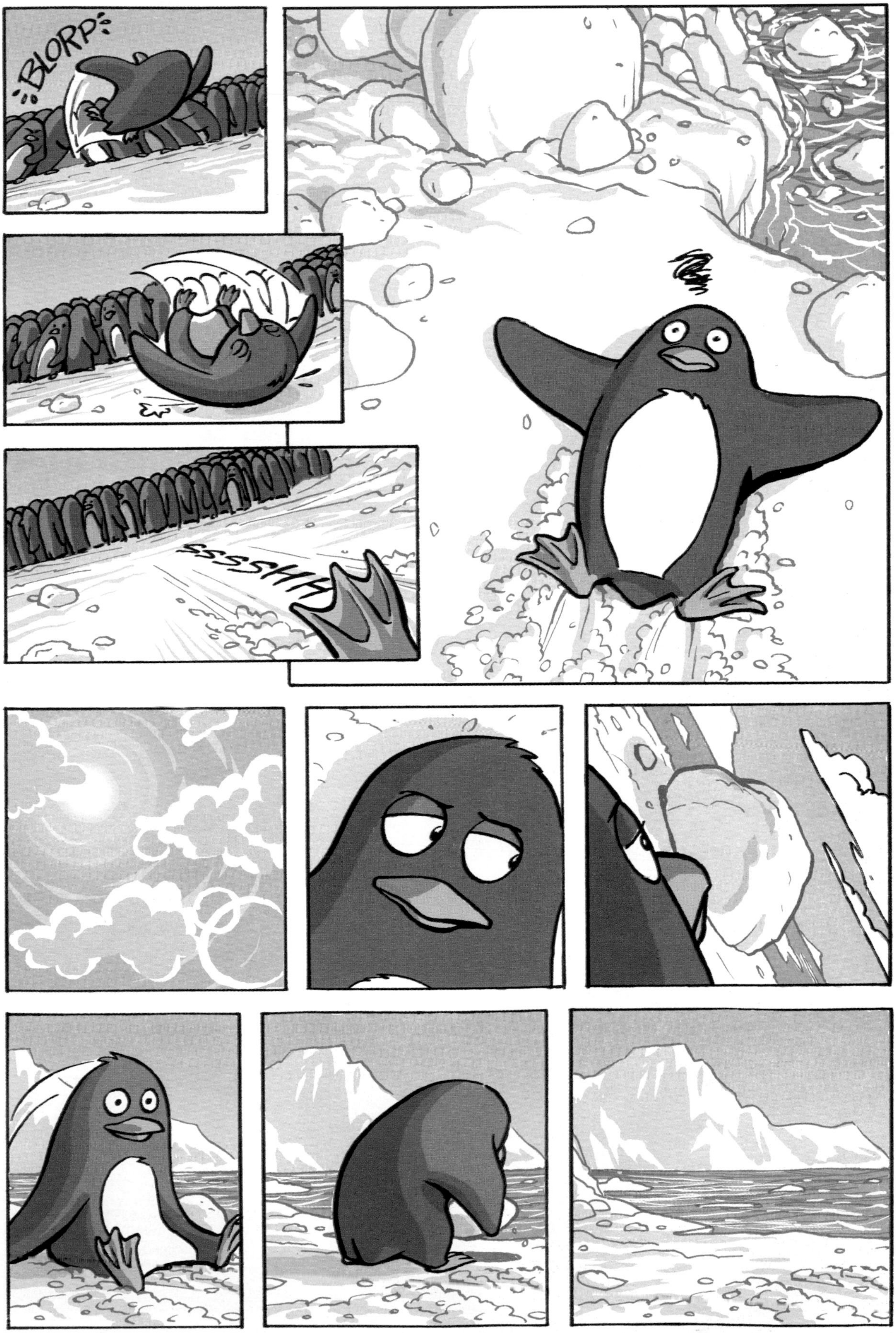
BLORP
SSSSHH

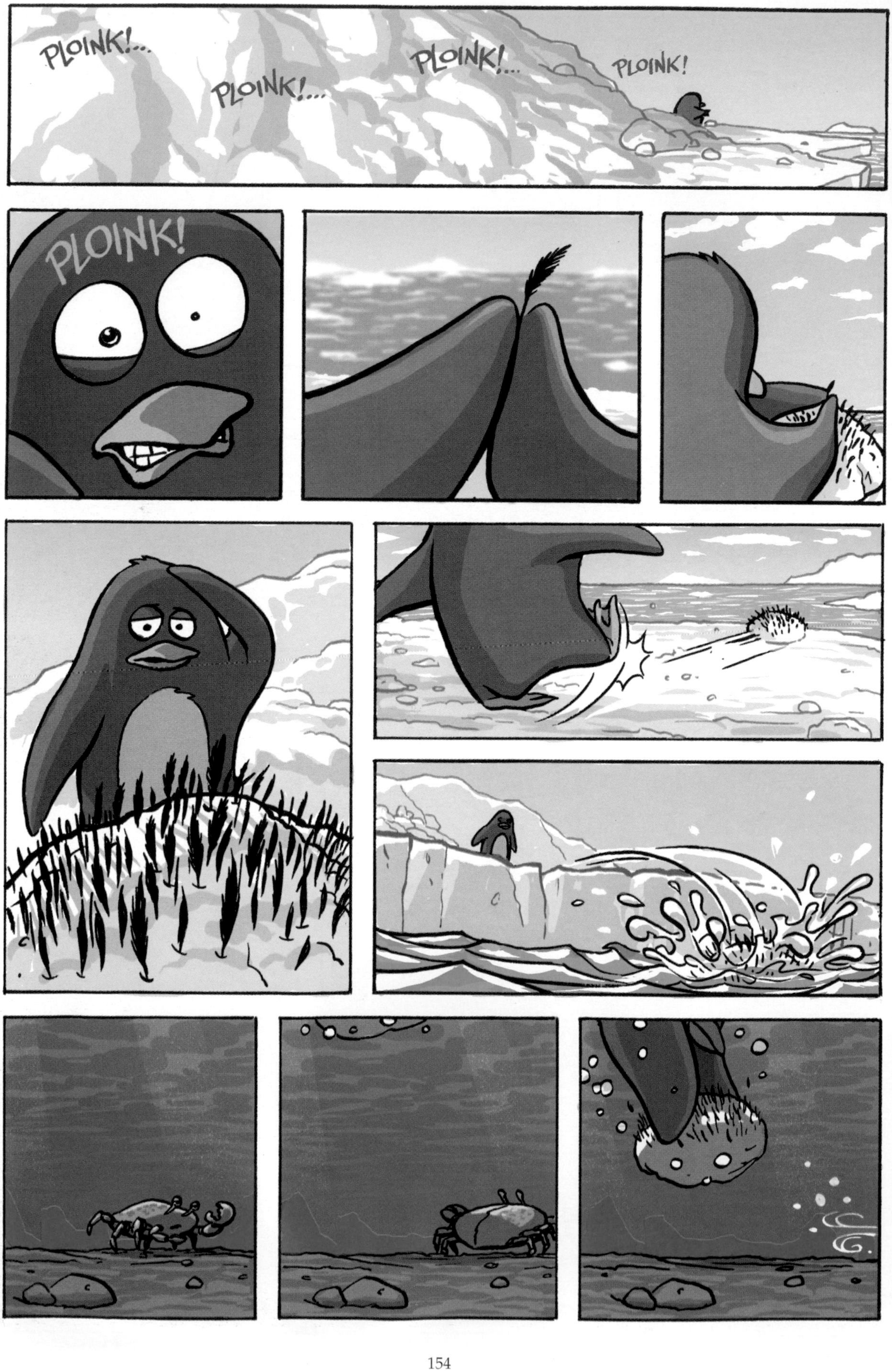
PLOINK!...
PLOINK!...
PLOINK!...
PLOINK!
PLOINK!

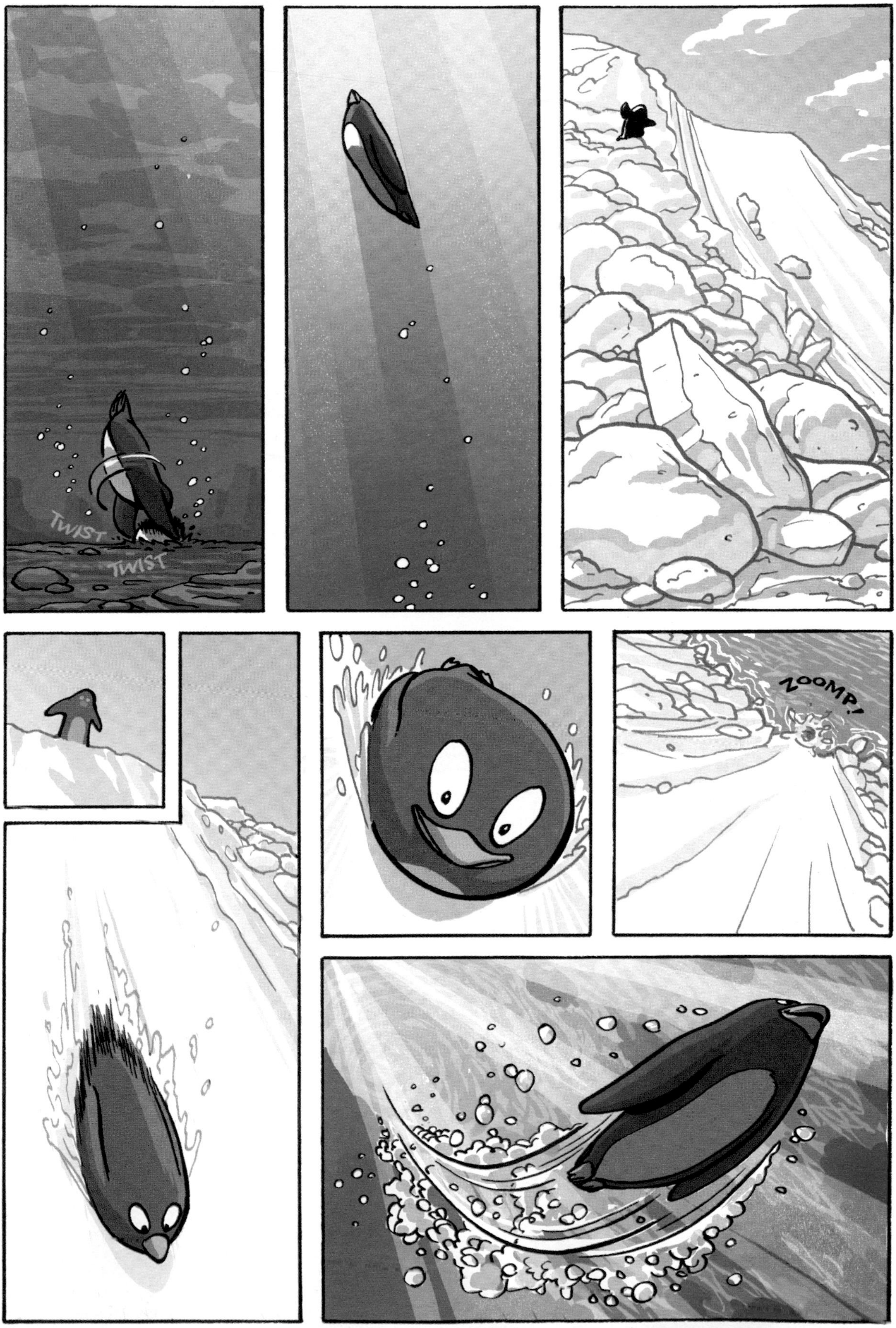
TWIST
TWIST
ZOOMP!

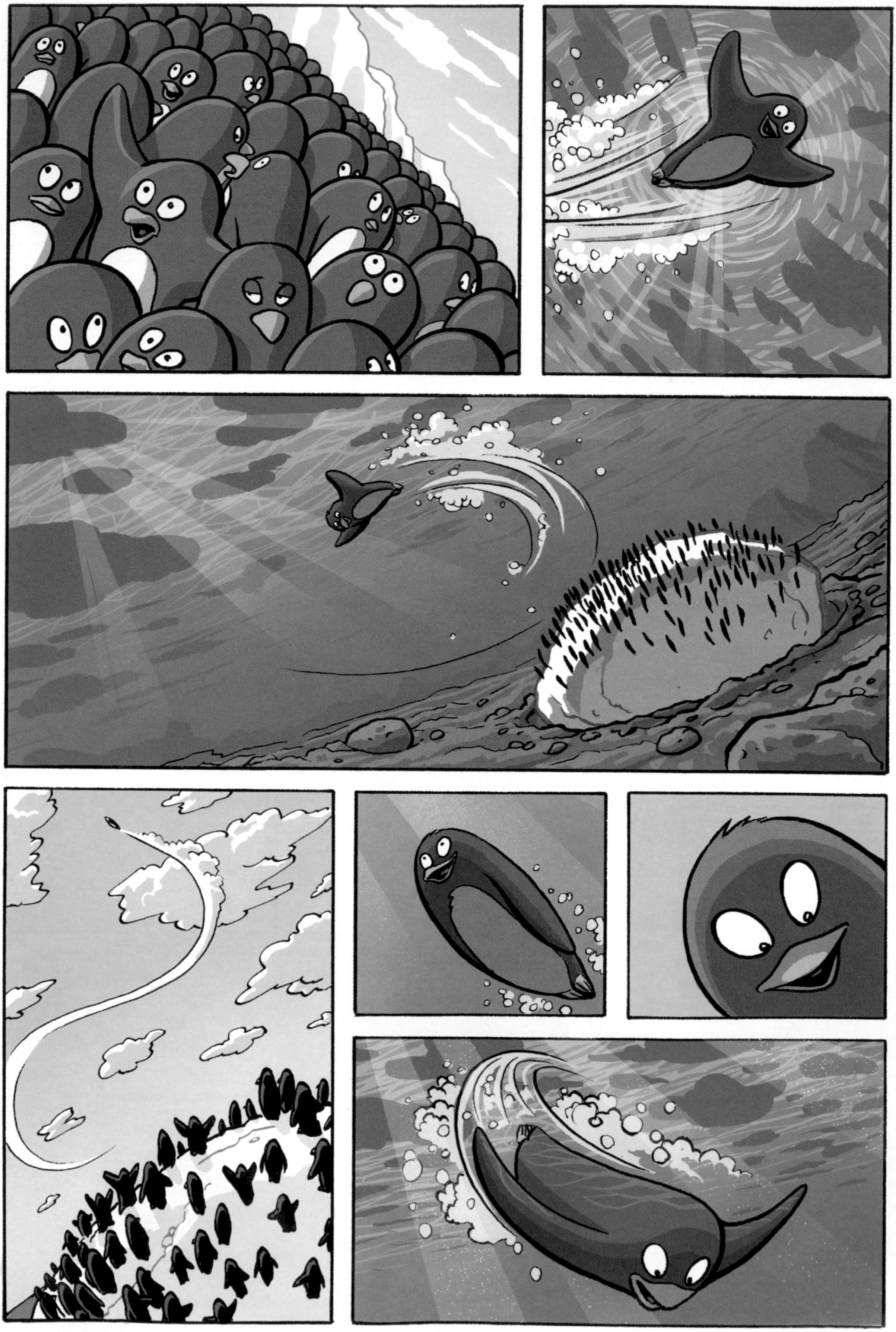

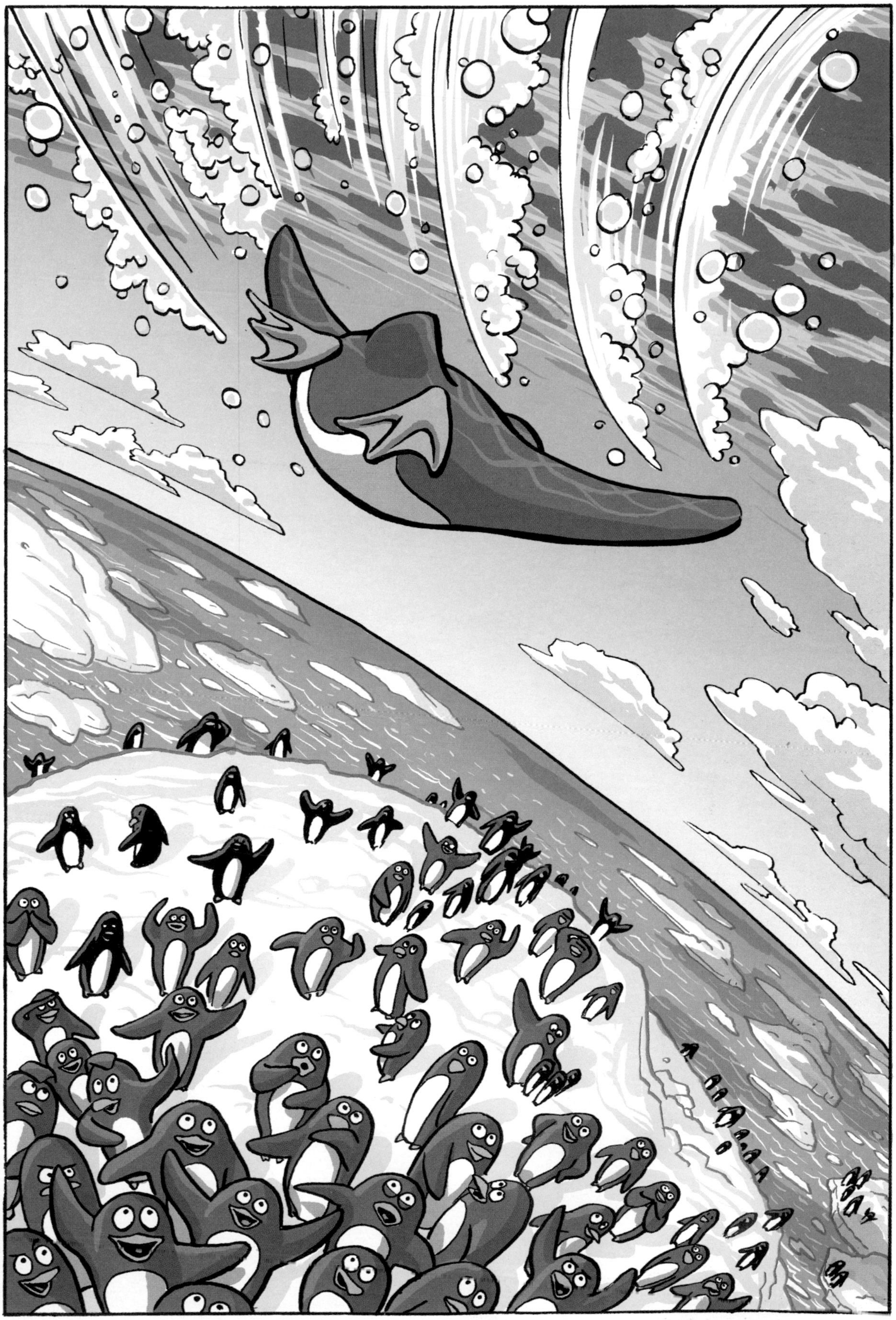

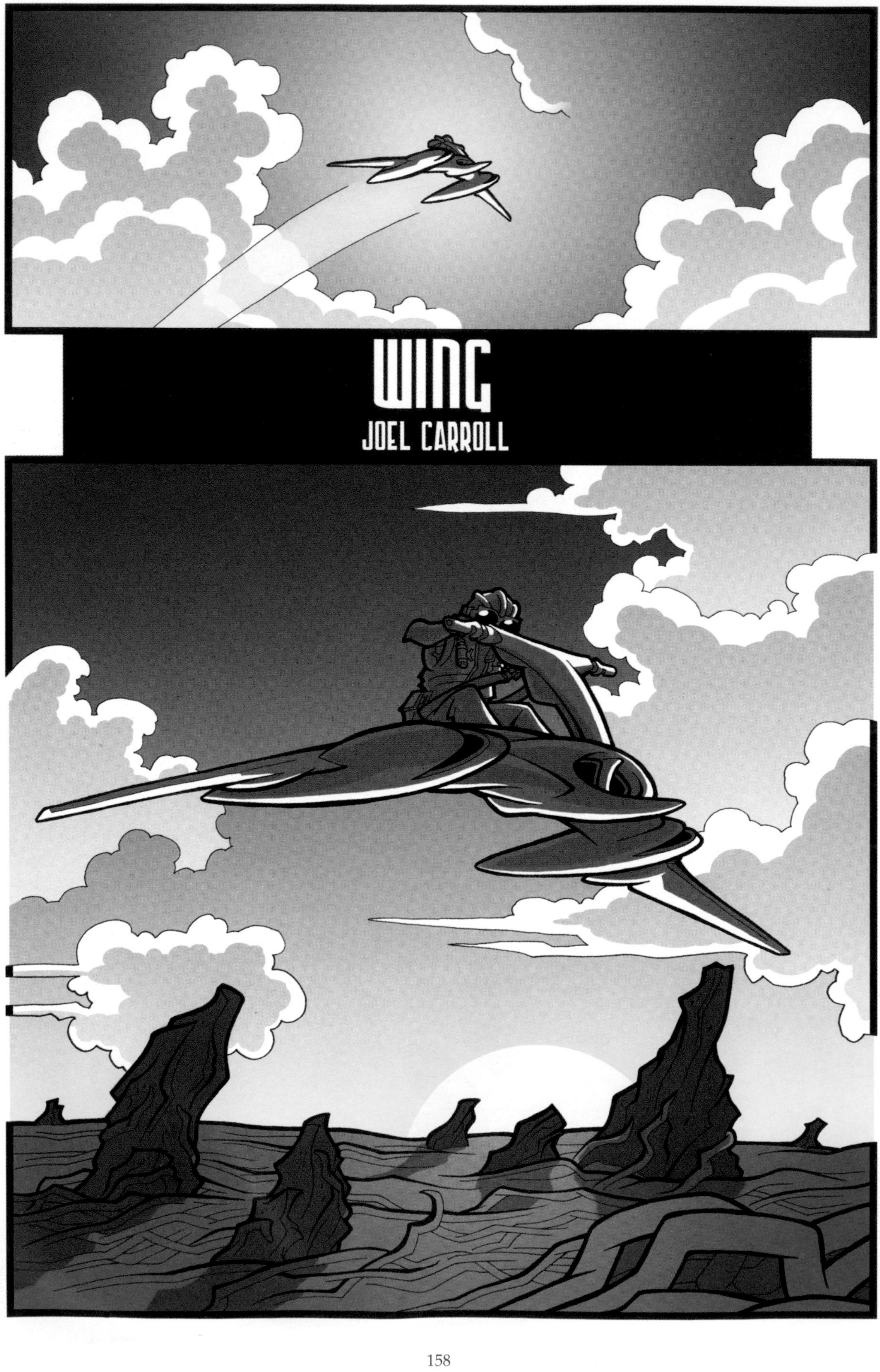
WING
JOEL CARROLL

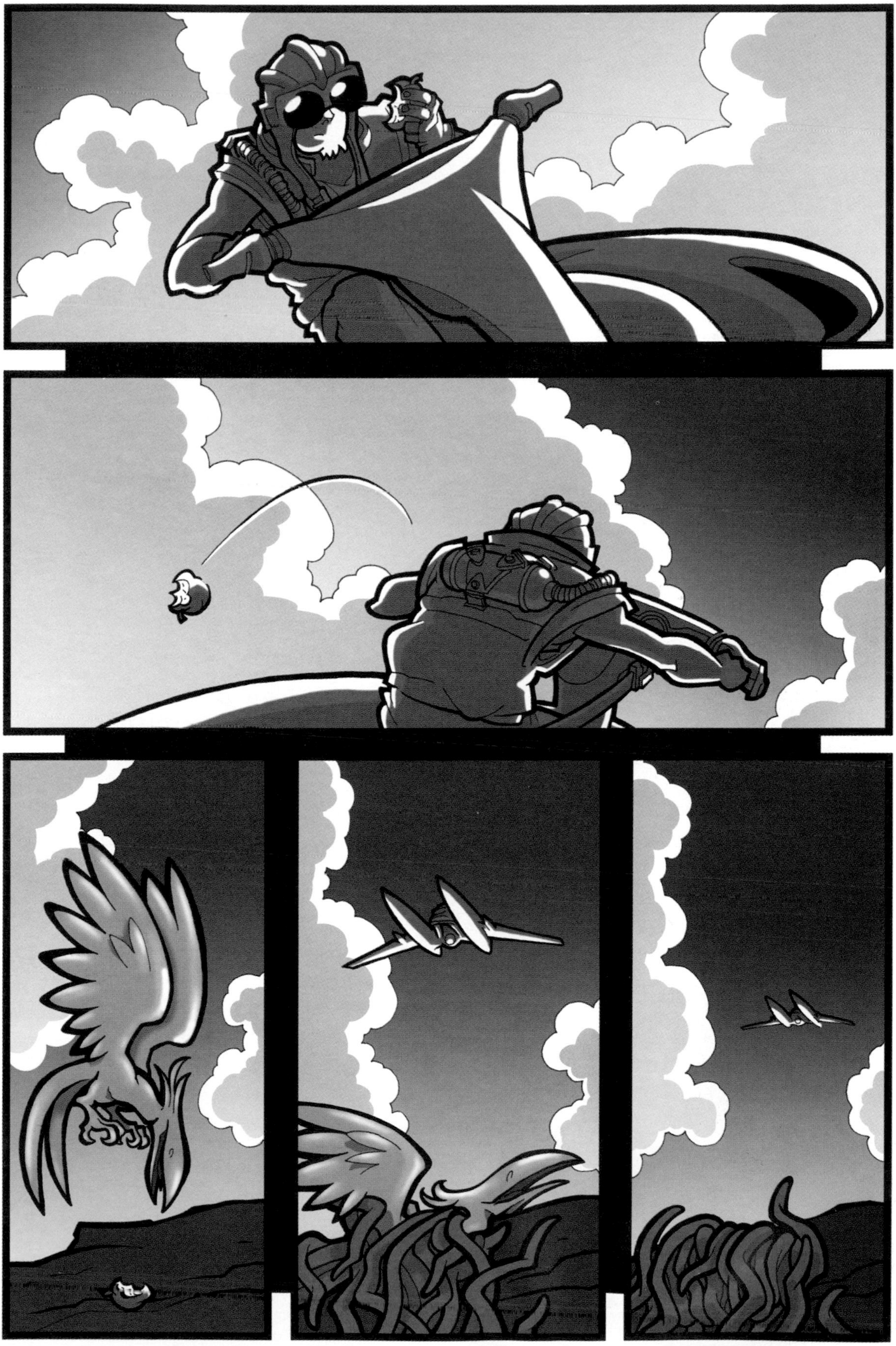

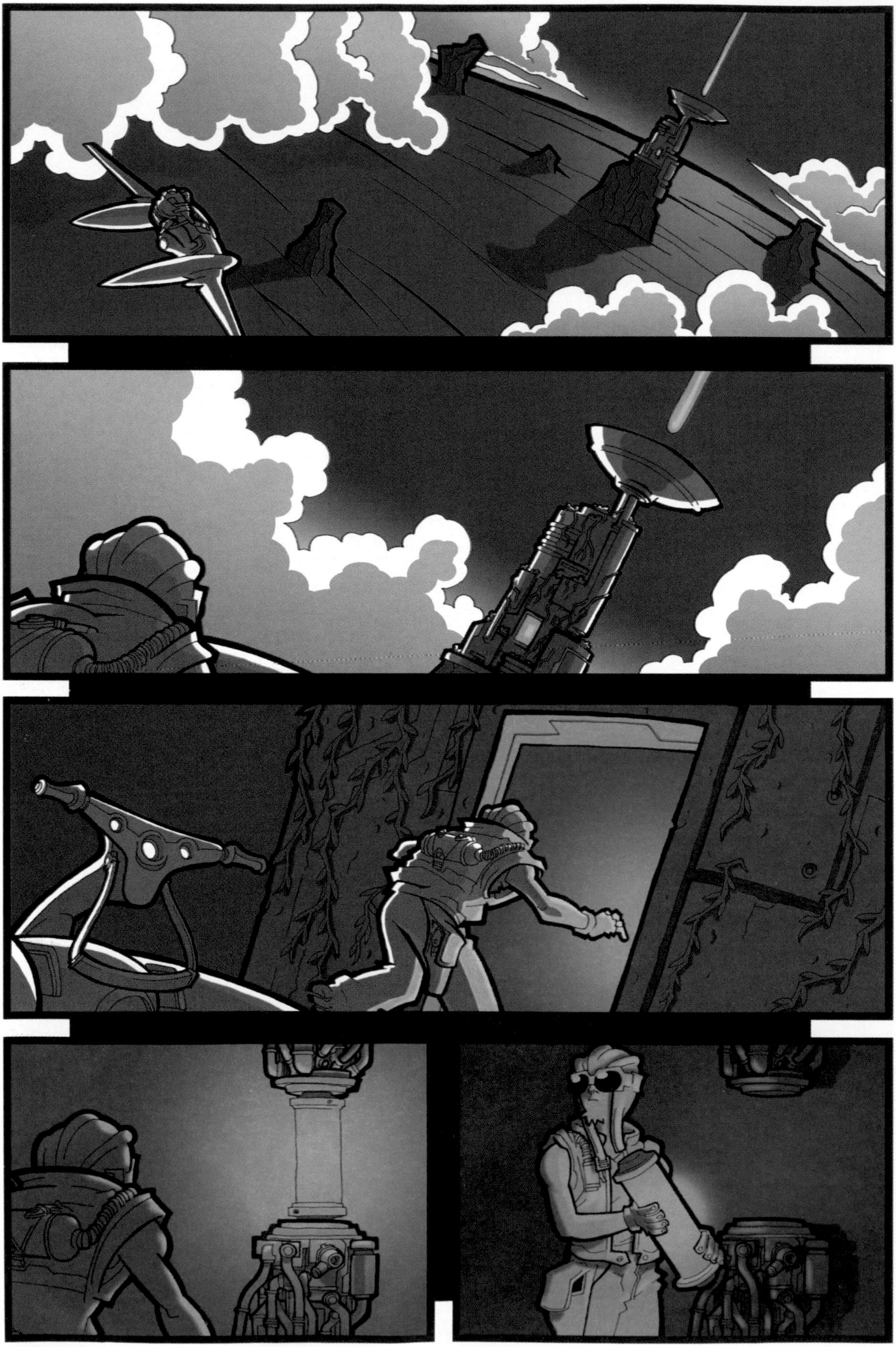

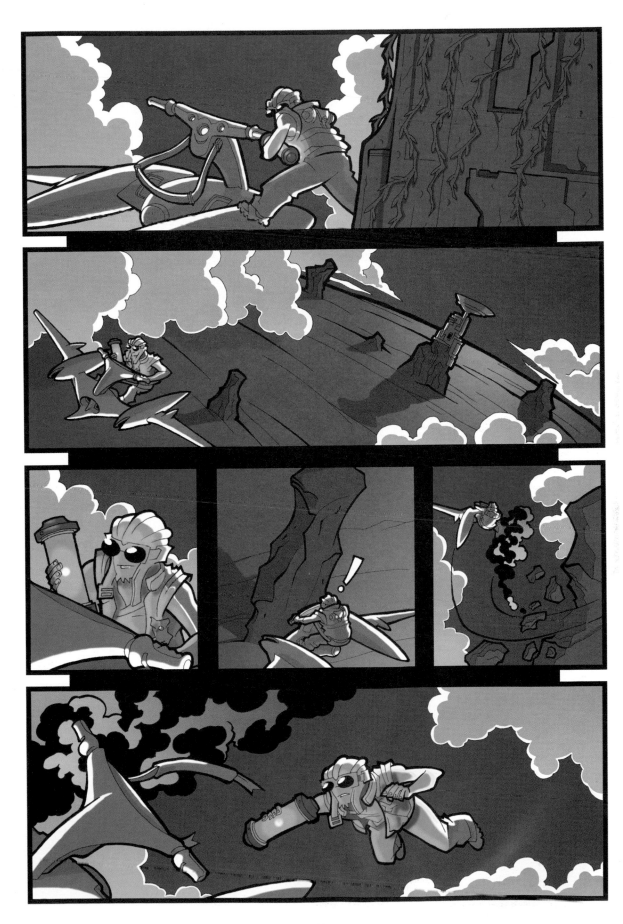

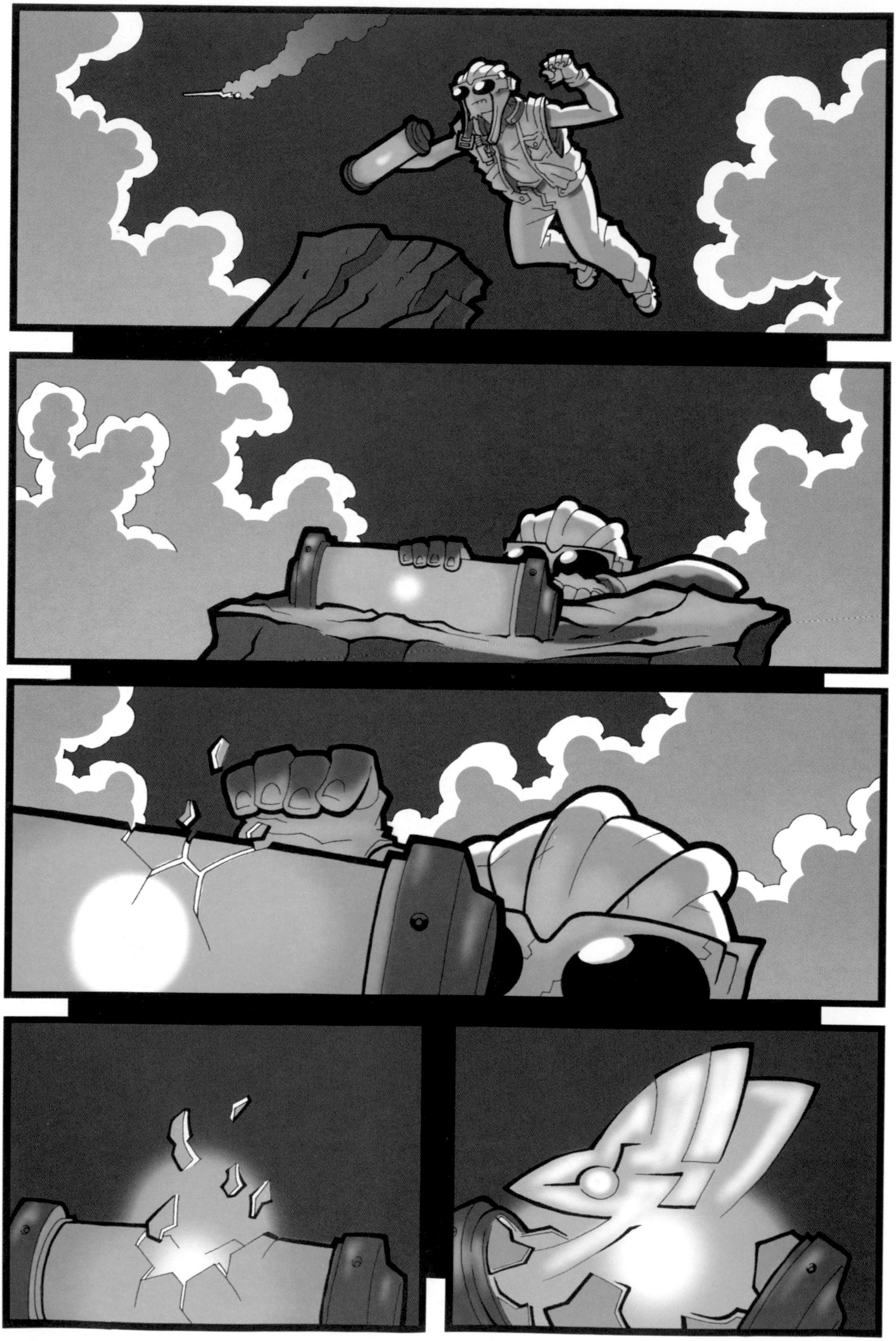

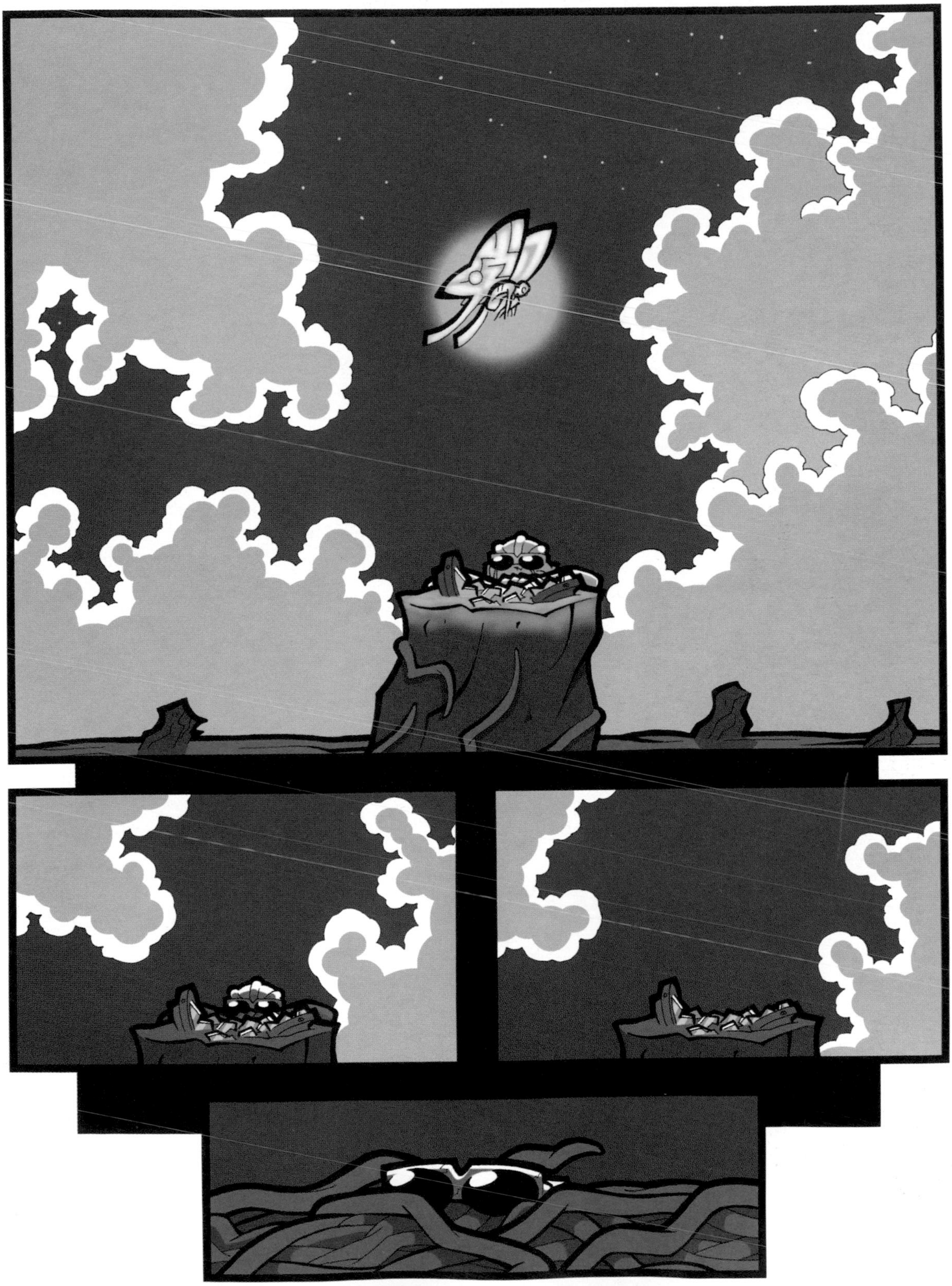

FIN

MIGRATIONS

by Kean Soo

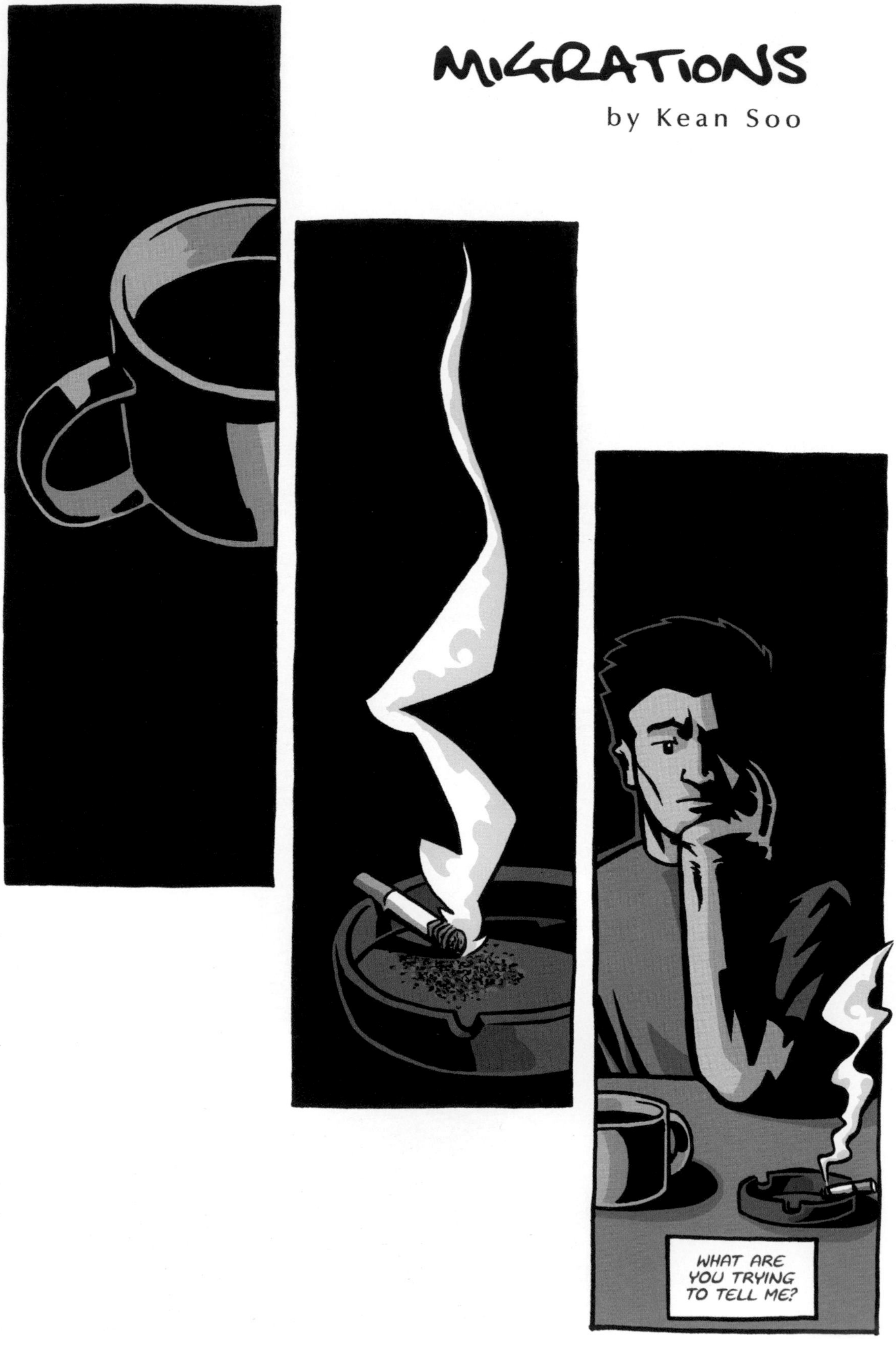
WHAT ARE YOU TRYING TO TELL ME?

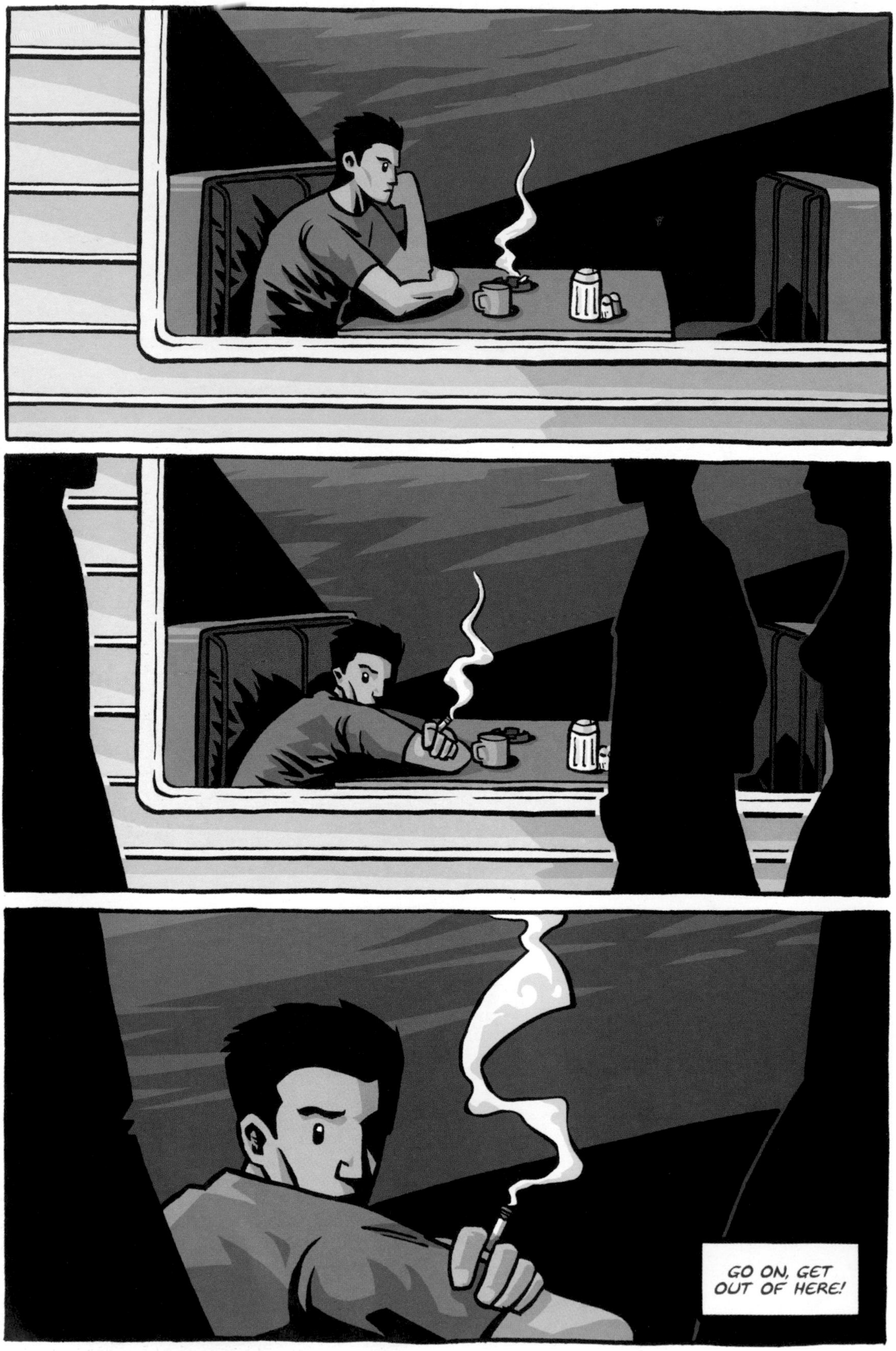
GO ON, GET OUT OF HERE!

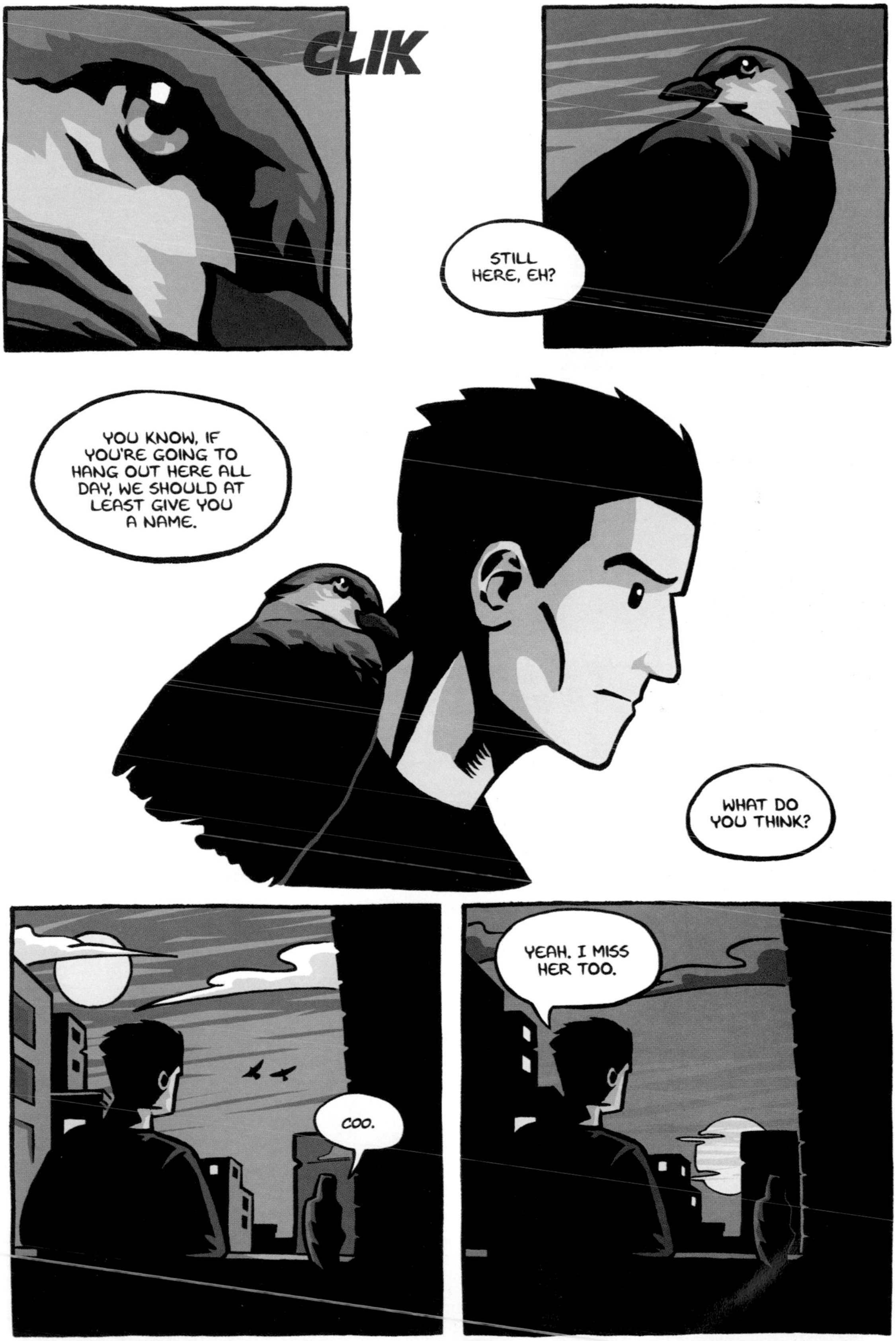
CLIK
STILL HERE, EH?
YOU KNOW, IF YOU'RE GOING TO HANG OUT HERE ALL DAY, WE SHOULD AT LEAST GIVE YOU A NAME.
WHAT DO YOU THINK?
COO.
YEAH. I MISS HER TOO.

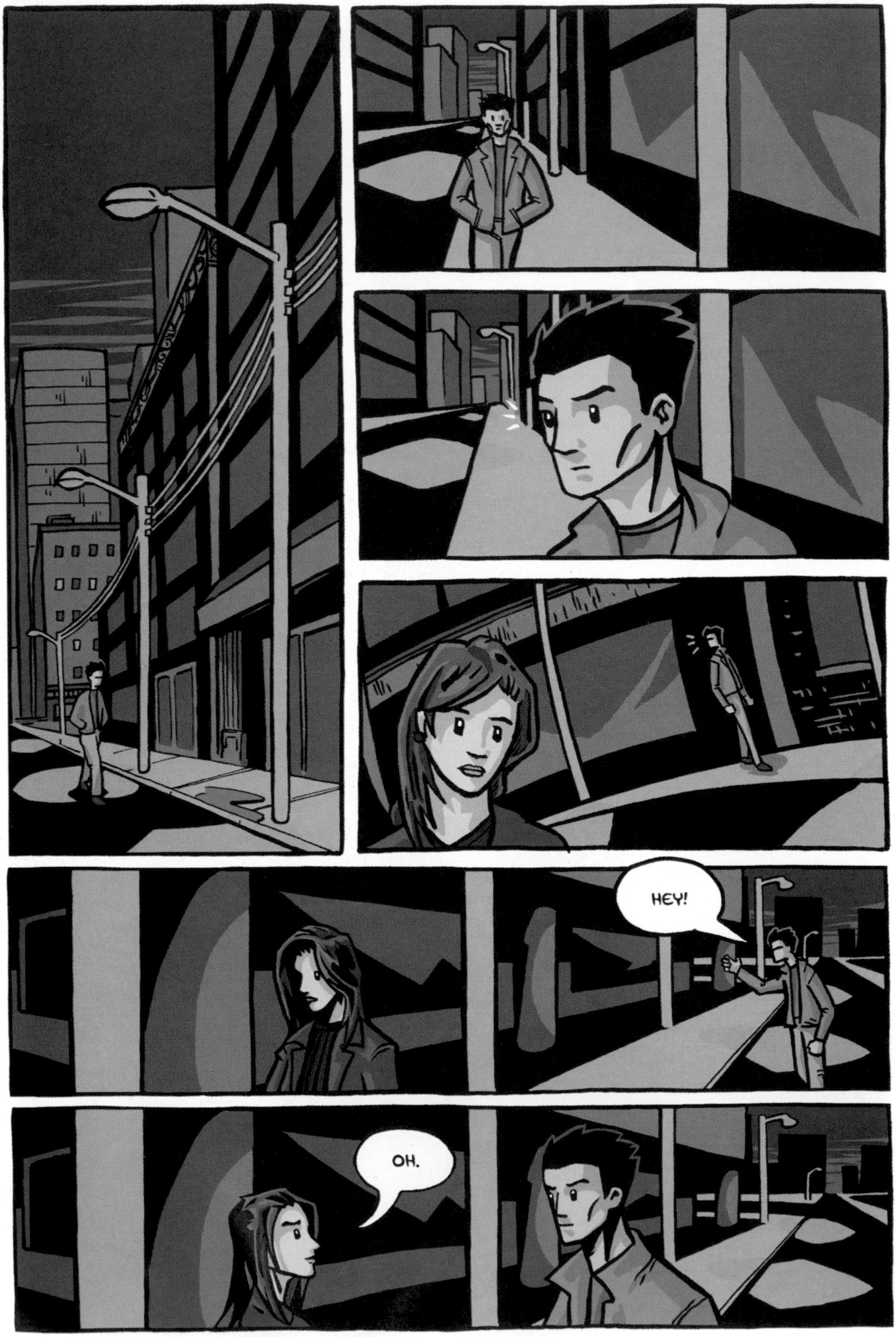
HEY!
OH.

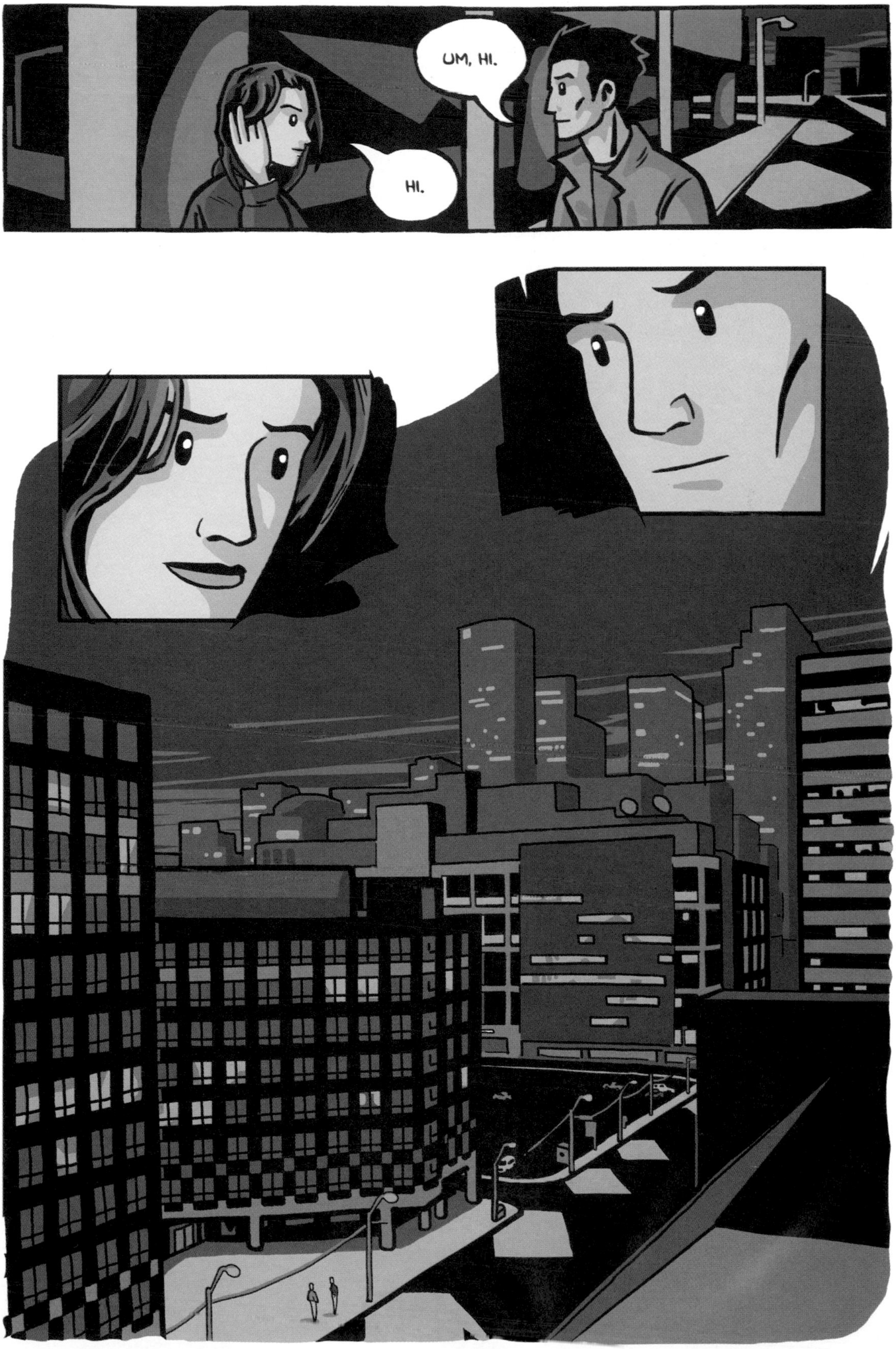
UM, HI.
HI.

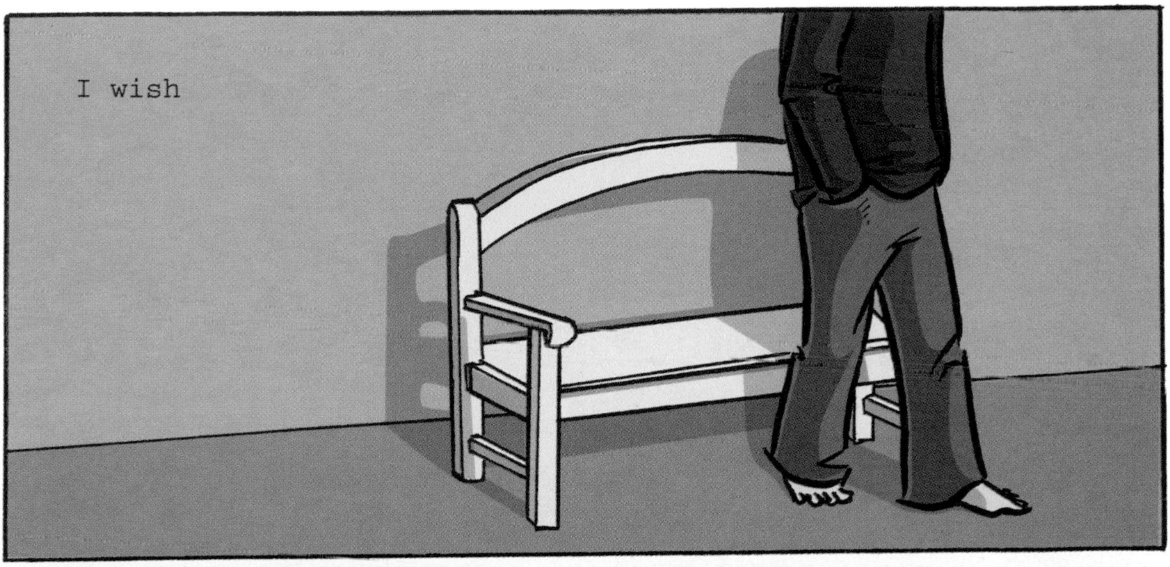
I wish

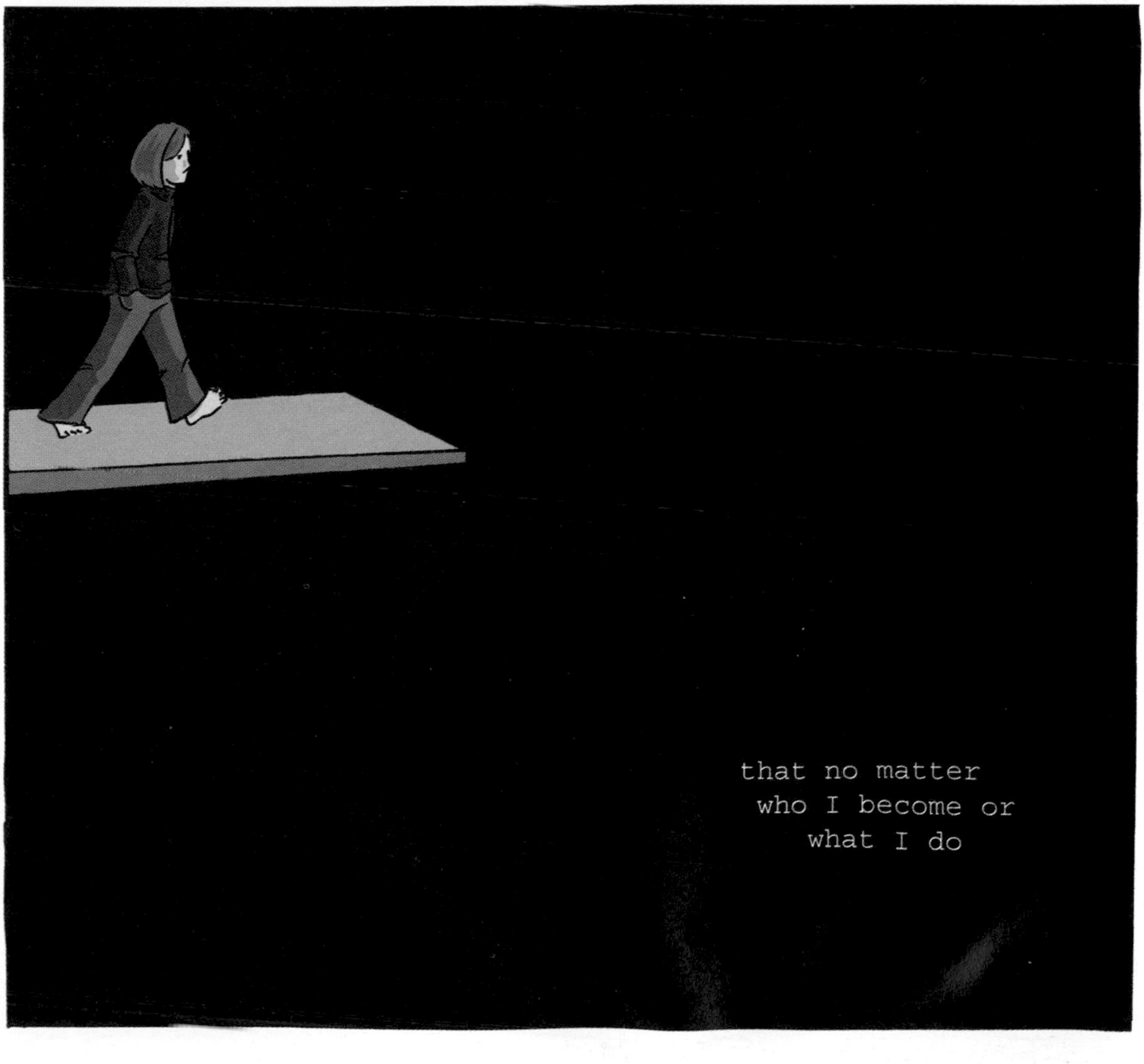
that no matter
who I become or
what I do

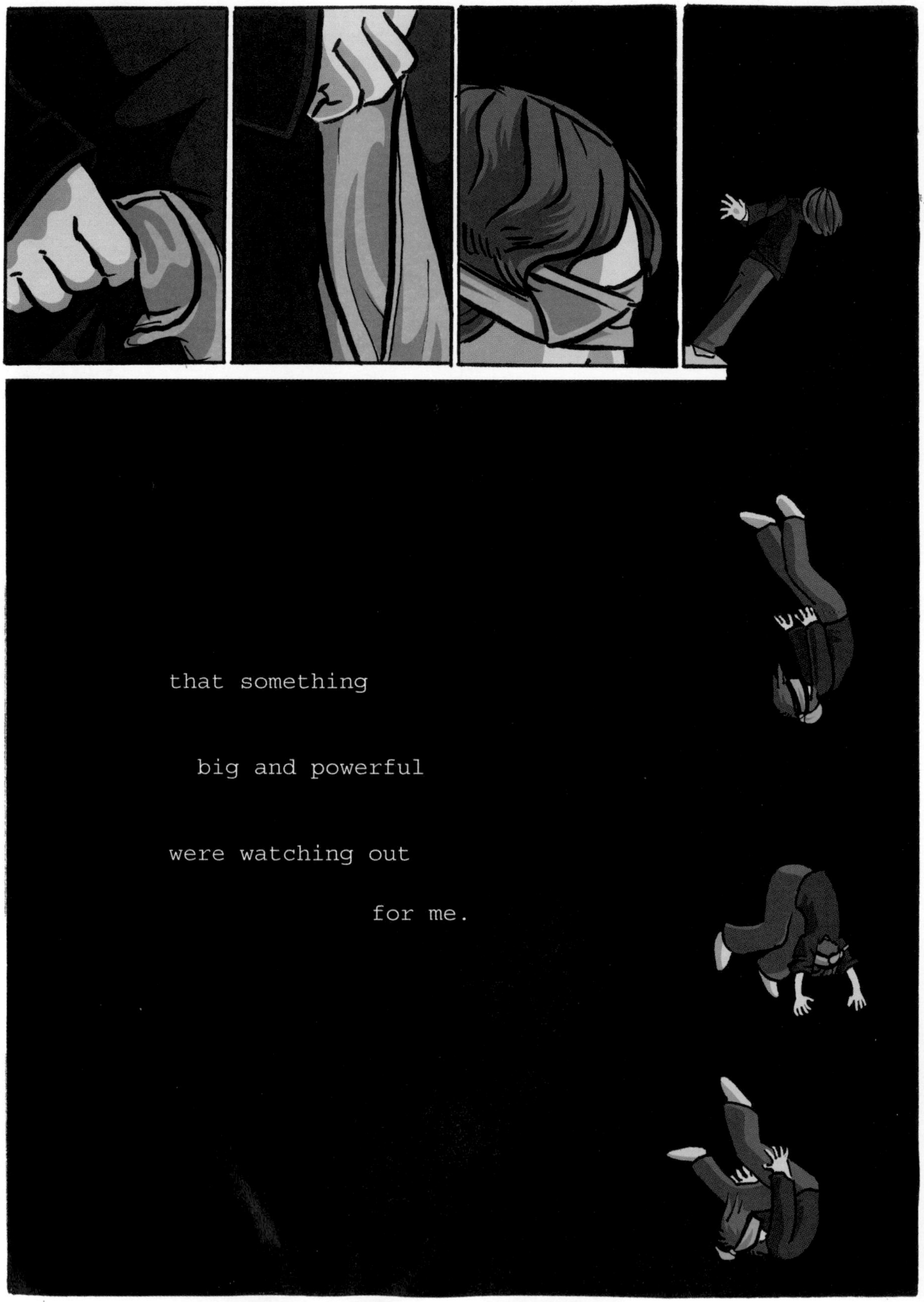
that something
big and powerful
were watching out
for me.

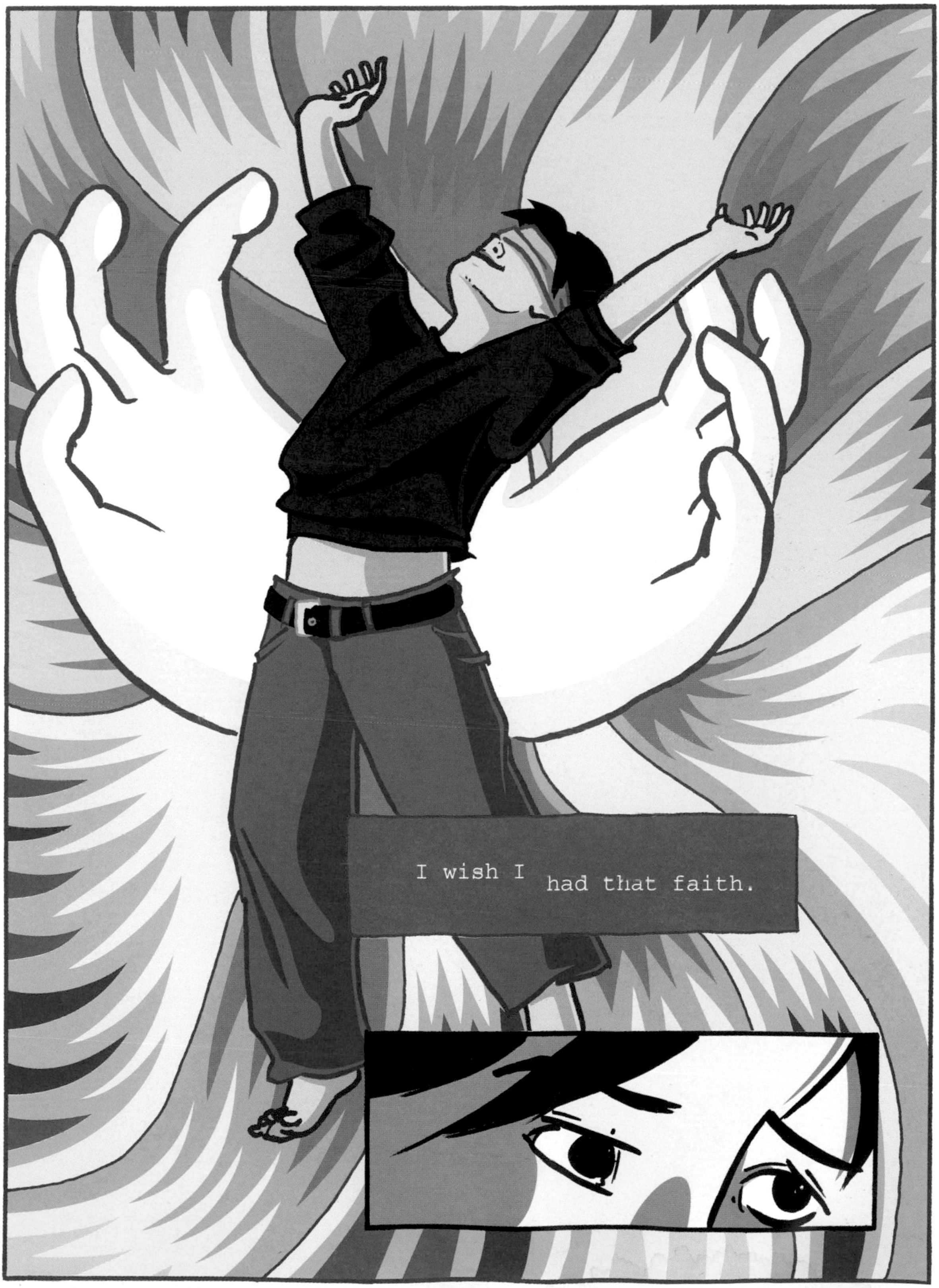
I wish I had that faith.

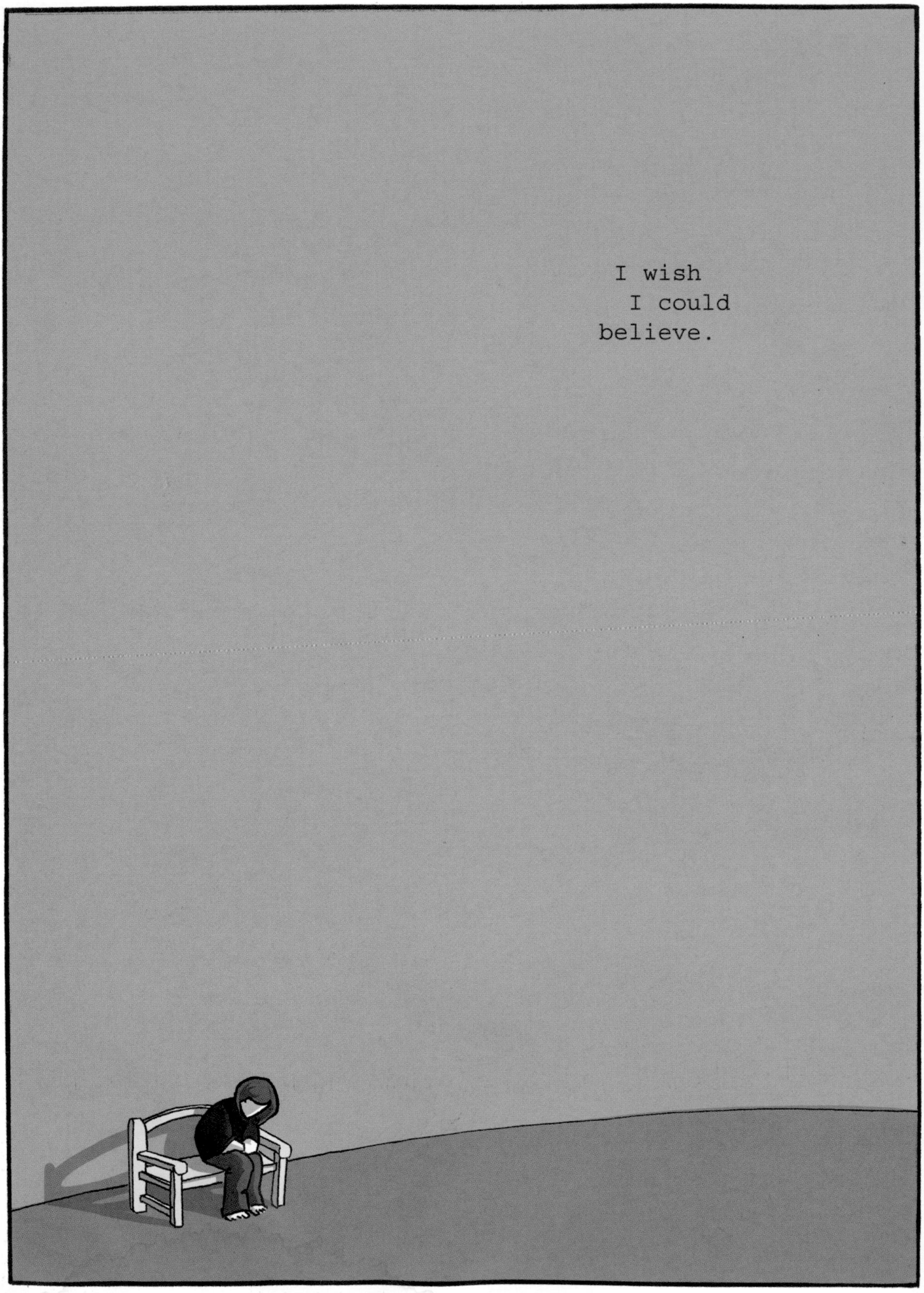
I wish
I could
believe.

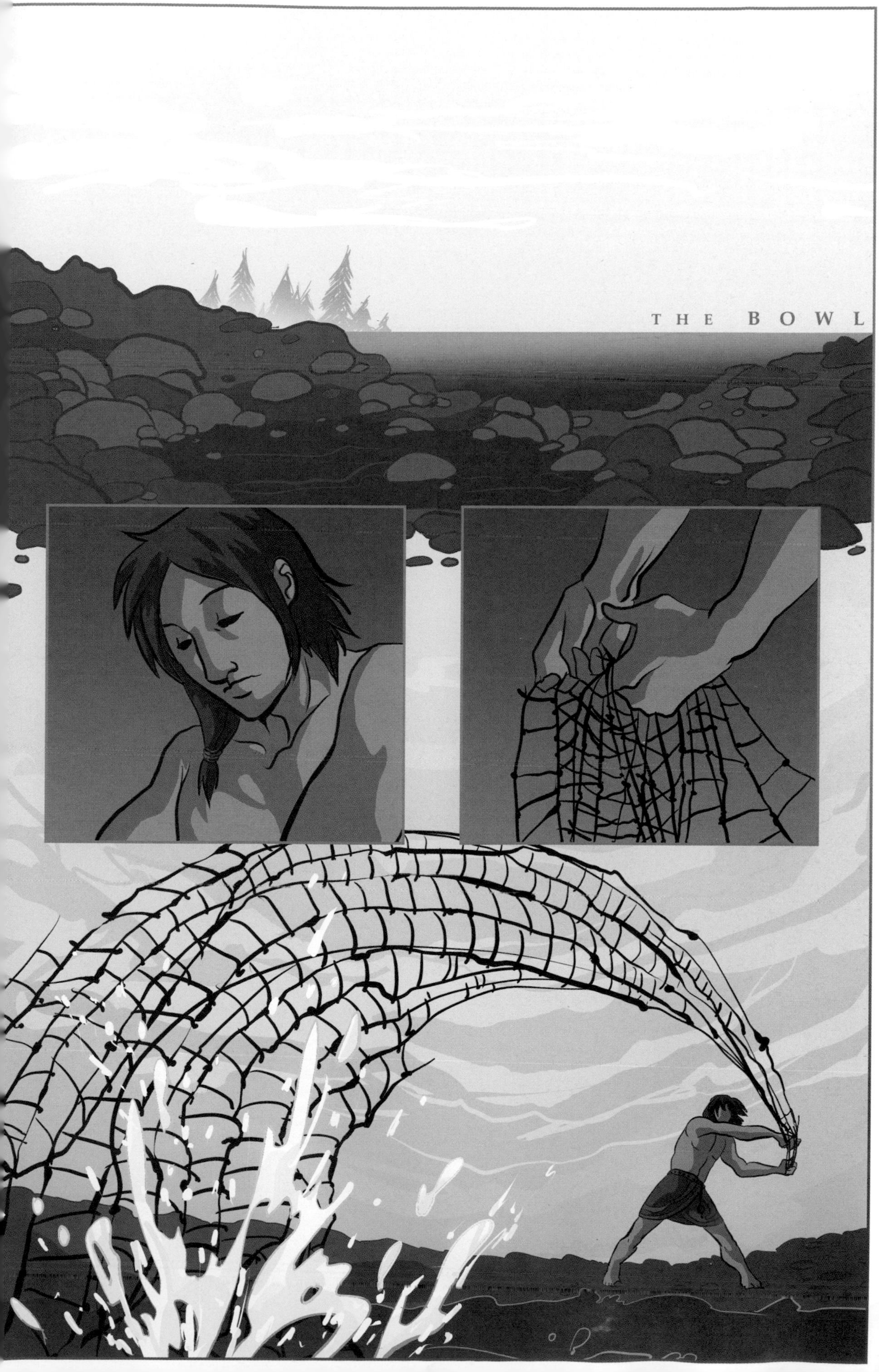

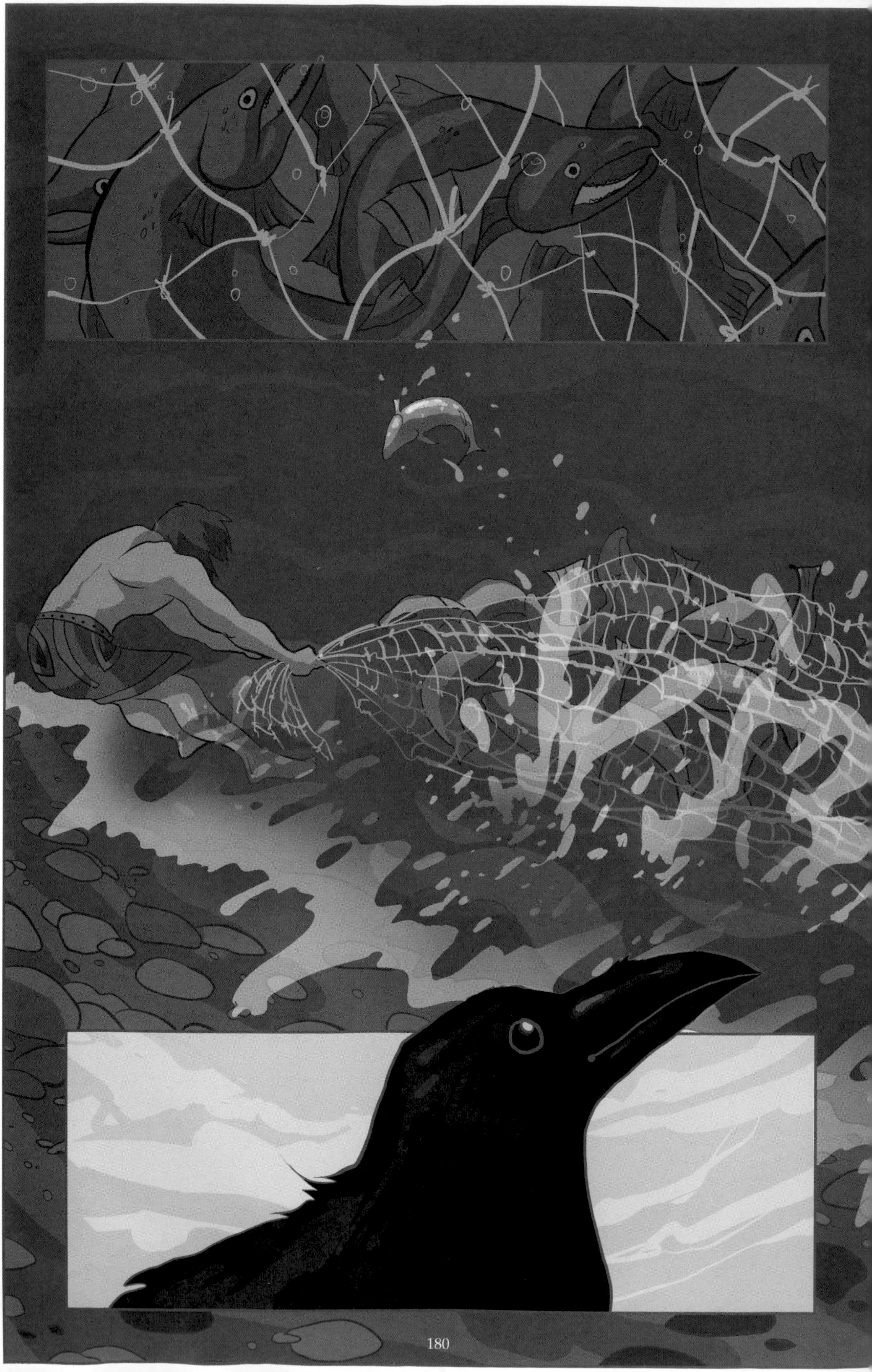

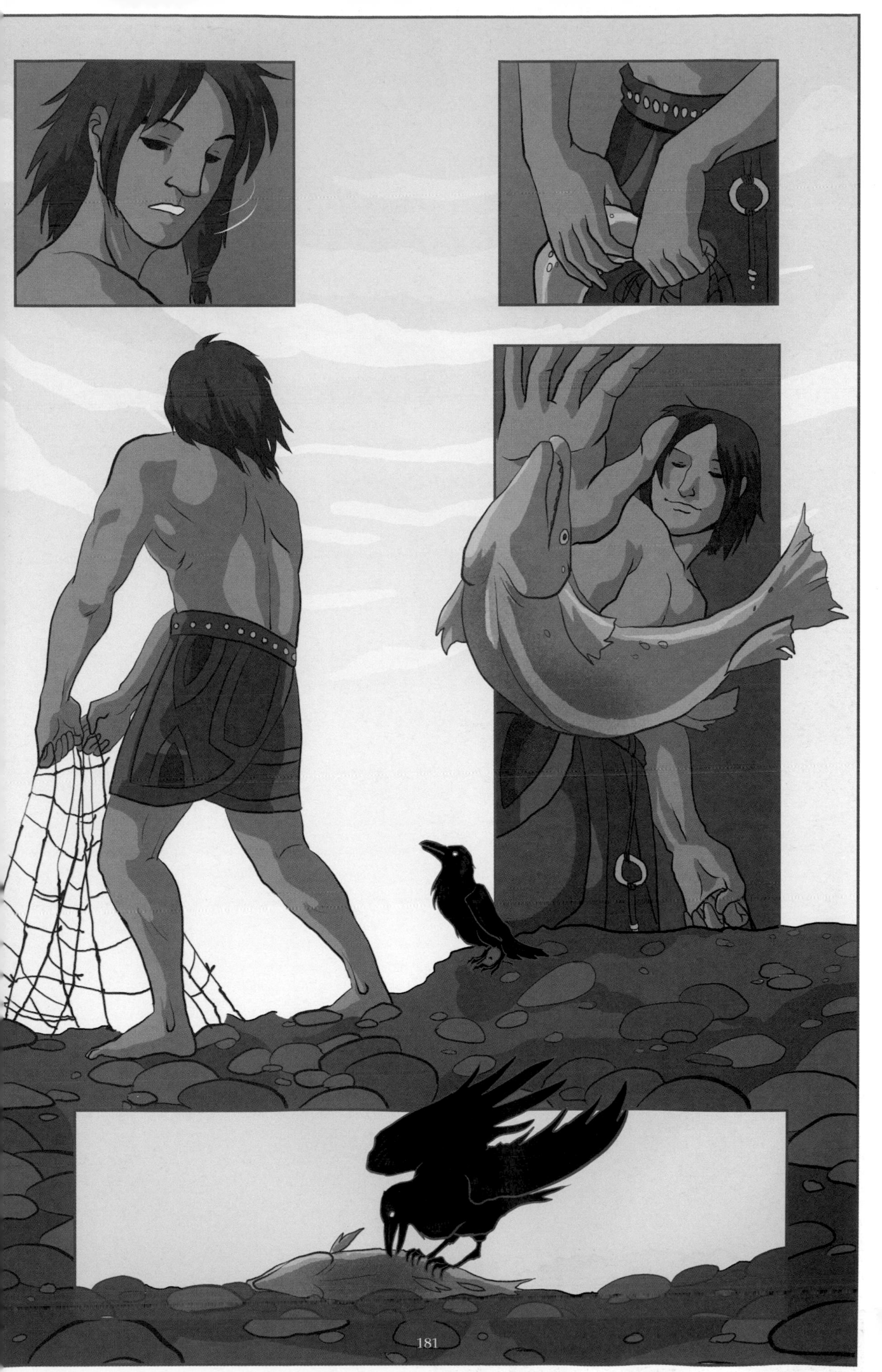

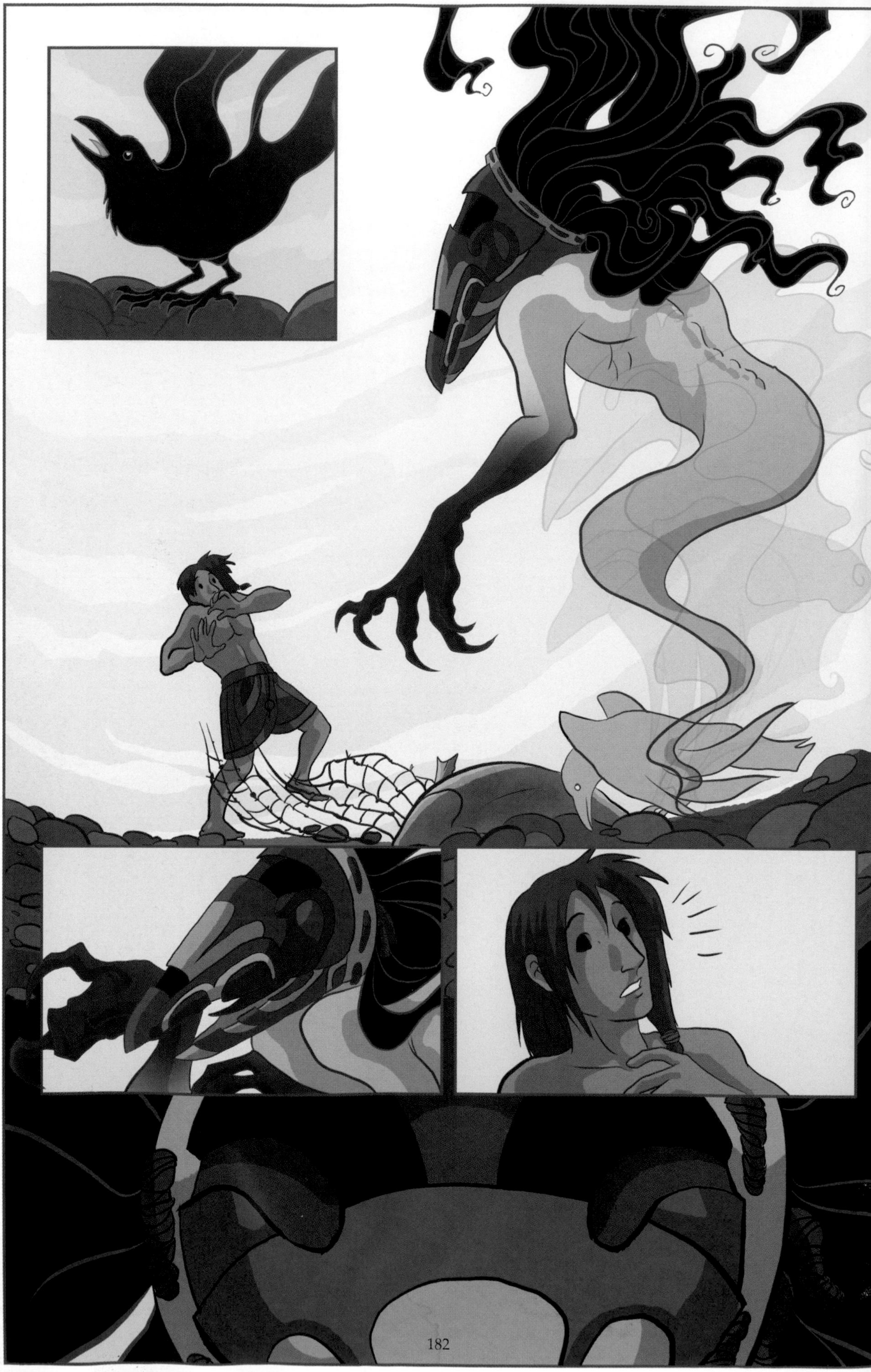

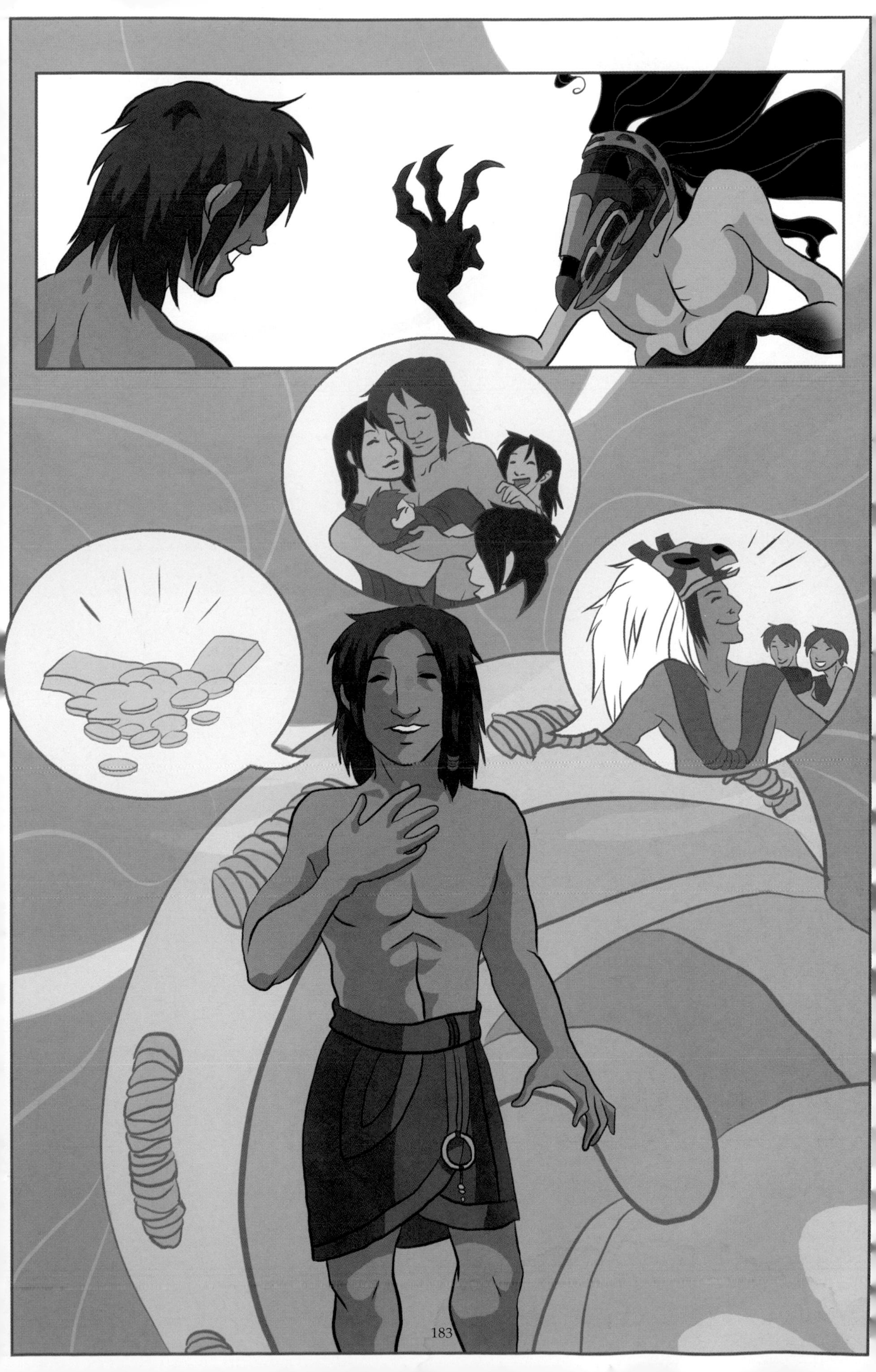

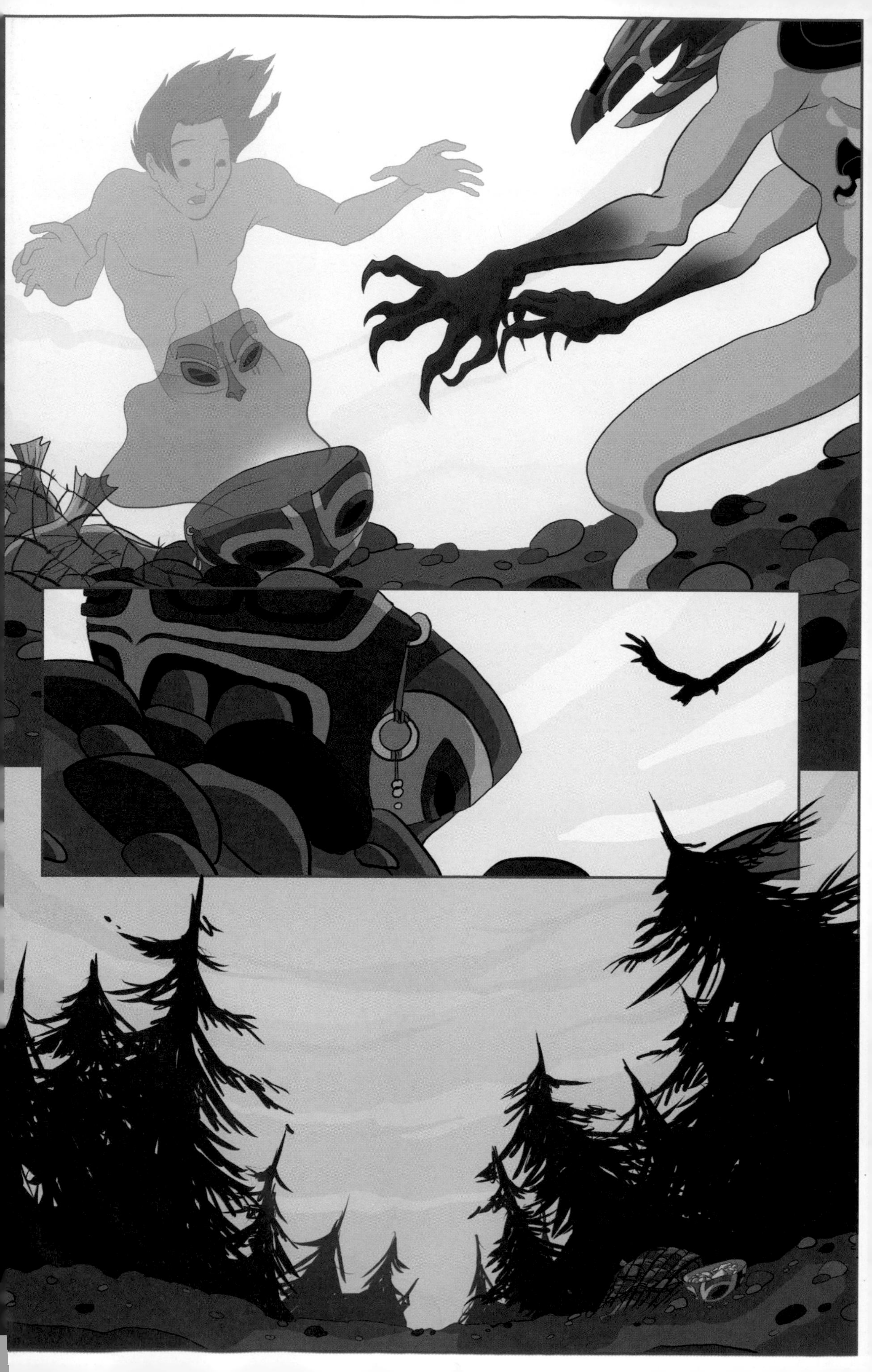

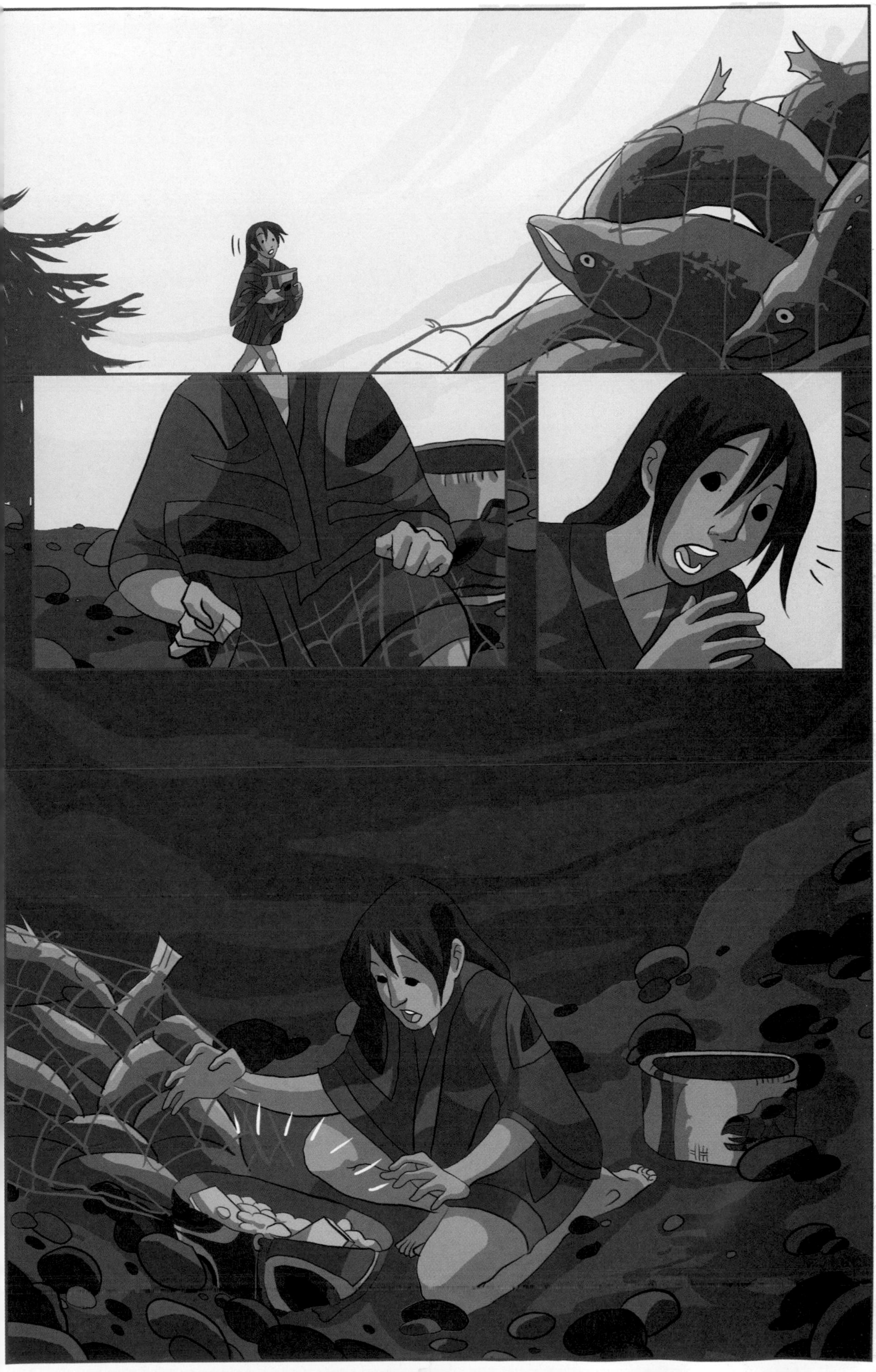

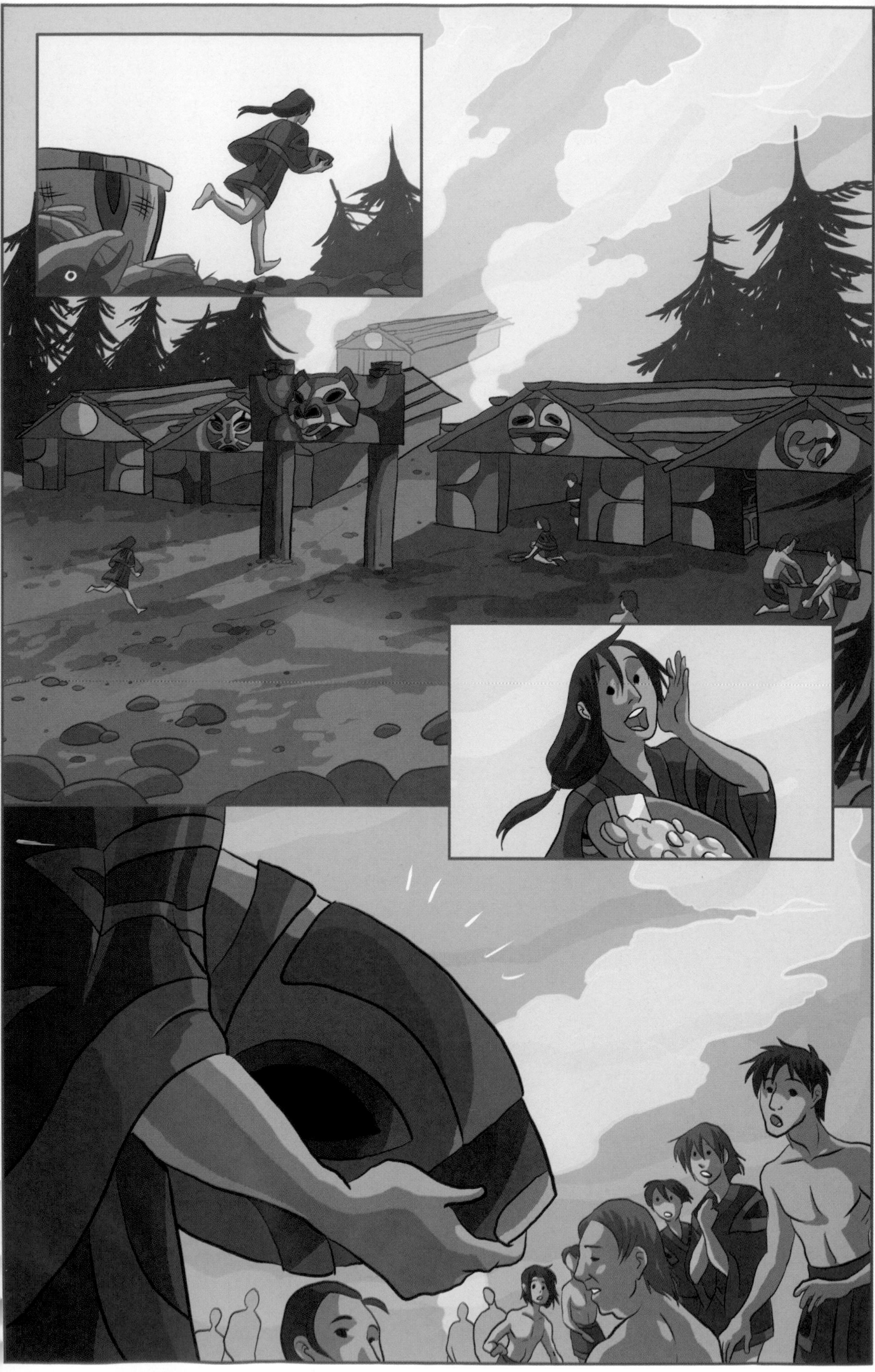

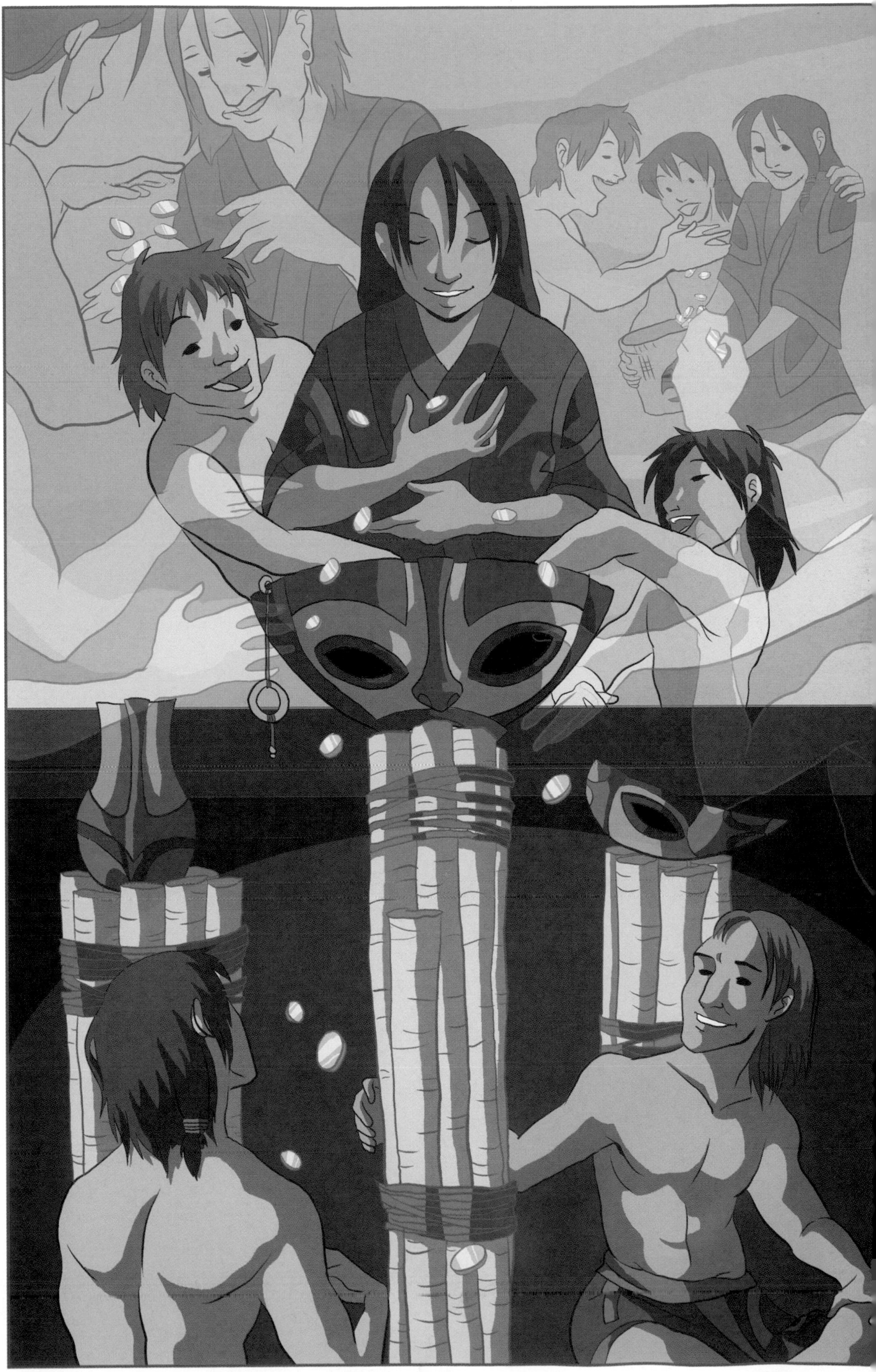

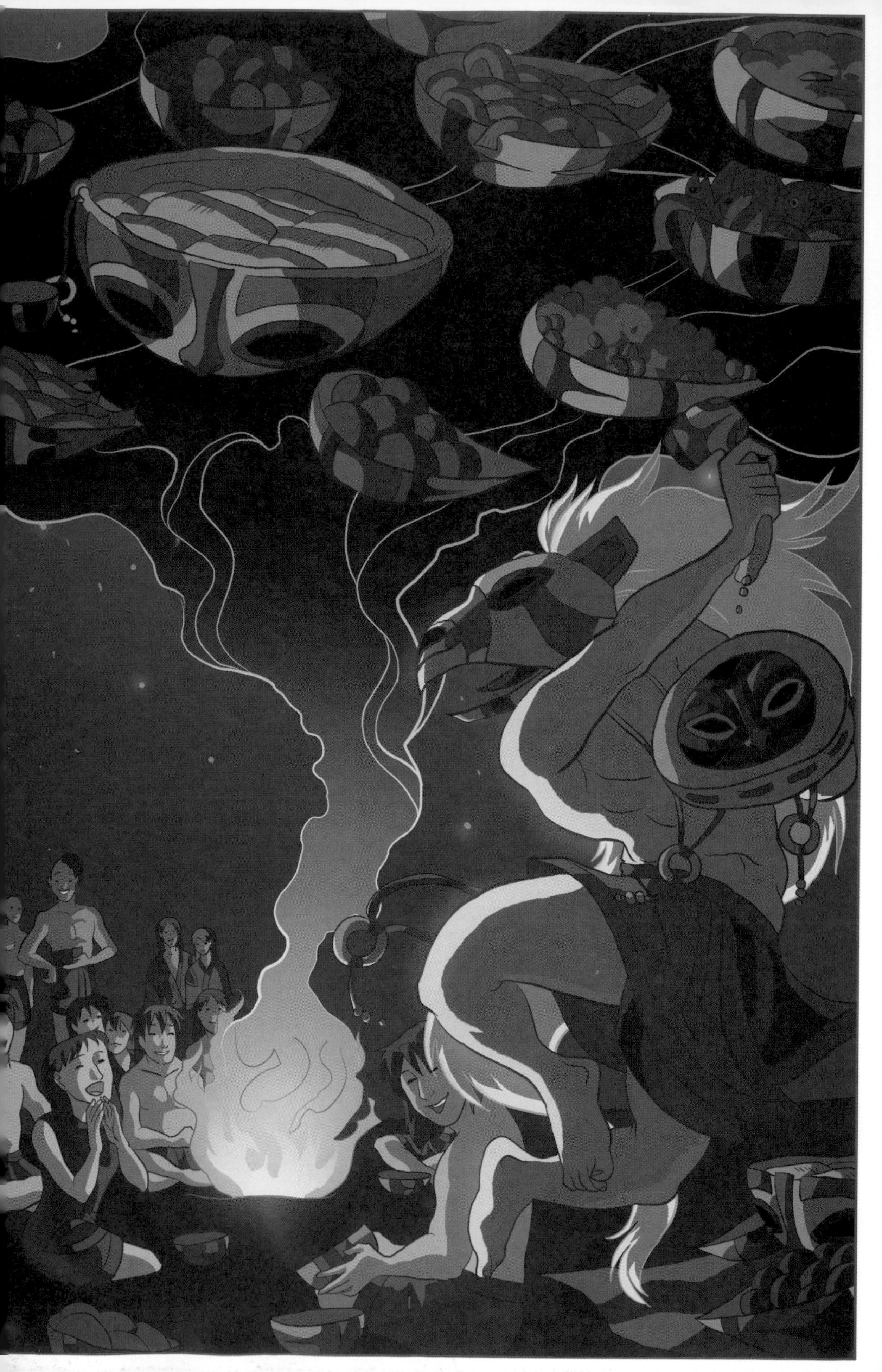

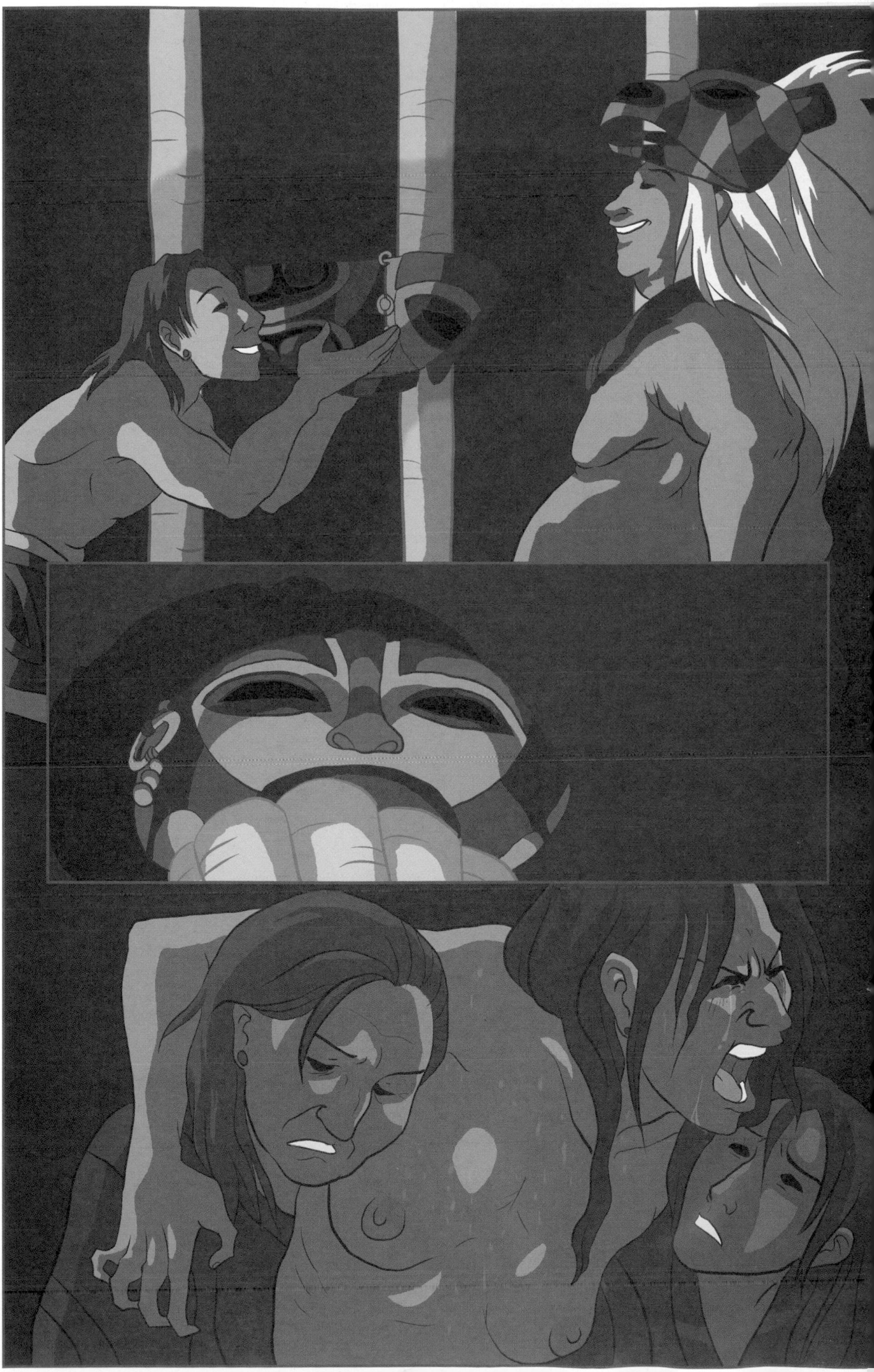

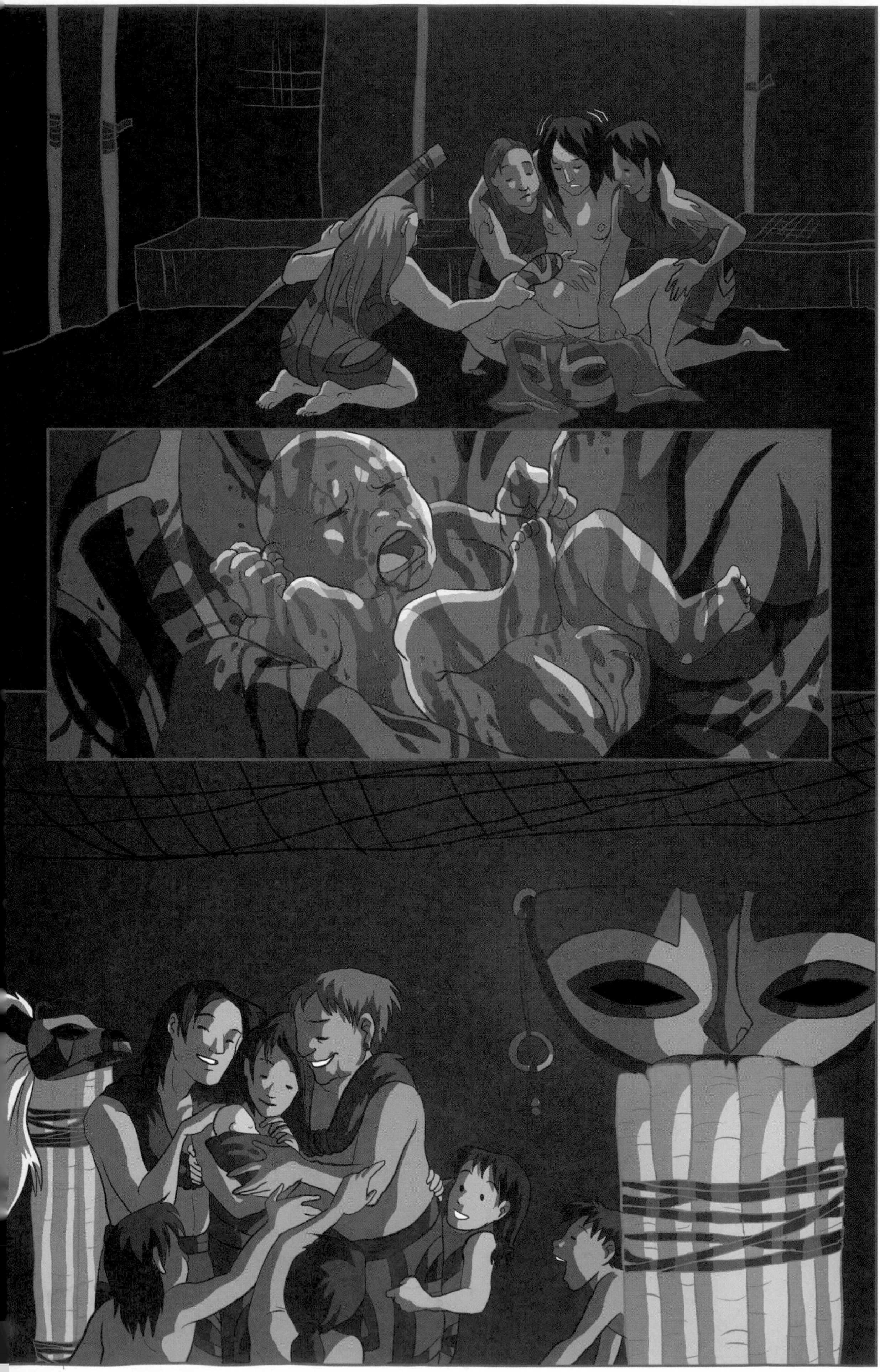

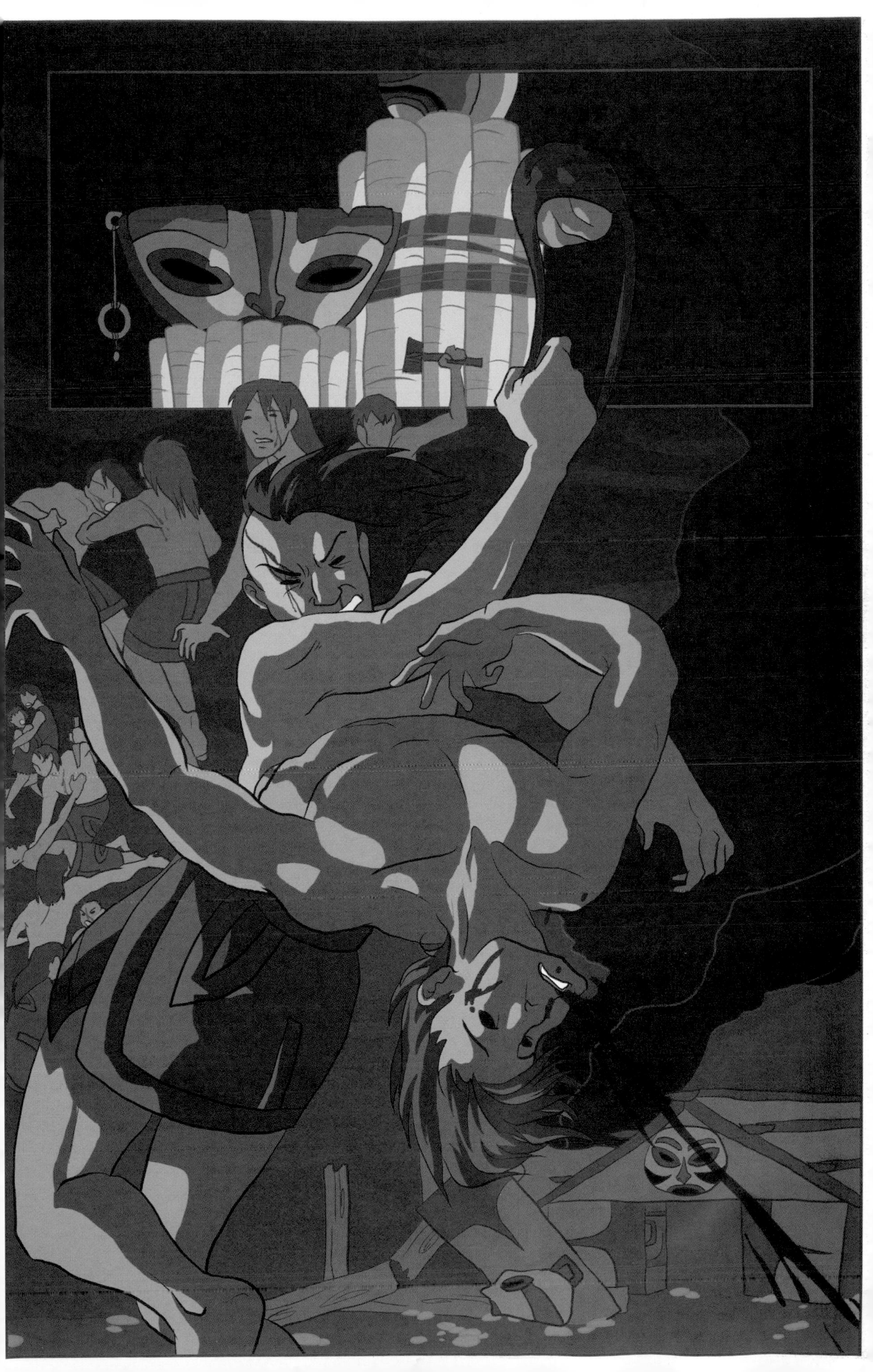

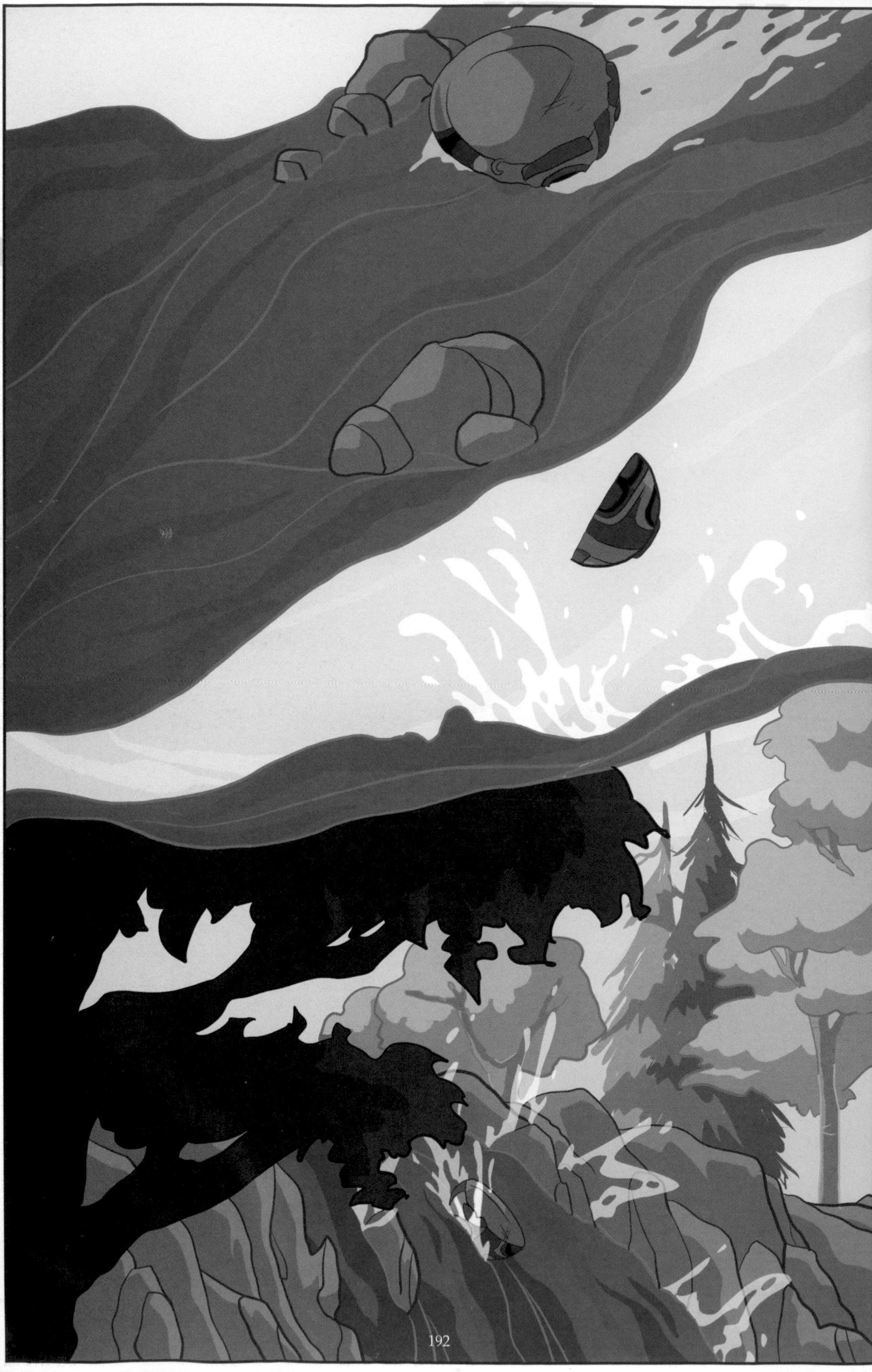

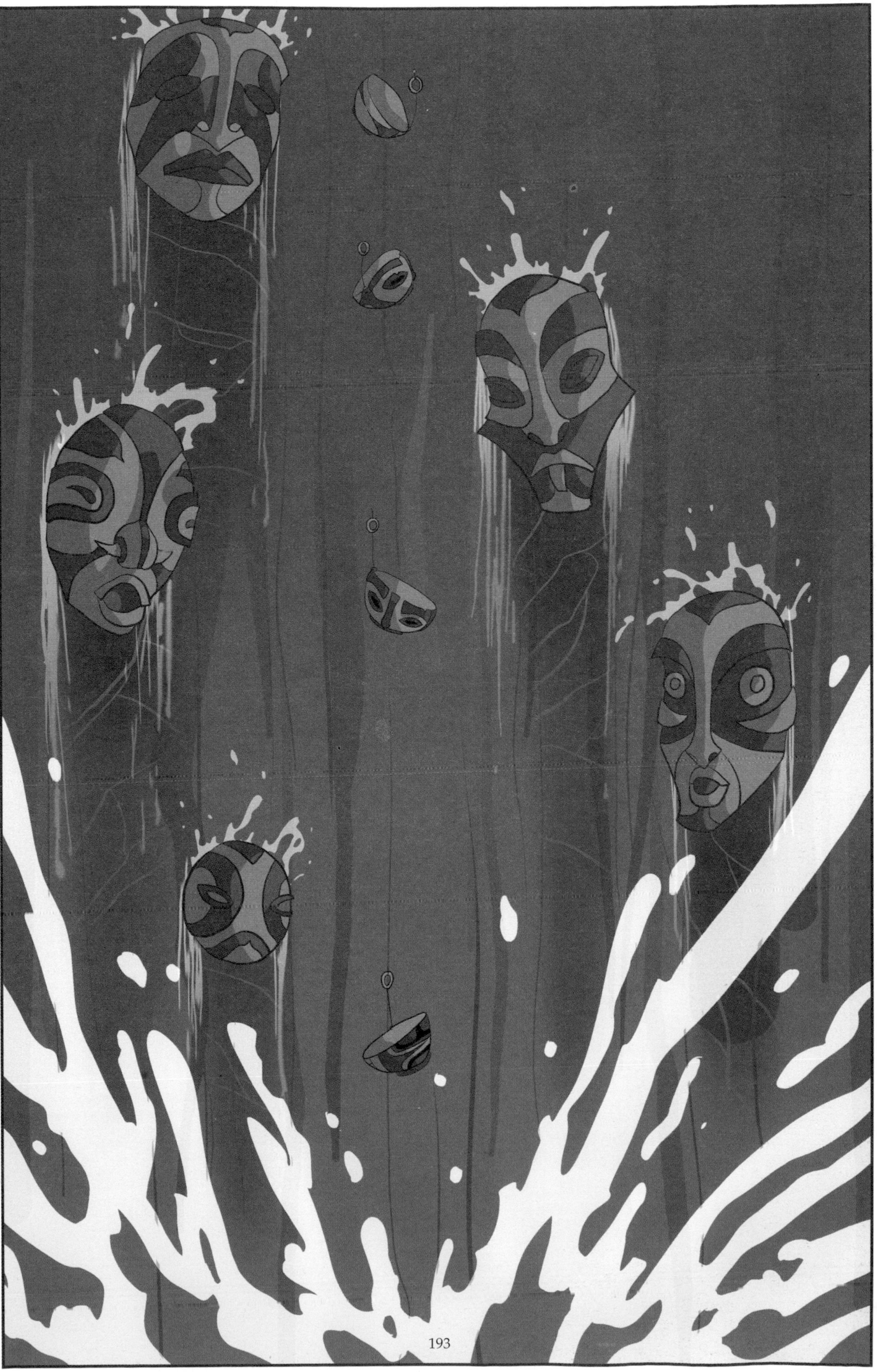

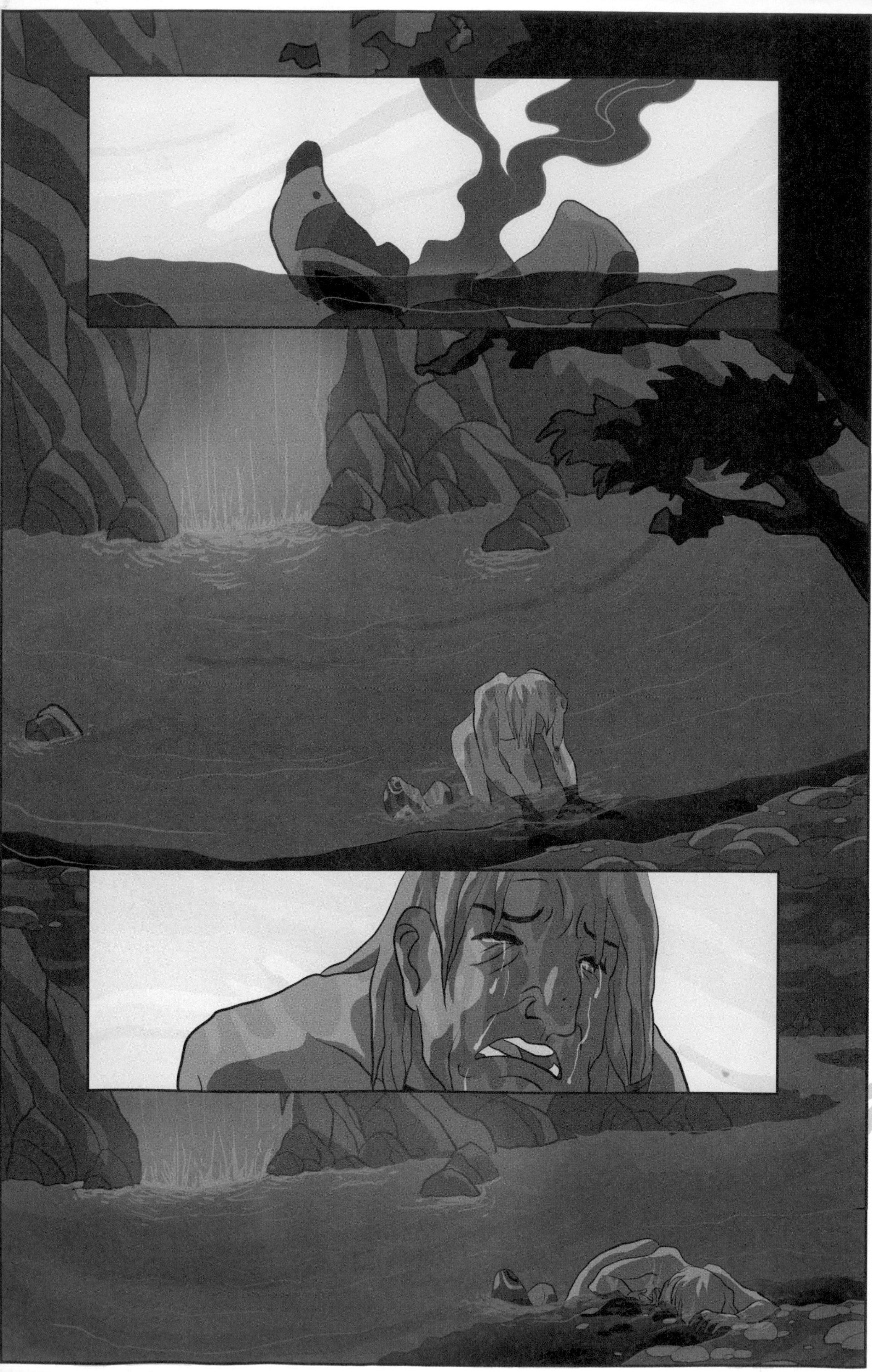

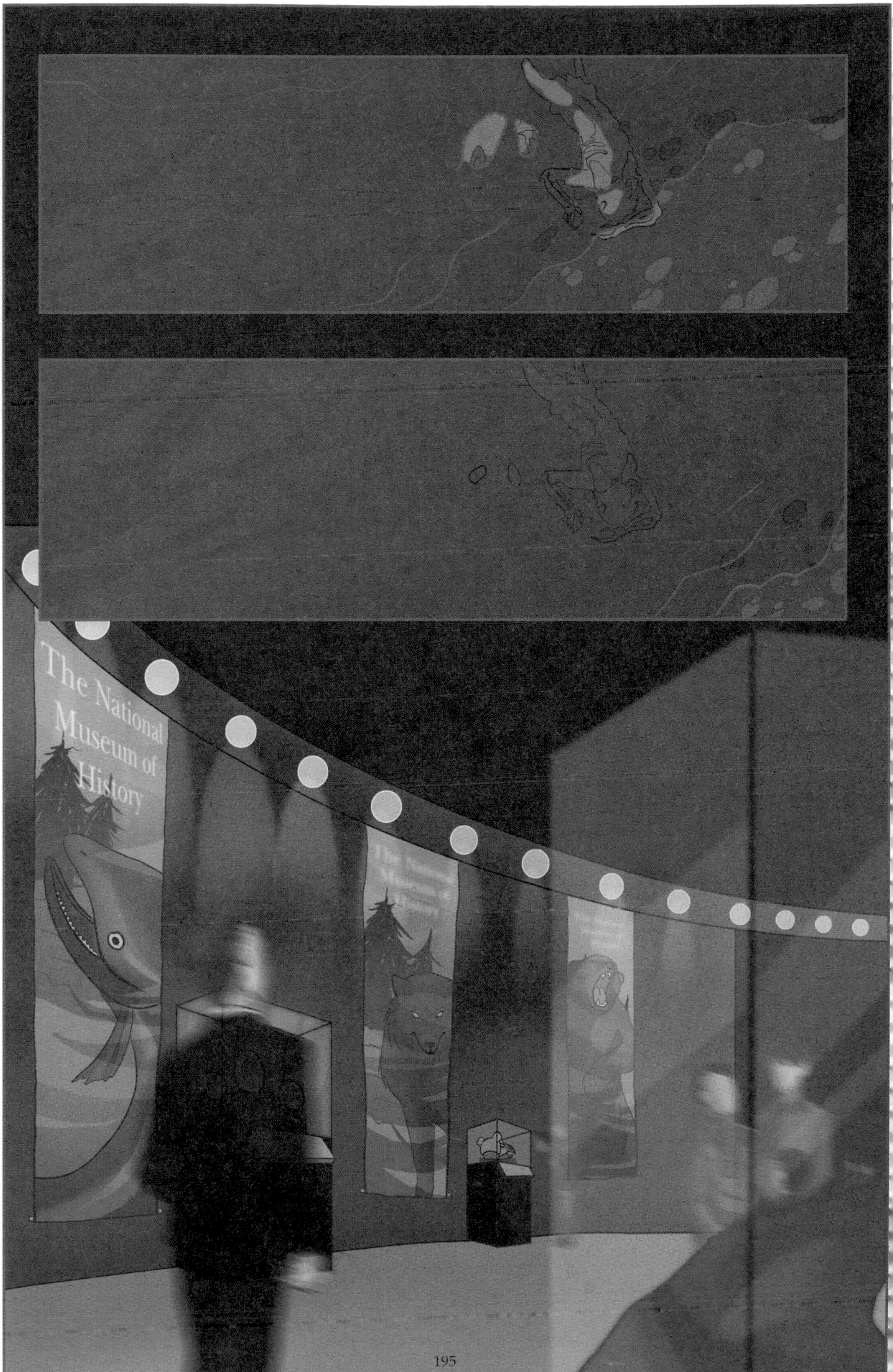
The National Museum of History

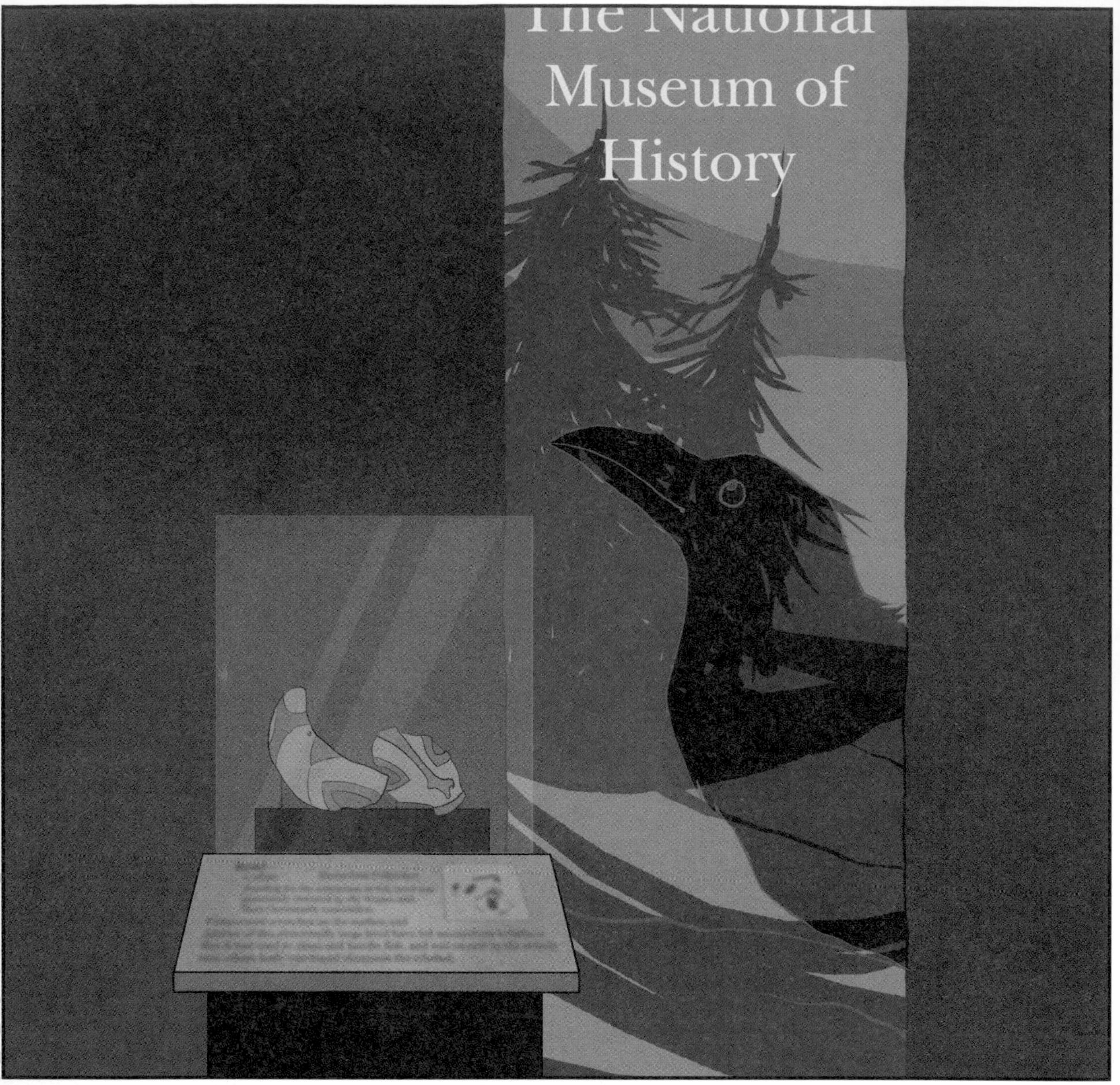
The National Museum of History

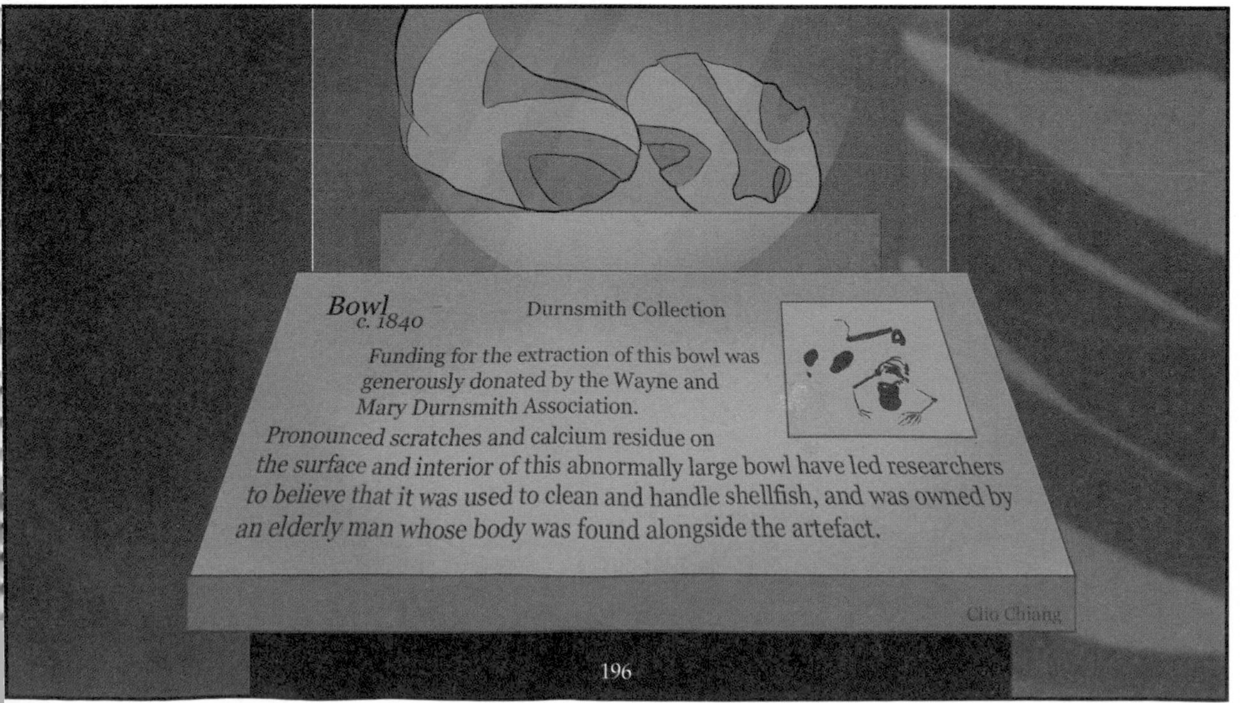
Bowl
c. 1840
Durnsmith Collection
Funding for the extraction of this bowl was generously donated by the Wayne and Mary Durnsmith Association.
Pronounced scratches and calcium residue on the surface and interior of this abnormally large bowl have led researchers to believe that it was used to clean and handle shellfish, and was owned by an elderly man whose body was found alongside the artefact.
Clio Chiang

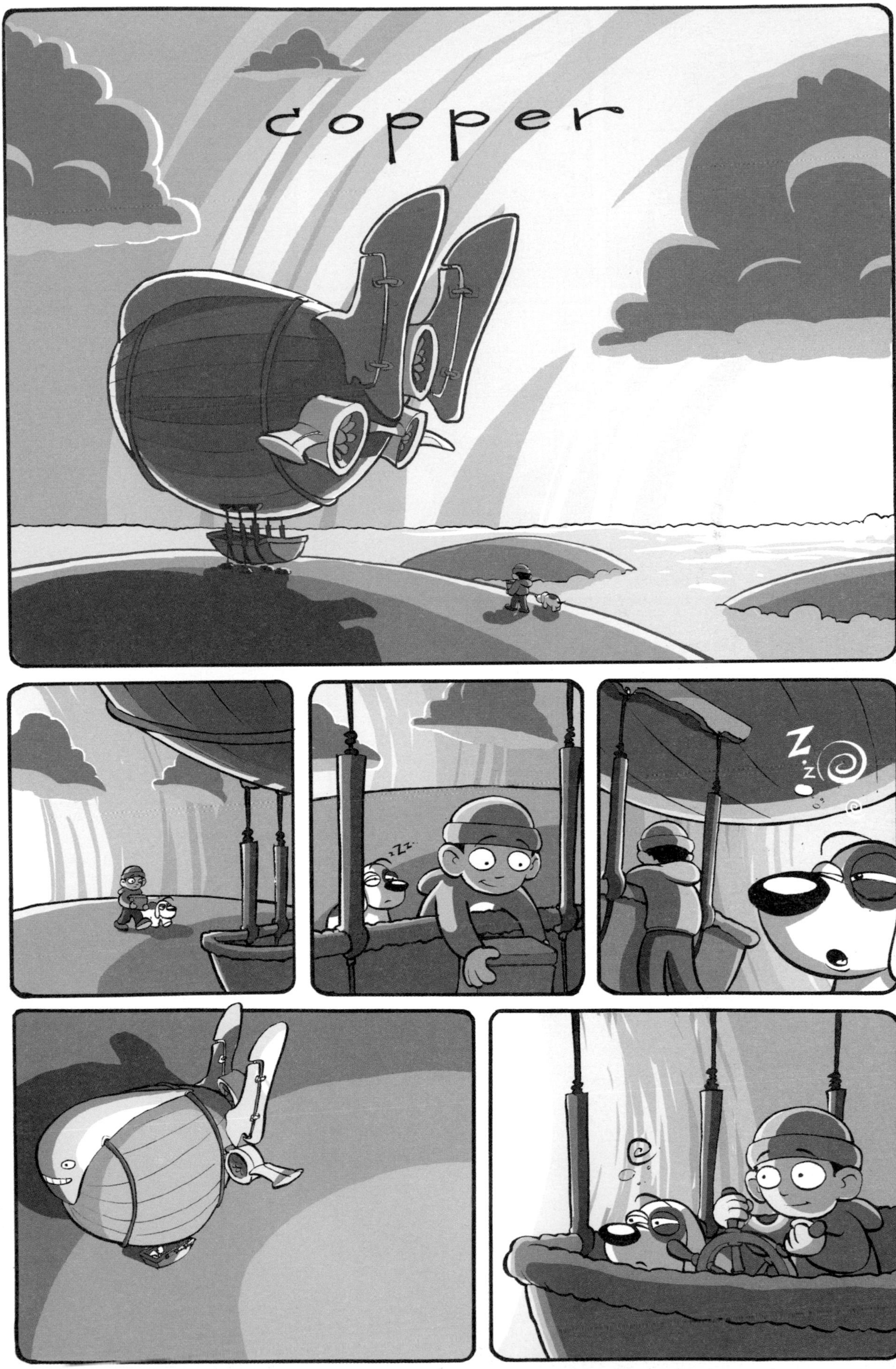
copper

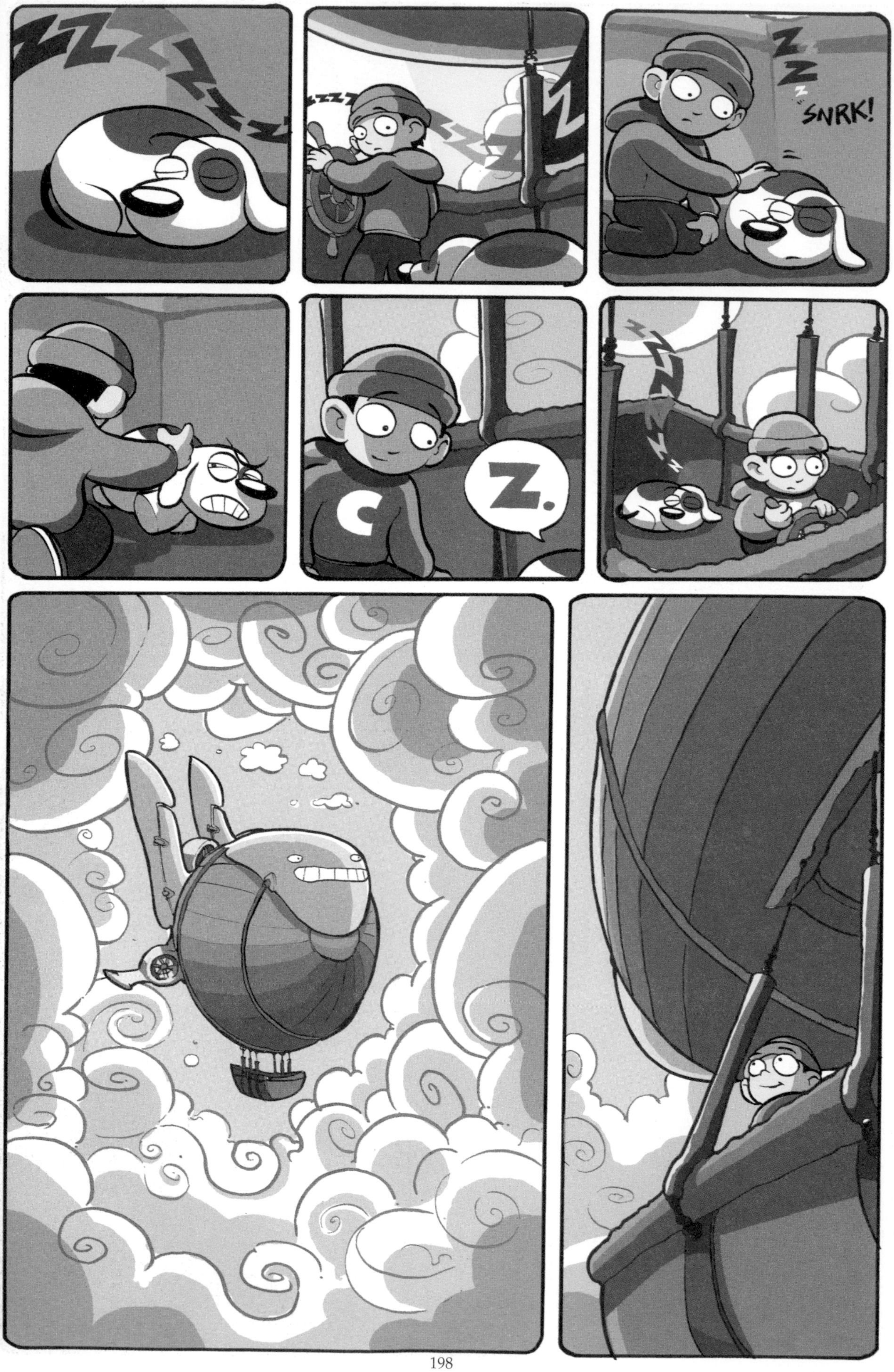
ZZZZZZ
SNRK!
Z.

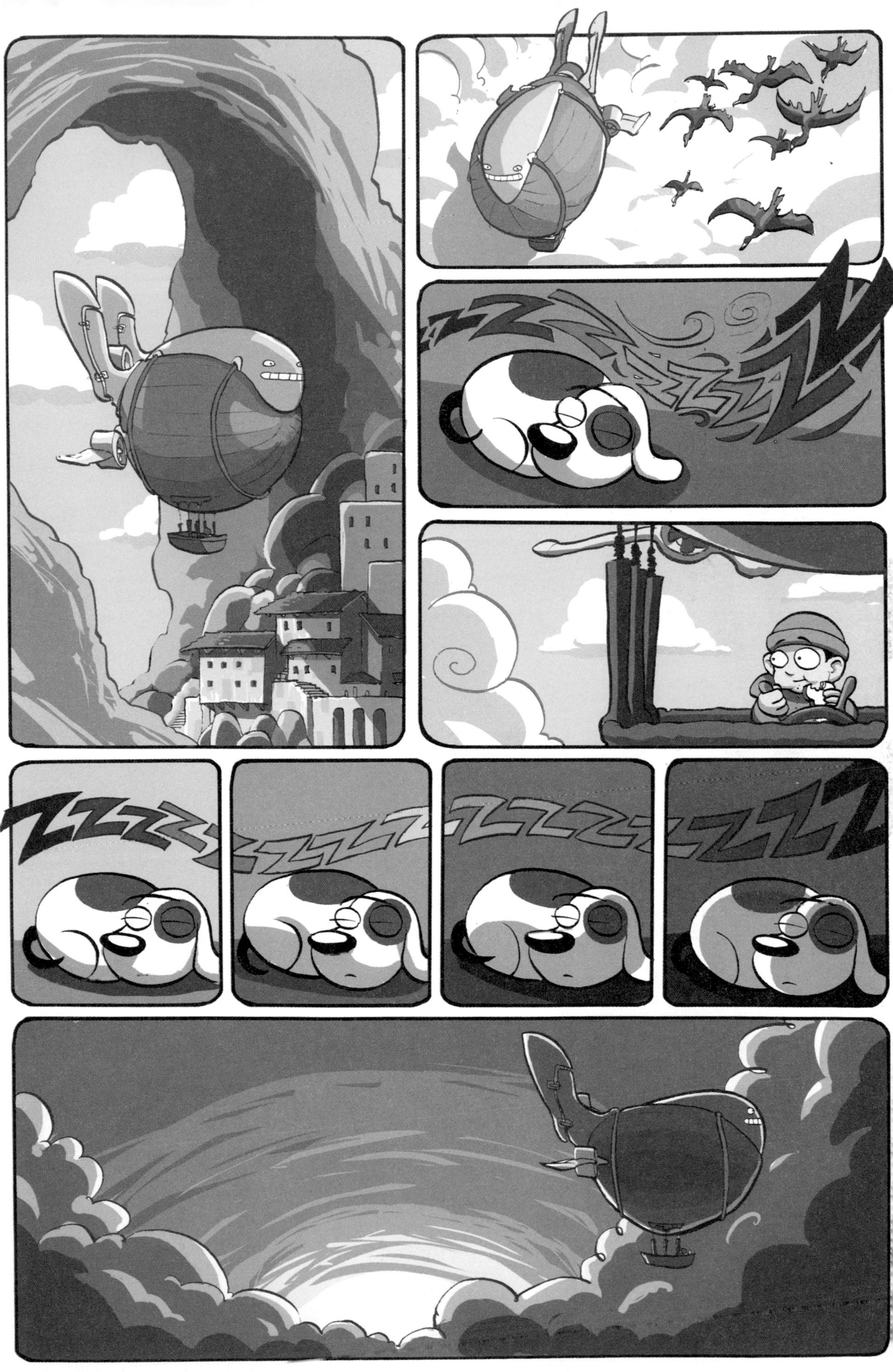

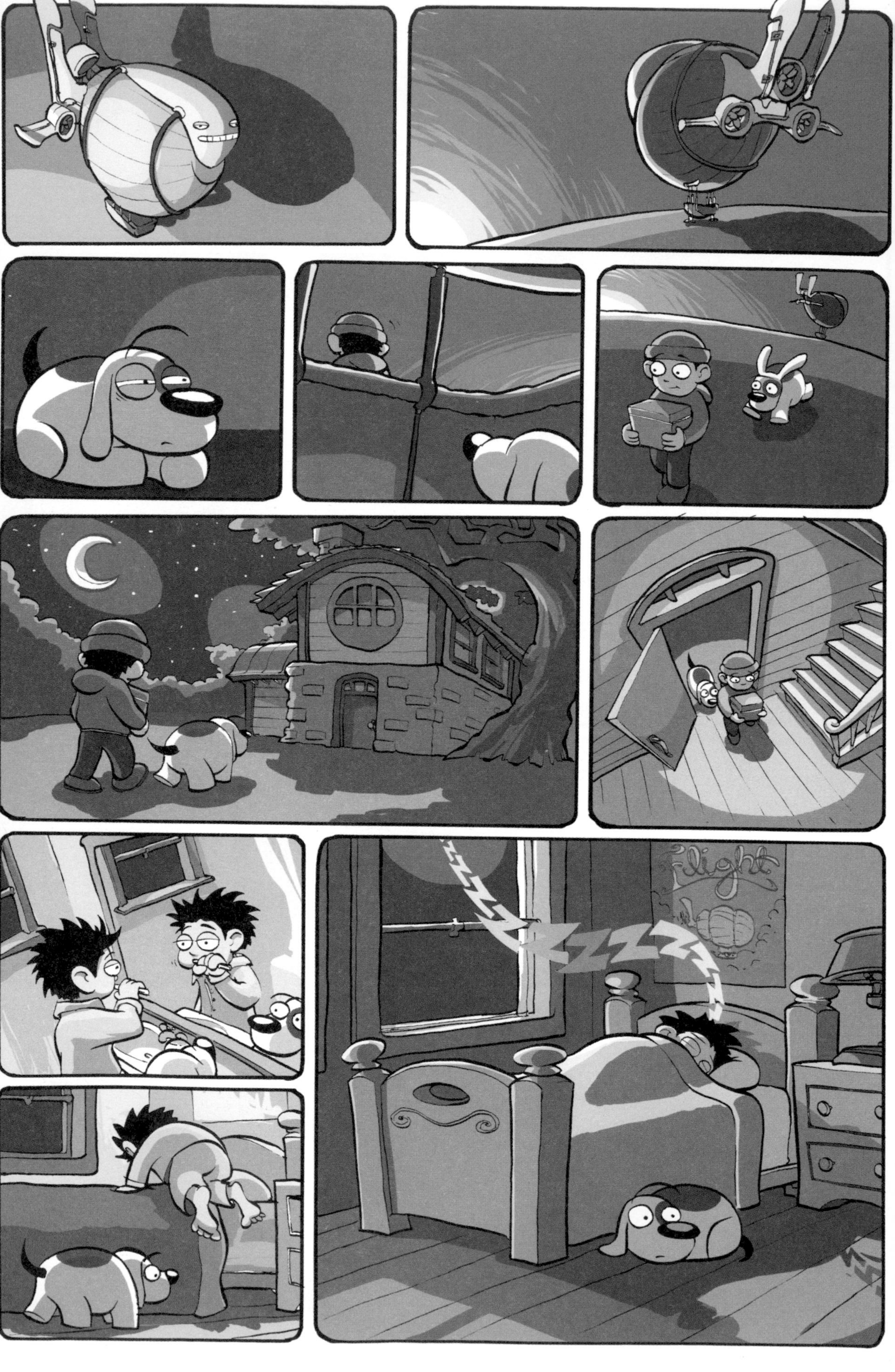
flight

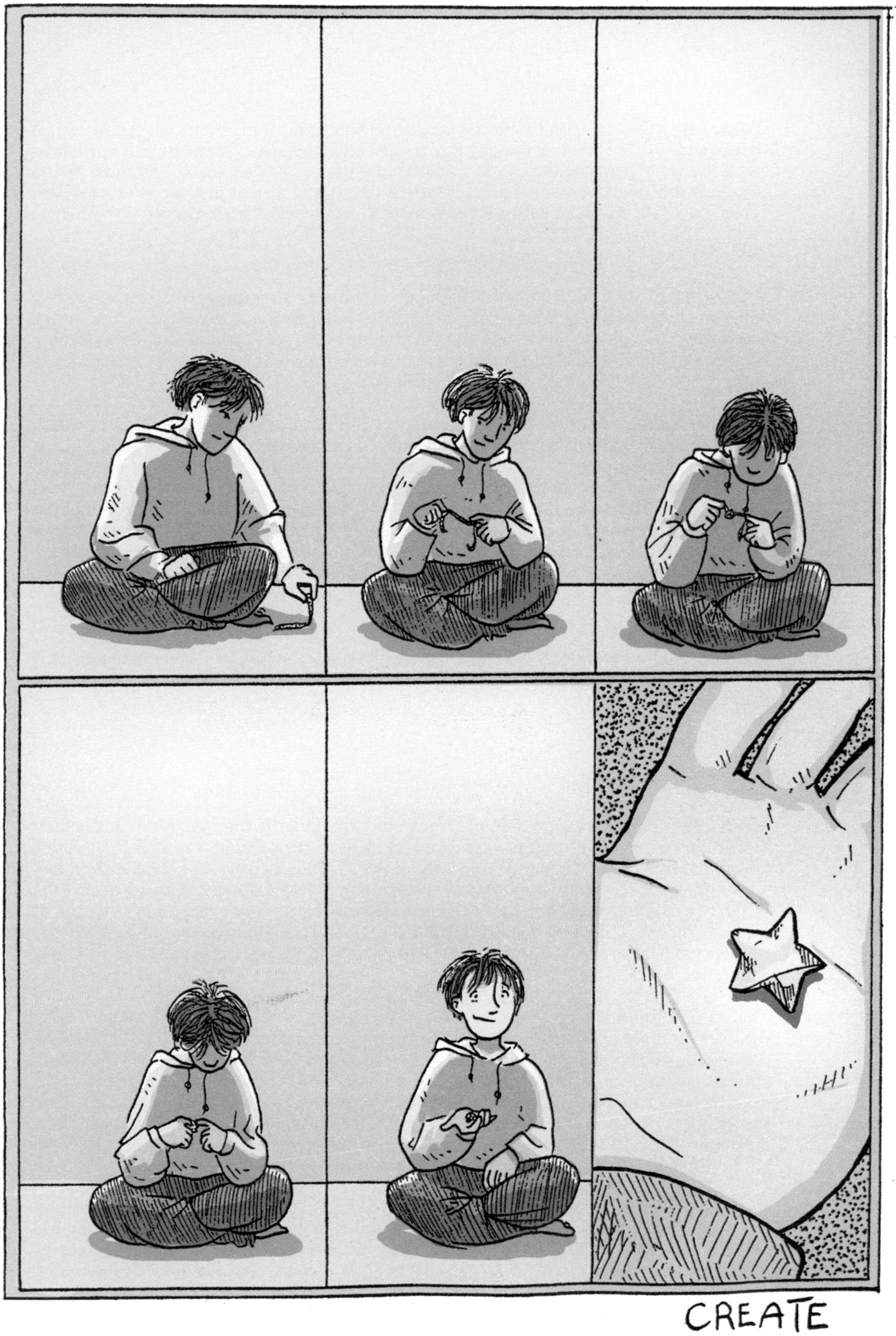

CREATE

THE YEAR COMICS TOOK FLIGHT

BY SCOTT MCCLOUD

Ah, 2004. I remember it well.

Today, fifty years later and with the benefit of hindsight, it's easy to see the historical significance of the Flight Anthology first published in that year. Many of its contributors would become giants of the comics industry not long after its release, and three would eventually become household names, yet in its day, it was seen as just one of several such books, noted for its high quality, but unremarkable in most other respects.

Little did they know.

In 2004, The American comic book industry was barely an industry at all. Just one in a thousand Americans read the comics magazines from their native land. Comics on the Web were beginning to proliferate and the graphic novel was gaining slightly in stature; but many of the best sequential artists, whether in print or online, tended to create comics more for the love of it than as a viable career.

Much has been made of the Comics Renaissance of the '20s (more properly 2017-2026) when comics first took their modern shape in the media landscape we know today. But in 2004, that generation was still in grade school, crowding into the manga sections of oversized turn-of-the-century book palaces decorated with giant portraits of dead poets and stocked with snacks and coffee costing a king's ransom. The young adult cartoonists of 2004 were fewer in number, gathering around their flickering primordial screens for the fellowship of each others' text diaries ("blogs" as they were known then), and gathering just once or twice a year at small comics conferences to break bread, converse and exchange quaint gifts such as hand drawings on napkins and homemade knitted articles of clothing.

Yet, few in number though they were, the generation emerging in 2004 managed in a single book to embody four of the most crucial turning points in early 21st century comics culture.

Turning Point #1: The Web Strikes Back.

Most of the contributors to Flight met each other through the Internet. Many made their reputations through their online work. And for most readers, Flight was their first printed encounter with these talented young cartoonists. Yet the barricades between print and webcomics that seemed so important to "Generation Zero" cartoonists like me made little difference to them. They didn't see print as a step up or step down; they didn't try print as the fulfillment of a lifelong dream; they didn't try it as a desperate compromise. Print was simply another way to connect with their readers and to express themselves in a new venue.

That said, it was an astonishing thing for us old-timers to see the way the project came together. Without a second thought, these twenty-one young artists had barreled ahead, completing 200 color pages before a publisher had even been found, secure in the laughably naive notion that good work would somehow find its level - which, of course, is exactly what happened. Conditioned by their experiences on the Web, none of them waited for permission to create these gems. Their attitude was simple. Step One: Draw the comic. Step Two: See what happens. It's an attitude we take for granted here in 2054, but to printed comics veterans in 2004, it was downright bizarre.

Most laughable of all was their attitude toward color. Color printing was still prohibitively expensive in the early 21st Century - and a hellishly complicated challenge to achieve the right effect in the finished product. Yet along comes the Flight team, accustomed to having color whenever they damn well pleased and - Boom! It's in color. Although it scared the crap out of many a prospective publisher, and certain contributors famously wept when they discovered print's sad inability to represent their beloved screen colors, it was nevertheless the right decision; and great care has been taken in this 50th anniversary commemorative reprint to faithfully reproduce that original book's colors as they were first seen those many years ago (along with the original editor's foreword by Dr. Kibuishi).

Turning Point #2: The Tribal shift.

In the Decade prior to Flight, most of the progressive wing of comics was dominated by the Iconoclast and Formalist Tribes. Walking through the turn-of-the-century expositions devoted to "small press" comics, visitors were greeted on one side of the aisle by roughly drawn "zines" about disaffected white youths with bad jobs, failed relationships and genital warts; and on the other by strange, multidirectional experiments and oddly-shaped cardboard constructions with day-glow silkscreen covers. I loved both types of comics (and make no apologies for my alleged complicity in the latter) but by 2004, a change was clearly in the air.

The return of the the other two tribes to independent comics found its focus in Flight. The Animists' love of pure transparent storytelling and the Classicists' attention to craft and enduringly beautiful settings was evident on many of the anthology's pages. While so many of the previous generation's revolutionaries had put raw honesty and innovation over straightforward plots and surface gloss, the Flight contributors tried to have it all-and in several cases succeeded. Flight gave readers something to read and something beautiful to look at again and again. For all the innovations of the rebel tribes, it was this kind of appeal to a broader readership that comics desperately needed in 2004. These artists delivered.

Turning Point #3: The Metabolization of Manga

Although Manga and Anime would have its strongest and most lasting effect on the generation that followed Flight, the artists in this historic anthology were among the first to have taken an early appreciation for Japanese story-telling and transcend it through their own, fully realized personal styles. As the great Japanese artist Hayao Miyazaki had gobbled up and fully metabolized the European world-building aesthetic of artists such as Moebius, so too did the Flight contributors gobble up and metabolize Miyazaki and his ilk. The result was markedly American in some cases, but also profoundly international in spirit-the beginnings of a trend that has continued to this day.

No big-eyed school girls or sword-wielding samurais were in attendance when these stories were conceived. No parodies. No slavish imitations of favorite styles. A few influences float to the surface here and there, but for the most part these are young artists who've learned from their heroes and moved on.

Turning Point #4: The Changing Face of Comics.

After an entire century of male-domination in the print comics field, the webcartoonist community was in the process of an astonishingly rapid correction in '04, and this was their first foray into the boy's club of print. Although not quite half of the contributors to Flight were women, the roster included several of the very artists that would quietly lead an army of their sisters onto the field just a few short years later (resulting to the male underrepresentation crisis of the late '20s, I might add... but let's not open that old can of worms).

The face of comics was changing in other ways too. In 2004 comics was ruled by the concepts of "mainstream" and "alternative" comics ("mainstream" at the time meaning a rather stagnant collection of companies specializing only in superhero comics perversely enough), but Flight turned the idea on its side, creating a work clearly designed to appeal to a broad audience, without merely aping the status quo of their day. It wasn't the first time such a thing had been tried, but it had never been tried so well. It was at this point in comics' development that a tipping point was reached and the explosion in diversity of genre that followed not long after may well have found its fuse in this book.

Four turning points of comics history in a single publication. Not bad, considering the casual spirit it was created in five decades ago! But we have the advantage of hindsight, don't we? 50 years of after-the-fact reasons to admire the book. Did it seem like a big event at the time? No. Not to most. Not at first. But it was to the contributors themselves. And it was to me, because I had an inkling of the revolutions it might trigger.

Ah, but I'd be lying if I said that aesthetics was the only reason that Flight was an important publication to me. Because unlike many of you, I had the privilege of meeting many of the contributors around this time, and now I remember them not just as industry figures and artistic demigods. I remember them as people.

I can see their faces even now: Dr. Kibuishi-still just "Kazu" to his friends-before all the Claire Danes stories threatened to eclipse his many accomplishments (and no, whatever you may have read, he did not lead her on in the least and the restraining order against Ms. Danes was entirely justified). Professor Meconis, still just an undergrad, but already writing up a storm, hand in a brace like everybody else that season, her great American graphic novel just some scribbled notes in a drawer. And the Legendary Mudron. Fresh-faced and cheerful; long before the Barcelona incident...

The world knows them as the grand old men and women of comics. Yet when this anthology was published in 2004, the average age of the contributors was just 24 years old-their whole careers still ahead of them. And that's how they're frozen forever in my mind. Laughing around a dinner table; karate chopping the air for passing cameras; or relaxing under a billowing white canopy beside a grand 20th Century convention hall on a long summer afternoon.

Fifty years ago, and it seems like only yesterday.

Scott McCloud's Brain
Sri Lanka, 2054